MW01698388

CLAIM YOUR CHILDREN BACK!

By Grant Agadjanian

Claim Your Children Back
By Grant Agadjanian

Transcribed by Allyson Livesay
Editor and Contributor, Arlene Hill
Cover and Layout by Anya Kinsley, TAITE+CO

Published by Creative Media Ministries
First Edition
Website: www.CreativeMediaMinistries.org
Phone Number: (951) 440-7688
YouTube: www.YouTube.com/ThePowerAtTheCross

Unless otherwise indicated, Scripture is taken from the New King James Version.

Printed in the United States of America.

To order more copies of this book, go to our website at
www.CreativeMediaMinistries.org
or contact (951) 440-7688.

ISBN: 978-0-9793409-6-3

Table of Contents

Forward

The concepts given by Pastor Agadjanian in this book explain and simplify this statement:

> "Those who are living upon the earth when the intercession of Christ shall cease in the sanctuary above are to stand in the sight of a holy God without a mediator. Their robes must be spotless, their characters must be purified from sin by the blood of sprinkling. Through the grace of God and their own diligent effort they must be conquerors in the battle with evil..." (*The Great Controversy*, p. 425, emphasis added)

If you have ever wondered what is meant by "diligent effort", this book will help. Have you tried to put away sin from your life, and given up in frustration, because your efforts never seem to last? Do you find yourself asking forgiveness for the same sins over and over? The "Biblical Principles of Spiritual Warfare" that Pastor Agadjanian describes will bring joyous vibrancy to your walk with Jesus instead of a vague yearning hope that you occasionally got "it" right. This book will also reveal the beauty of God's character, and that is exactly what can and will keep your children closer to God, and in the church.

You will want to share *Claim Your Children Back* with all your friends so that Prayer Groups in your churches can be trained and guided in effective ways to engage in spiritual warfare to claim not only your children, but everyone you know who needs to understand the process of righteousness through faith in Jesus, the Saviour of all humanity. A proper understanding of the birth, life, death and resurrection of Jesus will allow us to consent so that:

> "He will so identify with our thoughts and aims, so blend our hearts and minds into conformity to His will, that when obeying Him we shall be but carrying out our own impulses....When we know God as it is our privilege to know Him, our life will be a life of continual obedience." (*The Desire of Ages*, p. 668)

After learning these principles from his mentor, the late Bill Liversidge, Pastor Agadjanian brings his practical experience to encourage people who are still struggling with the battle that Jesus has already won for us. I pray that this book blesses and equips you as much as it has me.

Arlene Hill

Preface

Up to 85% of church members lose their children and grandchildren to the world. They are wounded by this fact, and grieve for these lost children and loved ones that are in the world and no longer in the church. This book, *Claim Your Children Back,* will change this by bringing healing, hope and encouragement to readers whose children and loved ones left the Lord. It will build their faith in the Word of God, will reveal and equip them with powerful Biblical principles for reclaiming their loved ones for God. It will also reveal to them how the Lord plans to save the lost prodigals and what He expects from church and family members.

You need not be disheartened! You will see the faithfulness of the Lord to His Promises to save our children and loved ones. *Claim Your Children Back* will bring unity among the believers, also it will reveal what can and will keep our children in the church and close to the Lord.

The Biblical principles in this book can be applied to reclaim any person dear to you, including missing church members that are no longer coming to church. This book will unite believers to start a powerful prayer ministry. The principles in this book will motivate believers to unite their prayers for loved ones. It is our united prayers that will drive Satan back and weaken his power and grip on our children and loved ones.

Isaiah 49:25 says, "But thus says the LORD: 'Even the captives of the mighty shall be taken away, and the prey of the terrible be delivered; For I will contend with him who contends with you, and I will save your children.'"

Jeremiah 31:16, 17 says, "Thus says the LORD: 'Refrain your voice from weeping, and your eyes from tears; for your work shall be rewarded, says the LORD, and they shall come back from the land of the enemy. There is hope in your future, says the LORD, that your children shall come back to their own border.'"

The inspiration for this seminar arose out of personal experiences and disappointments in my own life and family. I can identify with and feel the pain of every grieving parent and grandparent of children and family members who are no longer walking with the Lord.

Dedication

This book is lovingly dedicated to my family:

My wife Anne, the love of my life who stood by my side, in spite of my many shortcomings, in good times and bad times, and is always faithful and truthful.

Our son Grant Jr. who has a good heart and is a hard-working man who never gives up. He makes me a proud father.

And his loving wife Laureen, who loves our son and gave us **precious grandchildren Levi and Jewel**, the joy and love of our lives.

My prayer for all of you is that you will discover the beauty of God's character and Jesus will always be first in your life, and you will have the privilege to share the Good News—the Gospel of Jesus with people who do not know Him.

And my deep gratitude to all who made this book possible through their words of wisdom and their support.

About the Author

I was born in the Soviet Union during communism. At age 20, I graduated with an engineering degree but was required to take a test to determine if I was an atheist. I took it and passed. I was then drafted to serve in the Soviet Army and was sent to Siberia, although I had done nothing to deserve this. The climate was extremely harsh, with eight month winters of temperatures dropping to 45 degrees below zero, Celsius. I survived two years, but I became seriously ill and spent the next six years in and out of the hospitals. My parents spent their life savings for the best doctors, but ultimately they told me I had one year to live. Without hope of living more than a year, I began living carelessly but that only took me deeper into depression and physical pain. This became more unbearable especially after the medication stopped helping the pain.

One day while lying in bed with constant pain, the thought came, "This is the end of me." I thought of my young friends out there enjoying life, and I heard myself crying out "God, I don't want to die; Save me." I cannot explain this. How could that come from the lips of an atheist? I tell you, when you hit rock bottom, there is no atheist. God heard my cry. If God can hear the cry of an atheist, do you think he's too dull to hear your cries? How much more He hears the cry of His children? Have faith, my friends.

My older brother, Nelson arranged for me to meet with two Christian doctors who gave me a Bible and told me about God, and shared some of the health principles with me. While reading the Bible I began to have an appreciation of nature, and realized that there must be an Intelligent Designer of this beautiful and orderly world. I began to act on the Biblical principles and my health began to improve. Within a year, I was totally healed.

During that time of restoration, my wife, our son and I had a rare chance to enjoy a short stay at a resort near the Black Sea. My wife, Anne, noticed a lady with book stand selling books on the main street. My wife had an avid interest in health, so she bought a book called Family and Health. After reading the book, we thought the author is a contemporary educator. We were surprised to learn later that this book was written a century earlier, originally titled The Ministry of Healing. We began life style changes that resulted in losing friends since they thought we fit the Russian expression, "your roof has slid".

God arranged circumstances that moved us to the United States. There we studied with a Russian speaking Adventist pastor who opened to us the Biblical teachings of Seventh-day Adventism. We were baptized at the Loma Linda University church. As with many new converts, I did not have a grasp of the full Gospel, and eventually doubts crept in. I was focusing on my performance and became insecure and discouraged when I saw myself failing. I began to wonder if victory in the Christian life was ever possible. I was contemplating to leave the church.

God, in His great mercy directed us to a seminar called Victory in Jesus conducted by Pastor Bill Liversidge. I immediately realized that was what had been missing. The doctrines and the Gospel came together, so instead of leaving the church, I ended up in ministry. With God's gracious direction, and Pastor Bill's mentoring, I began to travel doing Gospel Revival presentations across the country.

My wife and I often wondered about the brave lady in Russia who sold us the Ellen White book. One day after conducting a worship service at a church in Oregon, I was invited to the home of a church member. They had a visitor from Moscow who had come to church but didn't speak English. They wanted me to share my personal testimony with her in Russian and she asked for details about my wife's experience buying the book. When I told her, she lifted her hands to heaven and proclaimed, "Lord, your ways are unsearchable." She explained that that was her book stand. They were selling books in spite of KGB persecution and threats of Siberian exile, jail, and taking away their children and homes. They risked everything just to spread the good news of the Gospel.

Dear Reader, thank you for your interest in this book. I pray that the Lord may use it to touch your heart. If He is calling you to any kind of ministry, I pray it will give you courage to answer that call. May God draw you closer to Him and bless you.

Grant Agadjanian

CLAIM YOUR CHILDREN BACK – PART I

WHAT CAN AND WILL KEEP YOUR CHILDREN CLOSE TO GOD AND IN THE CHURCH

"Those who wait for the Bridegroom's coming are to say to the people "Behold your God!" The last rays of merciful light, the last message of mercy to be given to the world, is a revelation of His character of love." (Christ's Object Lessons, p. 415-416)

CHAPTER 1

THE UNDISTORTED PICTURE OF GOD

An artist's daughter lost her eyesight in infancy. Her blindness was considered incurable. Not long after she was born, her mother passed away and her father was her constant companion. Then a new surgical technique was developed that promised to restore her vision. After surgery, while she lay recuperating in her hospital bed with her eyes bandaged, her brightest thought was: "Now I will be able to see my father!"

The day came when they took the bandages from her eyes. She opened her eyes and for the first time, she saw her father. As he embraced her, she exclaimed, "I have had a good-looking father all of these years and I didn't even know it."

My dear friends, we have such a beautiful Heavenly Father, and so many don't have any idea how gracious, loving, merciful, compassionate, forgiving, tender, holy, and just our Father is. This is because the true picture of God was distorted in the Garden of Eden. I praise God that picture was restored on the cross of Calvary.

You see there is a battle going on in this world today. That battle is not between you and Satan. That battle is between God and Satan over you. God's character was distorted by Satan. God allowed for this tragic drama to develop in this world. And He revealed His undistorted character so that every created being could make an intelligent choice. We as human beings will have to embrace either the lie of Satan about who God is or the truth about God.

I will attempt to draw the undistorted picture of God in this and the following chapters that will help you to make the right choice. As you behold the undistorted picture of God, you will not be the same. If you choose to come to the foot of the cross every day of your life to behold that undistorted picture of God, you will be changed into the likeness of what you behold. Let us come to the cross of Jesus together now.

I will begin with the statement from the *Gospel Workers* p. 315

> "The sacrifice of Christ as an atonement for sin is the great truth around which all other truths cluster. In order to be rightly understood and appreciated, every truth in the Word of God from Genesis to Revelation, must be studied in the light that streams from the cross of Calvary."

At the very heart of the Gospel message is the truth concerning the cross of Jesus Christ.

The Apostle Paul said,

> "For Christ did not send me to baptize, but to preach the gospel, not with cleverness of speech, so that the cross of Christ would not be made of no effect. For the word of the cross is foolishness to those who are perishing, but to us who are being saved it is the power of God." (1 Corinthians 1:17-18)

According to the apostle Paul, the power of God is in the message of the cross, so that message must be preached. The message of the Cross is the power of God. The Gospel is also the *"power of God"* (Romans 1:16). Then the Cross is the Gospel. And the Gospel is the revelation of God's character. The Bible tells us that God is love. That means that His power is exhibited through His love. As you read this chapter, you will experience the power of God.

To begin, we need to come to an understanding of the cross of Jesus from the Jewish perspective. Only then can we begin to grasp the meaning of His supreme sacrifice that was demonstrated by His infinite and unconditional love for us, of which apostle Paul tells us in Romans 5,

> "While we were still HELPLESS, at the right time Christ died for the UNGODLY… But God demonstrates His own love toward us, in that while we were still SINNERS Christ died for us… while we were ENEMIES we were reconciled to God through the death of His Son." (Romans 5:6, 8, 10)

God did not wait until we become strong, or godly, or righteous, or His friends. He did this while we were in that condition!

Have you ever wondered why the cross made such a tremendous impact on the disciples and early Christians? The disciples spent three and a half years with Christ. They traveled with Him, they heard Him preach, and they were taught by Him. At the end of three and a half years, even after witnessing the miracles, they were still a group of greedy and self-seeking men. Then came the cross of Jesus, and it totally transformed them. Now they were willing to be spent and to die for Jesus Christ. The Bible tells us that they turned the world upside down. It was because they understood what the cross meant. No wonder that the Apostle Paul said,

> "But God forbid that I should glory, save in the cross of our Lord Jesus Christ, by whom the world is crucified unto me, and I unto the world." (Galatians 6:14)

Paul makes another statement in 1 Corinthians 2:2, *"For I determined to know nothing among you except Jesus Christ, and Him crucified."*

What is it that made the cross the central theme and subject of New Testament preaching. I believe that if we find the answer to this question, the church would never be the same. But the problem is that the devil knows this too, and he does his best to enshroud the truth of the cross in darkness.

Let us dig into the light of God's Word and unfold more fully the truth of the cross so that we might experience the power of God that changes the hearts of sinners, and sets the captives free.

Apostle Paul says in Philippians

> "..And being found in appearance as a man, He humbled Himself by becoming obedient even to the point of death on a cross." (Philippians 2:8)

Why is Paul putting emphasis on even the *"death on a cross"*? The problem with most Christians is that they look at the cross from a very narrow point of view. We know that the Romans did the act of crucifixion, but somehow, we forget that they were fulfilling the desire of the Jewish leadership. And for the Jewish mind, the cross had a totally different meaning. Crucifixion was not a Jewish method of execution. The Jewish custom was stoning. So why were they crying, "Crucify Him?" Let's take a closer look at the cross from the Jewish point of view and not the Roman point of view.

Crucifixion was introduced by the Phoenicians over 600 years before Christ. Later on, it was adopted by the Romans as the highest form of punishment for the worst criminals, runaway slaves and rebels. The Jews hated crucifixion. Yet, in this case, they were shouting in one accord, "Crucify Him," and Jesus submitted to it, "even to the death on a cross".

What did the Jews have in mind when they shouted, "Crucify Him?

In Romans 8:32, Paul makes the statement that *"God did not spare His own Son."* What is it that God did not spare His Son from? He did not spare Him from death. Here we need to ask ourselves which death it was that Christ was not spared from. Was it the first death which Jesus called a sleep when Lazarus died? Or was He referring to the second eternal death?

In John chapter 19, we find Jesus in Pilate's court. Prior to this, Jesus had been tried by the Sanhedrin. The Sanhedrin was the supreme court of the Jewish nation, and they broke their own law over and over again in trying to condemn Jesus to be put to death.

Let's look at some of the Jewish law that they broke:

1. In Deuteronomy 19:15-21, if two or more witnesses in a case could not agree, and it was later proven that a witness was lying, the false witness was supposed to be punished with the same penalty that the person they falsely accused would have received. The Sanhedrin gathered several false witnesses, but their stories were inconsistent and did not agree. They did not punish false witnesses. They broke the law.

2. Then Caiaphas, the high priest, urged Jesus to tell them if He was the Son of God. Jesus could not lie and answered, "Yes." At this, the high priest tore his robe which was unlawful for the high priest to do upon penalty of death. (Leviticus 10:6, Mark 14:61-64). Rather than being put to death, he charged Jesus with blasphemy. They broke the law.

3. Jewish law does not take into account self condemnation which is what they thought Jesus had done by confirming He was the Son of God. The law says, "on the evidence of two or three witnesses he who is to die, shall be put to death; he shall not be put to death on the evidence of one witness." (Deuteronomy 17:6) Jesus was the only witness for Himself. They broke the law.

4. It was also contrary to Jewish law to try a person by night. It had to be by the light of the day and in the presence of the whole session of the council. They broke the law.

5. The Jewish law forbid putting people on trial during the time of the Passover. Jesus was tried during the Passover. Jewish law forbid putting anyone to death at the time of the Passover. They broke these and many other Jewish laws in order to put Jesus to death. Finally they condemned Him, but they could not put Him to death because they were under the Romans. And only Romans could put someone to death.

The Sanhedrin brought Him to Pilate's court, where he questioned Jesus and did not find anything in Him deserving of death. In fact, he acquitted Jesus three times: in John 18:38 and in John 19:4 and John 19:6. And in John 19:7 we read: *"The Jews answered him, "We have a law, and by that law He ought to die."* Now, what law are they referring to? The same verse gives us the answer, *"because He made Himself out to be the Son of God!"* That is, He made Himself equal to God.

Did they have a law that condemns the one who makes himself equal to God? The answer is "yes," the law of blasphemy.

God gave this law in Leviticus:

> "And whoever blasphemes the name of the Lord shall surely be put to death, and all the congregation shall certainly stone him, the stranger as well as him who is born in the land. When he blasphemes the name of the Lord, he shall be put to death." (Leviticus 24:16)

This law not only states that the person has to die, but it tells also how he has to die. To be stoned.

So the Jewish leadership is telling to Pilate: "We have a law and according to our law He has to die". The question is: Did they remember how person had to die, or they have forgotten their own law?

(Don't take my word for it. Read the scripture for yourself. It is vital that you test everyone who presents the Word of God with what God says, especially in the time that we are living in when we have been warned that there would be many false prophets).

There are many places that we can confirm this, but one of the shortest is found in John 10:30-31 where Jesus said, *"I and My Father are one. Then the Jews picked up stones again to stone Him."*

Now look at verse 33. *"The Jews answered Him, 'We are not stoning You for a good work, but for blasphemy; and because You, being a man, make Yourself out to be God."* This passage shows that they knew full well, the demands of their law for blasphemy is to stone. They knew the law, and they were intending to execute the law accordingly.

Why now they are asking Pilate to crucify Jesus, especially since the crucifixion was not a Jewish method of execution? The reason being, there was another law they were more interested in. You see, the Jews of Christ's day identified crucifixion with hanging on a tree. To the Jew, to be crucified meant you had committed the unpardonable sin and were being punished by the irrevocable curse of God, the equivalent of the second death of the New Testament (Revelation 20:6, 14). By crying out *"crucify Him"*, the Jews were asking God to pour out His wrath on Christ that He may experience the eternal death, goodbye to life forever. And we must remember one more fact, that the Jews did not believe in the immortal soul; that was a Greek pagan concept that crept into Christian church, and many believed this lie, that originated from the beginning in the Garden of Eden, when the serpent said to Eve: *"you surely will not die!"* (Genesis 3:4)

The law in which they were more interested is found in Deuteronomy:

> "If a person has committed a sin worthy of death, and he is put to death, and you hang him on a tree, his body shall not remain overnight on the tree, but you shall certainly bury him on the same day, so that you do not defile your land which the Lord your God is giving you as an inheritance; for he who is hanged is accursed of God." (Deuteronomy 21:22-23)

Now, let me give you a comparison between dying by stoning and dying by hanging on a tree. If a person is condemned to die by stoning, while he is being stoned and dying, he may still turn to God in repentance and have hope for eternal life. But if a person was to be hanged on a tree, that meant an irrevocable curse of God. No hope. That meant to be forsaken by the Life Giver. To be under the curse of God is the second death—eternal death.

Let me give you couple of references, one Biblical and the other historical:

1. When Joshua led the Israelites into the Promised Land, five kings joined their forces and fought against Israel. They knew what had taken place in Egypt. And also Abraham had witnessed to them about God, their Maker, four hundred and thirty years before. Now that God was bringing His people into the Promised Land, instead of opening the doors of their cities and their hearts to get to know their Maker, they joined forces and fought against God's children.

And whoever fights God's children—fights against God. So God gave the victory to the Israelites. Then Joshua captured the five kings and brought them before Israel, and said,

> "'Do not fear or be dismayed! Be strong and courageous, for thus the Lord will do to all your enemies with whom you fight.' So afterward Joshua struck them and put them to death, and he hanged them on five trees; and they hung on the trees until evening.'" (Joshua 10:25, 26)

These kings were enemies of the Most High God. Why did Joshua hang them on trees? He did this to show that the irrevocable curse of God was upon them.

2. As a direct result of The First Jewish Revolt in 70 AD, Roman soldiers under Titus besieged the City of Jerusalem destroying the temple and razing much of the city. The Roman soldiers, under the command of Titus were crucifying over 50 Jews a day, those who were fighting for the freedom of their nation. These people were heroes of Israel. Jewish historians do not mention in their writings the names of their heroes who were crucified, since they considered them to be accursed of God, as if they had never existed.

When Jesus was in the temple, He said, *"Destroy this temple and in three days I will raise it up."* (John 2:19) The Jews understood very well that He meant His own body. At the time of Jesus, the high priest was Caiaphas. He belonged to the party of the Sadducees. The Sadducees did not believe in the resurrection. Jesus challenged their belief by raising people from the dead.

By doing these things, raising people from the dead, and saying that He will rise in three days, the Sadducees became the most bitter enemies of Jesus. That is why they stirred up the crowd to cry, "Crucify Him." And Jesus submitted to it, even to the death of the cross.

By condemning Jesus Christ to be crucified, they wanted to be sure that He would never rise again and that even His name would not be remembered. It had been predicted, and the scripture was fulfilled. "

> "But I was like a gentle lamb led to the slaughter; and I did not know that they had devised plots against me, saying, 'Let's destroy the tree with its fruit, and let's cut him off from the land of the living, so that his name will no longer be remembered.'" (Jeremiah 11:19)

No man can conquer death. When Jesus arose from the grave, that provided the greatest evidence to the Jews that He is God, and when they still rejected Him, their house was left unto them desolate as Jesus had previously declared. That is how the devil's hatred of Jesus blinded the eyes of the leaders of the Jewish nation. That is why we must pray for the leaders of our country that the rays of Light would penetrate their hearts and minds.

So when the Jews were shouting, *"Crucify Him,"* they were asking God to pour out His curse and wrath on Jesus Christ. It was about this cup of wrath that Jesus was praying in the garden of Gethsemane three times *"O*

My Father, if it is possible, let this cup pass from Me; nevertheless not as I will, but as You will." (Matthew 26:39, 42, 44)

The question is: Did God pour His curse on Jesus on the cross or not?

The answer is "yes" and "no."

God did not pour out His curse on Jesus Christ on the cross for blasphemy, because Jesus is the Son of God. But the curse that rightly belongs to each one of us, God allowed to fall on Jesus on the cross. In that one moment two thousand years ago, God lifted the guilt, shame, sin and judgment from each one of us, even the second death, and He placed it on the One who did not deserve it and as the result of it – we have Great Good News,

Here it is: **THE SECOND DEATH IS NO LONGER IN YOUR FUTURE! ARE YOU REJOICING IN IT?**

> "As soon as there was sin, there was a Saviour. Christ knew that He would have to suffer, yet He became man's substitute. As soon as Adam sinned, the Son of God presented Himself as surety for the human race, with just as much power to avert the doom pronounced upon the guilty as when He died upon the cross of Calvary." (E. G White, *Advent Review and Sabbath Herald,* March 12, 1901)

The following statement agrees with the quotation above, was made by E. J. Waggoner when he was working with Ellen White:

> "This sentence of death was made known to Adam as soon as he was placed in the garden of Eden, as a warning against sin. When he sinned, he at once came under condemnation, doomed to suffer the threatened penalty. But right here came in the gospel. The sacrifice of Christ was just as efficacious the day that Adam sinned as it is today; He is the Lamb slain from the foundation of the world. For all practical purposes Christ was crucified as soon as Adam fell, for God 'calleth those things which be not as though they were.' Christ was given at that time. The sacrifice on the part of God to give His only begotten Son was already made; God loved the world then just as much as He did four thousand years later.
>
> "If it had not been that Christ was given for man's redemption, death would have ended all for Adam, and for all the human race. But the promise of a Redeemer carried with it another probation, and so the execution of the sentence was suspended until it should be seen what use men would make of that probation. God has

> appointed a day in which He will judge the world in righteousness by Jesus Christ (Acts 17:31) and until that time the sentence will be held in abeyance. Christ has suffered it, and all who receive Him, receive the penalty in Him, and his life answers for theirs." (E. J. Waggoner, *Signs of the Times,* August 4, 1890)

And how can we know that the curse that belonged to us has fallen on Jesus on the cross?

In Genesis God comes in the Garden of Eden after the fall of Adam and Eve. He speaks to Adam and Eve, and when He pronounces the curse because of their sin, He says,

> "Cursed is the ground because of your sake... both thorns and thistles it will bring forth for you...." (Genesis 3:17, 18)

What was on the head of Jesus on the cross? A crown of thorns was placed on His head. This is a symbol of the curse. This is the curse that was pronounced on our entire planet, including you and me. Jesus came to take that curse upon Himself. That curse, which is the second death, is no longer in your future. Does this make you rejoice? Christians must be the happiest people on the planet earth, as those whose death sentence was just canceled!

Let me reinforce this fact with another scripture. Galatians says,

> "For all who are of works of the Law are under a curse; for it is written: 'Cursed is everyone who does not abide by all the things written in the Book of the Law, to do them.'" (Galatians 3:10)

This includes every person that has ever lived on this globe. We are all under the curse. This is really bad news. Unless we understand how bad that bad news is, we will never appreciate how really good the good news is. So, you've heard the bad news. Now I'm going to give you the good news.

> "Christ redeemed us from the curse of the Law; having become a curse for us—for it is written: 'Cursed is everyone who hangs on a tree.'" (Galatians 3:13)

Christ became the curse for you and me. He humbled Himself and became obedient to the point of death, "even the death on the cross". Do you see now the meaning of the death on the cross? *"Cursed is everyone who hangs on a tree."*

When Jesus was on the cross, He cried, *"My God, My God, why have You forsaken Me?"* (Matthew 27:46; *cf.* Psalm. 22:1)

Do you know what the Father did? In accordance with Isaiah 53:6 and Isaiah 59:2 the Father looked down at Jesus on the cross, and He turned His face away from Jesus and let Him die.

Why would the Father do this? I will answer this question. But in order for you to appreciate the answer, we need to answer another question first. This will be a seminary level question. WHEN ADAM SINNED, WHERE WERE WE? Turn in your Bible to Hebrews 7.

> "Even Levi, who receives tithes, paid tithes through Abraham, so to speak, for he was still in the loins of his forefather when Melchizedek met him." (Hebrews 7:9-10)

This is the concept of biblical oneness and corporate solidarity. Once you understand this concept, you're going to see it all through the Bible, and you will appreciate the Gospel on a deeper level. Even though Levi wasn't born yet, he was in Abraham's loins, the Bible is telling us that when Abraham paid tithes to Melchizedek, Levi did it also, even thought he was not yet born. Here is the same concept in a simple form:

God created all men in one man, Adam. The devil ruined all men in one man, Adam. God redeemed all men in one man, Jesus Christ. This is the same concept of Biblical oneness, or Biblical solidarity.

> "For as in Adam all die, so also in Christ all shall be made alive." (1 Corinthians 15:22)

Now, to apply the principle in these two verses, when Adam sinned, where were we? We were in Adam, in his loins, in his seed, just like Levi was still in the loins of Abraham when he paid tithes to Melchizedek. And whatever happened to Adam happened to us. In one man the devil ruined the whole human race, but God had a plan. God placed the human race in another Man, and that Man was the Lamb slain from the foundation of the world. My friend, before God created this world, before sin entered the human race, God had a plan to save us!

Hallelujah, praise God! What a God we have.

And when the fullness of time came, God sent His Son in the likeness of human flesh. Jesus Christ became the second Adam.

The Bible tells us that God put us in Christ.

> "But it is due to Him that you are in Christ Jesus, who became to us wisdom from God, and righteousness and sanctification, and redemption." (1 Corinthians 1:30)

The book of Ephesians is full of these statements. Jesus lived a sinless life. Both Adams are under every aspect of the same law. That is whatever happened to the first Adam because we were in him happened to us. And whatever happened to the second Adam because God put us in Him, now He considers that it happened to us. Have you ever heard the statement, "righteousness by faith?"

And Apostle Paul tells us in Colossians 2:10 that *in Him* we are complete.

Then God took the whole human race in the flesh of Jesus Christ and brought it to the cross to meet the justice of the law. All mankind was represented in the humanity of Christ that died on the cross.

When He was on the cross and cried out, *"My God, My God, why have You forsaken Me?"* The Father turned His face away from Jesus and let Him die. Why did the Father turn His face from Jesus? What did the Father see on the cross that made Him turn His face from Jesus? Who did the Father see on the cross?

He saw you. He saw me. He saw each one of us in Christ, and He turned His face away from Jesus Christ, His only Son, and let Him taste our second death. That is why the second death is no longer in our future. Jesus not only took your sin to the cross, He went to the cross as you. He not only died on the cross instead of you, He died on the cross as you. On the cross of Christ, justice and mercy kissed each other. A tremendous collision took place on the cross of Jesus between God and man, where all of the pain was absorbed by the heart of God so that, whatever happened to Jesus, God now considers that it happened to you and me.

Oh how merciful God is to us! He did not allow us to go through such agony of the curse/second death. He put us in Christ and Jesus Christ took all our punishment for the sin problem.

Jesus was not a sinner, but He invited God to treat Him as if He was a sinner so that we who are sinners might be treated as if we were righteous. That's how God treats us. If you are contemplating leaving God and the church, please look at the cross of Jesus. Look at the love of God. You are loved with an everlasting love.

The Cross of Jesus is the Gospel, it is the power of God. And it is the Gospel, not "do's" or "don'ts" that fills our hearts with gratitude to God and we will WANT to do what He says. We will do all of it out of gratitude. This is the only true motive to serve the Lord.

If we want to retain our young people closer to God and in the church, WE MUST GIVE THEM THE GOSPEL!

Why would God go through so much agony to save sinful, wretched human beings like us?

I will give you two answers to this question:

First of all, there was a sin problem. Many of us are still playing around with sin, forgetting that sin put Jesus, the Son of God, on the cross. The mentality of people who play that game is like the antediluvian people before the flood. All of them heard the message. Many believe, but many were thinking in their minds, "We can still enjoy the pleasure of sin a little longer, and when we see the clouds and the rain coming, we'll jump on board the boat." It didn't work that way. The boat sailed, and they were not on it. Right now, my friend, if you hear His voice, don't let your heart become hardened. Today is the day. Tomorrow may never come.

Let me give you a radical definition of sin. Sin is a blatant mutiny against God. And either sin or God must die in your life. Both cannot exist in your heart. If sin rules in you, it will kill the life of God in you. If God rules in you, sin in your life will be killed. The culmination of sin on this planet was the crucifixion of Jesus Christ. What was true in the history of God on this planet, will be true in your history and mine. That is, sin will kill the presence of God in us.

Now the second answer to the question "why God had to go through such an agony?" Scripture tells us, *"God so loved the world*—the human race—*that He gave His only begotten*, one–of–a–kind *Son."* (My paraphrase) What does it say next? "That whosoever is *good* should not perish?" Some may say "yes" today. But God's Word says, *"That whosoever BELIEVES in Him should not perish, but have everlasting life."* (John 3:16) That's the love of God.

It is the revelation of His character of love–the Gospel, that will lead people to repentance.

Let me unfold for you the depths of God's love.

In John 17:23, Jesus was praying to His Father in the presence of His disciples. He said, *"...Father, that they may know that You love them, as You love Me."* Let me paraphrase this and bring it home. What is Jesus actually saying? He is saying that God the Father loves you no less than He loves His Son, Jesus Christ. Let that sink in. And in John 15:9 Jesus said: *"Just as the Father has loved Me, I also have loved you."* (John 15:9) There you have it. God the Father loves you infinitely, and God the Son loves you infinitely. Then Jesus went to the cross, and there He signed it with His own blood.

While He hung on the cross, He was tempted three times to come down from the cross if He was the Son of God, and save Himself. (Matthew

27:39-44; Luke 23:35 & 37) Could He have done it? Absolutely. But could He, by coming down from the cross and saving Himself, save us at the same time? The answer is—no, He could not save us at the same time. He had to make a choice. And the choice He made is, to save mankind, you my dear reader and me.

This must speak loudly to every human heart something very profound.

One day I was contemplating God's Word about the cross and meditating on the scenery of the cross and what actually took place there. I still remember where I was and what I was doing, when God spoke to my heart and mind. It broke me into tears when I realized what actually happened on the cross. I called that the last words of Jesus from the cross to me.

When our children, our youth, and our prodigals embrace this message, it will keep them in the church and hold them fast to Jesus. Once this is in place, it's not easy for Satan to take them out of Christ's hands.

It is a sad fact that in the United States we are losing up to 85 per cent of young people to the world. What has taken place in our country and in our churches?

The good news is, God's power is sufficient, and His power is the Gospel. The Gospel is the revelation of God's character which is what you will be hearing repeated over and over again in this book.

I invite you to use your sanctified imagination and come with me back two thousand years to the foot of the cross. Picture Jesus as He is being scourged by a whip that has sharp bones of animals and metal pieces attached to it. Up to forty times He has been whipped and beaten, bruising His body and ripping His flesh. Then He is forced to carry the cross to Calvary, where His flesh is pierced as He is nailed to the cross. Can you see the blood running down His face as the Roman soldiers force a crown of thorns on His head that went deep into His scalp, ears and forehead….

As you standing at distance and watching Jesus hanging on the cross, He lifts up His head, opens His friendly eye and He looks at you with so much love and kindness in His eyes. And you know He wants to say something to you. But for that He had to lift His body on the nailed hands. The weight of His body hanging from His arms impeded His breathing and speech, so He must push down on His nailed feet and pull up with His nailed hands, causing intense pain to be able to speak to you. And as you watch, He lifted His body on the nailed hands, He took His last breath and spoke His last Words to you. Have you ever wondered what those last words of Jesus could of been to you if you were there? I have heard those words in my heart and in my mind, and I was not the same person anymore. I want to share these words with you.

Jesus didn't actually utter these words, but His action speaks louder than any words can. Anytime, from now on when you see the cross, you should hear the Words of a Gentleman, Jesus Christ through His act of staying on the cross. This is what He speaks to every human being today and through the centuries:

"Whoever you are, whatever country you come from, it does not matter. No matter what the color of your skin is, no matter what you have done in the past, it does not matter. I can come down from the cross and save Myself, but I cannot save Me and save you at the same time. I choose to stay on the cross because I love you more than I love Myself."

And He died….

Dear friend, that's who your God, your Creator is. This is the undistorted picture of God.

And YOU ARE LOVED!

Don't let Satan deceive you with his lies.

Today Jesus is calling every human being from the cross, revealing His love to humanity. Have you given your heart to Jesus? Maybe you are coming to church, but you have some reservations. You've never fully committed your heart to God and have never entered into the Lord's covenant expressing publicly that you identify with Christ's death through baptism. Maybe you are saying to yourself at this moment, "If He is that kind of God, there is nothing to hold me back". You had so many reasons that were preventing you, and today as you are hearing and seeing the beauty of God's character and His love for you, you understand that God loves you more than He loves Himself, and He doesn't want to spend eternity without you. Do you want to open your heart to Him? If your answer is "yes", heaven is rejoicing over you right now. "*…For the joy that was set before Him,* (to save you) *He endured the cross, despising the shame….*" (Hebrews 12:2) The joy of Jesus is to restore us back to His righteousness and eternity with Him. The cross of Jesus was to lose His existence. Dear friend, the joy of your restoration was so much greater than the perspective of Him losing His existence. This is your God, dear friend. Never forget that.

It is with this concept of God, with this undistorted picture of God, the Everlasting Gospel – the Power of God, the Bible tells us that the apostles turned the world upside down.

This very thing God wants to do it through us today, because that same Power of God is available to us today. It is the Everlasting Gospel that will turn the hearts of sinners to God, and we will stop losing 85 per cent of our young people, your family members, children and grandchildren.

That is the focus of Creative Media Ministries, to reveal and proclaim the undistorted picture of God to the world, to retain our young people in the church, to bring the prodigals back to the Father and to help our church members to live an extraordinary Christian life.

My prayer for you, dear reader is:

Loving Father, Lord Jesus, I praise You for loving us that much. You gave Yourself up to save sinners like us. You expressed on the cross that You love us more than You love Yourself. This is the kind of love that captures our hearts. Anoint the reader with the Holy Spirit so that the fire of love You have given to them today, will never go out. Pour your oil upon that fire continuously. May they fall deeper in love with You every day of their lives. Bless their families and make them light bearers for our world.

I pray in Jesus name. Amen!

CHAPTER 2

LOST IN THE FATHER'S HOME

Friends, would you agree that the last several years have brought great changes to our world? We as Christians should not be taken by surprise. Ellen White wrote, "Great changes are soon to take place in our world, and the final movements will be rapid ones." (9T11) May I suggest to you that "soon" is already here with us, and what is next? The last day events, they will be rapid ones. Are you ready for it? We cannot afford to be foolish virgins or spectators. We must have oil in our vessels.

THE FULLNESS OF THE HOLY SPIRIT

A young man asked me, "I want to have the fullness of the Holy Spirit. How can I have it?"

Let me tell you his story.

I was in one of our Adventist churches here in the U.S. providing a series of meetings. As I was waiting in the church office, the pastor burst in with tears in his eyes and asked, "Would you please pray for my nephew, Daniel?" His nephew was this young man who would later ask me how to get the fullness of the Holy Spirit. We still had about thirty minutes before the morning service, so I asked him to tell me the story.

Daniel was raised in an Adventist Christian home during the time of the Soviet Union. When it fell apart, his family moved to a country in Western Europe. By then, Daniel was in his late 20's and spoke five languages fluently. He was active in the local SDA church, but for some reason he became interested and began to study about Buddhism. He found aspects of it attractive, and even visited a Buddhist temple. During this visit, something unusual happened to him, he got a spirit, but not one anyone would want to have. After that experience, his father noticed something about him had changed.

Shortly after the visit to the Buddhist temple, Daniel had been at home alone one day. He was standing on the balcony of their second floor apartment. As he looked down, suddenly there was a strong push from behind him. He flew off of the balcony and landed on the ground. He couldn't move, and immediately realized, he was paralyzed. At the hospital, x-rays and scans confirmed that there was a break in his spine. Curiously, the doctors were convinced from the findings, that his spine wasn't broken from the fall. They told the family that the break was consistent with a very hard push from behind. Remember, there was no one at home with him.

These evil spirits are real things, my friends. And if you are walking with Christ, you need not even to fear them, but anything you do that invites them in will be used as a channel into your mind. It is dangerous to experiment.

The pastor went on to tell me that his nephew was now paralyzed from the waist down. He had been lying in bed for almost six months. He had deep sores on his back. His eyes were infected and draining, and he could not tolerate the light. He had to be in a dark room. He was hearing demonic voices and seeing visions of ugly creeping creatures dragging him from his bed into a dark pit and calling Satan their daddy. This young man was cursing God and cursing his parents.

Again, the pastor asked if I would pray for him. We called his father, who was this pastor's brother. The father put the phone on speaker and for 10 minutes I presented to Daniel Jesus Christ crucified. His family was also with him, so I prayed for him and the whole family.

After we had finished praying, Daniel asked if he could call me from time to time. We began a spiritual journey together over the phone, between Europe and the U.S. Every Friday, I studied with him and his family, and in time, the group began to grow. For over three years we did not miss one Friday. Even when I was traveling, being at airports around the US, I would find a quiet place and present another study. The relatives began to join. The focus of every study from the scriptures was the character of God. We used stories from the Bible and the encounters of Jesus, to unfold the Gospel which is the revelation of God's Character. The more we studied, the more his faith grew.

One day, I asked his father if he would consider calling the pastor and elders to come and anoint his son. It was during the COVID lockdowns and the father told me that pastors were forbidden to visit their parishioners. Rather than allow governmental regulations interfere with spiritual ministry, I said to him, "You told me you are the elder of the church." He said, "Yes, I am." I told him, "I am also an elder, so let's do it long distance over the phone."

Daniel agreed, so we studied the fifth chapter of James over the phone. The healing described in that chapter suggests that physical healing is the result of spiritual healing. Jesus's method was to address the spiritual need for healing first, and the physical followed.

After the study we prayed and I asked his father to anoint his son, which he did. Then I asked him to anoint every window and door in the apartment, which he did also. We declared it to be the safest place in the entire town.

Two days later, the nurse came to change the bandages covering the deep sores on his back. As the nurse turned him over and took off the old bandages, she was shocked. The sores were healed. We attributed it to the spiritual restoration that was taking place.

We continued with the studies. Daniel was still hearing some demonic voices and seeing demonic visions. This continued for some time even while he was coming back to God. I told him it would go away and that as he came into the fullness of the light, the darkness would disappear. Do not be afraid of the Light! As we continued studying, the darkness did leave him. The voices and the visions were gone. Why? Darkness cannot exist in the presence of the Light.

Today, although he is still paralyzed, Daniel is in ministry. He is ministering to people who are going through trials in their lives. He is doing this for people around the world in five languages. He preaches in his local church and is helping people in many different ways. He is part of the online church that was formed because of Pastor Bill Liversidge's book, *Victory in Jesus.*

When *Victory in Jesus* was translated into the Russian language it spread like wildfire. It has been reprinted a number of times and does not stay on the shelf. As a result, a group of people began to study the principles presented in these books and the benefits of the death and cross of Jesus. It gripped them. They organized a group, and it began to grow. Since this was during the pandemic, this was an online church, and Daniel and his family became active within this church. He is also translating Christian literature into different languages.

Today, this online church is reaching 12 countries with over 2,300 members. We did an evangelistic series online through YouTube and Telegram for this church. We had thousands of people attending. Another church of 1,300 grew out of this. The people don't just meet on Sabbath. They meet twice every day and have a 24/7 prayer line.

Returning to Daniel's question, "How can I have the fullness of the Holy Spirit?" I asked him to turn in his Bible to John 15:26-27.

> Jesus said, "But when the Helper comes, whom I shall send to you from the Father, the Spirit of truth who proceeds from the Father, He will testify about Me. And you also shall bear witness, because you have been with Me from the beginning." (John 15:26, 27; *cf.* Acts 1:8)

Are you hearing this? The availability of the Holy Spirit is in direct proportion to our willingness to witness about Jesus Christ. Seeking for the fullness of the Holy Spirit is seeking to witness about Jesus and being used in Christ's service. If the Holy Spirit is going to witness through me about God, then I must know God. Then the questions arise, "What is my concept of God? What kind of God do I believe in? What is my picture of God?" That is why it was necessary for Daniel to study and understand the undistorted picture of God which is the Gospel in its simplicity.

Continuing in John chapter 16:

> "They will put you out of the synagogues; yes, the time is coming that whosoever kills you will think that he offers God service." (John 16:2)

People can kill others thinking they are doing a service for God. Something went wrong in their concept of God. Why do you think there are so many people in the world that don't like God? Is it possible that we might have people in churches that have a distorted picture of God? That applies to all Christian churches, including our own. Because we are losing up to 85% of our young people to the world, this is a legitimate question to ask.

I was raised an atheist and I became a Seventh-day Adventist Christian in the United States through a study of the Word, and I could not argue with the doctrines. They are all Biblical, so I joined the church. After some years, doubts crept in. I began to ask myself, "Am I good enough? Will I make it to heaven? Why am I falling into the same sin over and over again? Is victory possible for the Christian?" I almost left the church, but God in His mercy brought me to a Victory in Jesus seminar that Pastor Bill Liversidge was presenting. It was here that the Gospel and the doctrines came together in such a way that rather than leave the church, I ended up in ministry.

Now I understand both groups, those who have left the church, and those who are still in the church but are struggling and unhappy. The reason is the same for both groups, the absence of the Gospel! We are robbing our youth of the Gospel. They do not hear it and they do not experience the Power of it. Now, what is the Gospel? It is *"the power of God unto salvation for everyone who believes...."* (Romans 1:16) Friends, the Gospel is the manifestation of the *power* of God—delivering sinners from their sins and planting in them God's righteousness. There is nothing at all wrong with doctrines in our church, they are Biblical. But they need to be presented Christ centered. And because we were described as "dry as hills of Gilboa" the fullness of the Gospel was given to us. And God is waiting for us to take hold of it—for it is the Power of God.

Pastor Liversidge presents this practical Gospel message with simplicity and clarity in his book, *Victory in Jesus.* Through this Good News Gospel message, the Holy Spirit has moved upon the hearts of prodigals who have been enslaved by the enemy in all sorts of vice to draw them back to the Lord. It speaks to our youth in the church and to those who are spiritually dead. You must have this book for yourself, and for the sake of your children who are prodigals, and those who are lost in their home church. This book brought revival to many in our church and brought many prodigals back to God's fold. A number of prodigals who read *Victory in Jesus* went into ministry.

The book, *Victory in Jesus,* was originally focused on Seventh-day Adventist believers who failed to experience the power that is in the Gospel.

It was later edited, and a second edition under the title *Overcoming Through Jesus,* was printed. This edition can be shared with people of all faiths and non-believers.

Both versions are available on our website at www.CreativeMediaMinistries.org.

Let us now move from the prodigal Daniel to the topic of our study, Jesus' parable of the prodigal son.

THE PRODIGAL SON

Please open your Bibles to Luke 15, where we find three parables. The third parable is the story of the lost son whom we most often refer to as the prodigal. You know the parable. In this story we are going to discover the undistorted picture of God—which is the Gospel, Good News for everyone. You will be drawn closer to God, whether you are a prodigal or whether you are lost in your Father's home.

> "Then He said: "A certain man had two sons. And the younger of them said to his father, 'Father, give me the portion of goods that falls to me.' So he divided to them his livelihood. And not

many days after, the younger son gathered all together, journeyed to a far country, and there wasted his possessions with prodigal living." (Luke 15:11-13)

This parable is the tale of a father and his two sons. The passage immediately draws our attention to the younger of the two sons. What comes to your mind when you think of a younger son? The word the "younger" suggests that he did not have as much of experience with the father as the older son.

Let's give a definition to the prodigal. It is the one who, in spite of experiencing the father's love allowed the tempter to take him captive.

How can this happen? Here are at least two answers:

1. Misunderstanding of the Father's character.
2. Determination to follow the dictates of his own inclinations.

These two will do it. I pray that the character of God will come out for you in this parable in crystal clarity, so that you will have a closer relationship with Him and this will not allow the tempter to take you captive.

The younger son said to his father, *'Father, give me the portion of goods that falls to me.'* What do we hear in his words? He feels no obligation to the father. He has no respect or gratitude for the father, but still claims the share of his father's possessions.

He is not thinking of the future, but only present time pleasure.

In Jewish society you cannot get inheritance while the father is alive. The father was not dead, nor was he dying. But he asks the father for his death benefits, which, in this situation, would be one-third of his father's estate. A double portion of the estate would go to the older son, as was the custom then. The father was under no obligation to give anything to his son at this time. How this must have pained the father's heart. What the son was saying to his father is, "I want your money more than I want you. I wish you were dead." What must he have thought of his father that would cause him to disrespect him this way? I pray this is speaking to you and that the character of our heavenly Father will come out in crystal clarity, that you might have a closer walk with God, and that you will not allow the tempter to take you captive.

In the next verse (13) we find the three missteps of the prodigal:

1. He gathered everything together,
2. He went to a far country, and
3. He squandered it all.

My friends, this is relevant today to so many life stories. Perhaps you have experienced this, or your children have done something similar. This is the way of the sinner. When a person is selfishly controlled by the sinful desire to indulge in pleasure without control, he separates himself from God.

The scripture says, "He went to a far country." He went far away from the father and his principles. Nowadays that would be like running to Las Vegas. As sinners, we want to get as far away from God and His principles as we can. By the way, do you think he had some fun? Of course he did. He had a lot of money and no one to control him. How long did he have fun? That depends on how much money he had and how fast he was spending it. But it didn't last, and that was the end of his fun.

> "But when he had spent all, there arose a severe famine in that land, and he began to be in want. Then he went and joined himself to a citizen of that country, and he sent him into his fields to feed swine. And he would gladly have filled his stomach with the pods that the swine ate, and no one gave him anything." (Luke 15:14-16)

I would call this double trouble. He ran out of money, and inflation hit the country. He joined himself to a citizen of the country who sent him into the field to feed his swine. A Jewish boy feeding swine! He was so desperate he would gladly fill his stomach with swine's food, but even that was not given to him. And for a young Jewish man, could you fall any lower than that? He had hit rock bottom.

> "But when he came to himself, he said, 'How many of my father's hired servants have bread enough and to spare, and I perish with hunger! 'I will arise and go to my father, and will say to him, "Father, I have sinned against heaven and before you, and I am no longer worthy to be called your son. Make me like one of your hired servants."' (Luke 15:17-19)

He finally acknowledged the reality about his father that was always there. The Father had not changed.

A few points are emerging in this story.

POINT NUMBER ONE – HE CAME TO HIS SENSES

What causes a person to come to his senses?

- A trial brought him to his senses.
- He hit the bottom.
- He was in need, and others did not understand his need and were indifferent. They didn't sympathize with him.

- Loss of wrong friends.
- He was in a far land.
- Memory of the father's home, how good he had it at father's home. The Bible tells us that it is "the goodness of God" that leads sinners to repentance. (Romans 2:4)

What do you think the father was doing all the while his son was gone? He was praying.

What was he praying for? He was praying for the son to come back.

What was it that would bring the son back? The trials.

Didn't we just read in Romans 2, that it was the goodness of God that would bring him back? True, but let's think this through. Sometimes genuine love is tough. We call it "tough love." We can come to a logical and radical conclusion here, that the father most likely was praying for the trials in his son's life. This wise Father knew that while the son had money, he did not even remember his father. The father loved his son and was not happy that his son would have to suffer in order to come to his senses. It is sad that so many must learn these lessons the hard way, but that is better than never coming to an understanding that their Father truly loves them. How does this speak to you, dear parents? Perhaps we need to pray a little wiser. Maybe we need to pray radical prayers that our children will experience all or some of these difficult circumstances, that they will lose their wrong friends and remember how good they had it back home where they were loved.

> "But when he came to himself, he said 'How many of my father's hired servants have bread enough and to spare, and I perish with hunger! I will arise and go to my father, and will say to him, 'Father, I have sinned against heaven and before you, and I am no longer worthy to be called your son. Make me like one of your hired servants.' And he arose and came to his father. But when he was still a great way off, his father saw him and had compassion, and ran and fell on his neck and kissed him. And the son said to him, 'Father, I have sinned against heaven and in your sight, and am no longer worthy to be called your son.'" (Luke 15:17-21)

The son decided to return home and tell his father that he is no longer worthy to be called his son; rather, he should just treat him as a hired servant.

The son has lost his identity. He did not know or understand his father. He wanted to go back to his father's home, where he was raised and loved, and ask to be treated as a servant. He failed to realize that his wise, loving, generous, compassionate, and forgiving Father would never demand the eternal groveling required for his son to become a slave just to survive.

I want to suggest to you, that he was lost in his own house before he left the house. With pain in his heart, the father had let him go. The son never understood the character of his father, who, in this story, represents God and His character. So it is with many Christians today. And God's character is good news—very good news!

Let's see what we can discover about the character of the father from these next verses.

> "And he arose, and came to his father. But when he was still a great way off, his father saw him and had compassion, and ran and fell on his neck and kissed him. And the son said to him, 'Father, I have sinned against heaven and in your sight, and am no longer worthy to be called thy son.' But the father said to his servants, 'Bring out the best robe and put it on him, and put a ring on his hand and sandals on his feet. And bring the fatted calf here and kill it, and let us eat and be merry; for this my son was dead and is alive again; he was lost and is found.' And they began to be merry." (Luke 15:20-24)

Look at the actions of the father that portrays his character! The passage says, "When he was still a long way off, his father saw him."

- The father saw him. The word "saw" is a verb. It is an action word.
- The father had compassion on him.
- The father ran.
- The father fell on his neck.
- The father kissed him.
- The father ordered the best robe to be put on him, the ring and the sandals.
- The father ordered a celebration for the return of the prodigal son, the son who did not want his father in his life.

These are the actions of the father. Underline them in your Bibles. These actions are the portrayal of the character of our Heavenly Father. Jesus through this parable is revealing the character of our Father. That is why Jesus came to this earth, because the character of God was distorted by the serpent in the Garden of Eden.

Now the son says to his father, *"I have sinned against heaven and in your sight. I am no longer worthy to be called your son."* How does the father respond? First of all, the father ignores this because it simply is not true. There is nothing the son can do to change the fact that he is the son of his father.

Again, the father takes action. He tells his servants to bring out the best robe and put it on him, and to put a ring on his finger, and sandals on his feet. He tells them to bring the fatted calf and kill it, so that they can eat and have a celebration. He declares that his son was dead and is alive again. He was lost, and now he is found. And what a celebration it was!

Thinking back to the time when the son left the home, what do you think the household went through? What was your family going through when your children have left God and the church and are out in the world? Are you mourning and grieving, having pain for loss? Are you ashamed? God knows what you are going through, dear friends. Before this crisis hit you, God already had a plan and a solution for your crisis. There are Biblical principles to reclaim your loved ones back that will be presented in the second part of this book.

The scripture says that the father *ran*.

POINT NUMBER TWO – THE FATHER RUNS!

Authorities do not run in Jewish society. They walk with dignity. In this case, we see the father abandon his dignity. He acts recklessly and scandalously generous towards his prodigal. Why do you think the father ran? The father knew the regulation in Deuteronomy:

> "If a man has a stubborn and rebellious son who will not obey the voice of his father or the voice of his mother, and who, when they have chastened him, will not heed them, then his father and his mother shall take hold of him and bring him out to the elders of his city, to the gate of his city. And they shall say to the elders of his city, 'This son of ours is stubborn and rebellious; he will not obey our voice; he is a glutton and a drunkard.' Then all the men of his city shall stone him to death with stones; so you shall put away the evil from among you, and all Israel shall hear and fear." (Deuteronomy 21:18-21)

Jewish law required that when a son rebelled against his parents, he was to be stoned to death by the community. Why do you think the father was running? *The father was running to protect the son from the judgment required in the Scriptures!* Please hear this!

And so is God—He takes our judgment upon Himself. Dear prodigal, once you decide to return to God, He runs towards you. Do you know what else He does? He embraces you and kisses you. He rejoices in your return. Heaven is celebrating! If you've been given a distorted picture of God, I beg you, please give Him a chance to love you!

In what condition was this young man when he came home? When the young man returned home, he had come from working in a pigpen feeding dirty pigs. He hadn't had anything to eat. There weren't any nice hotels for him to stop at and clean up. He was dirty, stinky, hungry, and poor. That's what the sinner is, what sin has done to us. We are all in that condition. We are all destitute of the righteousness of God. Please notice what the father does.

POINT NUMBER THREE – THE FATHER KISSED THE DIRTY STINKY SON!

What a God we have! The moment the prodigal turns his face and heart toward God, God is ready to embrace him. No matter how we look, no matter what bad choices we have made in the past, it doesn't matter how dirty we are. God doesn't ask us to go wash first before He will kiss us. Romans 5 tells us that while we were still helpless, ungodly, sinners and while we were still dirty, stinky enemies of God, He reconciled us to Himself through the death of His Son. Dear friends, that includes our young people, our prodigals, all of us. We must understand the character of God.

So the father commanded his servants to bring out the best robe and put it on the son. Why would he command that the best robe be put on his dirty, stinky son? He wants no one to mock his son for the condition that he was in. So it is with God. He accepts the sinner in this condition. He waits for us and asks us to come as we are. But He will never leave us the way He found us. Instead, He clothes us with the rich robe of Jesus' righteousness the moment we come to Him.

Some translations include the word "quickly". It happens quickly when you come to God. No probationary time is needed. You are declared righteous! And while you are in the process of growing, you are not under condemnation!

This reminds us of the message given through the sanctuary. When the Jews of the Exodus came out of Egypt the Bible says there were about 600,000 men alone. If you add women and children, it would be almost two million. Imagine how large an area you would need for two million campers. That is not a tiny crowd. That is why God, in the pillar of fire by night and the cloud by day, was leading them, and searching for the adequate place to camp His children.

Then the tabernacle was placed in the center of the camp. There were three tribes on each of the four sides. The nearest Israelite tent was about half a mile away from the tabernacle.

Let's say that I have done something wrong in my tent. What do I need to do? I would have to take a lamb and walk a half mile in open space to reach the sanctuary. What is everyone going to think about me? You would think that preacher has done something wrong, wouldn't you? And rightly so. But the moment I enter the doorway into the courtyard no one can see me. The walls of the sanctuary were over eight and one-half feet tall. They were made out of white linen, a symbol of the righteousness of Jesus. The moment a person came into the sanctuary (through the door, Jesus is the door…) no one can see that person. The only thing they could see is the white linen – the symbol of the Righteousness of Jesus. That person is hedged with the righteousness of Christ. What a beautiful message. The moment the prodigal comes to God, he is clothed with the rich robe of Jesus' righteousness. Are you a prodigal reading this? Would you like to come back? He is waiting for you with the rich robe of Jesus' righteousness to cover you with it.

To what status was he elevated? Servant /hired man, slave or sonship? He will be restored to the honor of sonship! And so it is with you dear prodigals. Your Heavenly Father is waiting for your home coming.

POINT NUMBER FOUR – YOU MAY COME TO GOD AS YOU ARE, BUT HE WILL NEVER LEAVE YOU THE WAY HE FOUND YOU

What else was given to the prodigal? The ring. The ring was a sign of authority.

Do you know that the moment you come to God, you are clothed with the rich robe of Jesus' righteousness, and authority is given to you to represent the Father! You are not in church just to enjoy the doctrines and the fullness of the truth. No, God has given us the authority and responsibility to represent Him in this world around us.

The prodigal was also given a pair of sandals. According to Ephesians 6:15, sandals are symbols of being ready to proclaim the Gospel, which is the undistorted character of the Father. "Go tell the world" about your Daddy. The servants in the home of the master did not wear sandals or any kind of footwear. Only members of the master's household were privileged to wear sandals.

Jesus says He does not call us servants, but friends, and He has sandals for every friend. Be ready to put them on, because every day that you go out of the house you're not meeting people on the streets by accident. If you take the time, you will find that those people are putting up a facade while going through deep trials. Begin to talk to them, and they will open up to you. They crave your prayers. Befriend them and give them Bible studies focusing on the character of their Heavenly Father.

Help them to see it, to discover it and to fall in love with the Lord. The rest of the doctrines will be received automatically. "Do not put the cart before the horse," as my dear friend Bill Liversidge often said.

Now, put yourself in the shoes of the prodigal. The gracious actions of the father revealed his true character. What effect would that have on the son who has now returned? Let's make a list of what the prodigal felt and realized and what was awakened in him:

- True repentance
- Unworthiness
- Surprised
- Genuine love for the father
- Peace
- Joy
- Desire to serve the father out of gratitude
- Right motive to serve the father
- Realized the grace of the father
- True obedience
- Relief
- Loyalty
- Faithfulness

My dear reader that is exactly what the Gospel does! Nothing else will produce these results. And the Gospel is the revelation of God's character. The Gospel is the "Power of God for salvation to everyone who believes…." (Romans 1:16) The Gospel is the manifestation of the power of God at work, delivering sinners from their sins and planting in them His own righteousness.

Most likely, because of his father's unconditional love and forgiveness, the son's guilt, shame, and regret gave way to tears of joy and acceptance, and trust was re-established. Now that he was reinstated as a son, and his love for the father was awakened, we can imagine that he had the desire to serve and obey his father out of gratitude, with the right motive. There was genuine repentance, and the authority that came with the ring his father gave him empowered him to prove himself worthy of that trust.

This is exactly what the Gospel of Jesus Christ does, my friends. Nothing else but the revelation of His character will produce this result! It is the goodness of God that leads sinners to repentance, which means a 180 degree turn.

God revealed the plan of salvation, the Gospel, through the sanctuary model, which teaches us how God saves mankind from sin. That was its purpose. That model was first given to the Israelites, but they became legalistic, exclusive and self-righteous which perverted the Gospel message of the sanctuary. They did not understand the Gospel in the Sanctuary and this led them into apostasy.

The early Christian church had the sanctuary message, the Gospel. But as the apostles died out, and the church fell into the hands of the church fathers who were Greek, they saw no value in it. The church went down, down into darkness. That's how the Dark Ages came about. The plan of salvation was darkened until the Reformation began restoring it, and the light began to rise up again.

In 1844, this very message of the Gospel in the sanctuary was restored by the understanding given to a group that later formed the Seventh-day Adventist church. Around that same time the enemy of souls inspired another teaching that was brought into Christianity, called dispensationalism. This theory taught that before the cross, you were saved by keeping the law and after Christ's death, you were saved by grace and that the law is no longer valid. In other words, you may now go kill, steal, fornicate, lie, worship idols, take God's name in vain, disrespect parents, and all this is now okay, and it will not affect your salvation. Isn't that ridiculous?

Over time, The Adventists strongly defended the importance of the law, and we became good at it! We took pride in proving the validity of all God's commandments from the Bible, but sadly, along the way we lost the Gospel emphasis. It is the devil's plan to keep Christians in one of the two ditches, cheap grace or legalism. The Lord in His great mercy began bringing us back into balance with the enhanced understanding of Christ our Righteousness that began to occur around 1888. During the years leading up to the General Conference held at Minneapolis the Lord sent warnings that we were over-emphasizing the importance of the law.

Jesus gave the commission to his disciples to "Go into all the world and preach the gospel to every creature" for a witness. (Mark 15:16) How does the Three Angels Message of Revelation 14 begin?

> "Then I saw another angel flying in the midst of heaven, having THE EVERLASTING GOSPEL to preach to those who dwell on the earth—to every nation, tribe, tongue, and people" (Revelation 14:6)

This is the main emphasis of the three angel's message. No one will fear/revere God without understanding His character which is the Gospel. That is why the Gospel must be understood and presented first to reveal the undistorted character of God, to undo the work of Satan. When the fullness of the Gospel, the beauty of the character of God was presented at the General Conference in 1888, Ellen White strongly supported it. In a letter written to General Conference President, O. A. Olsen from Australia in 1895, she made the following statement which was later published in the *Testimonies to Ministers* compilation:

> "The Lord in His great mercy sent a most precious message to His people through Elders Waggoner and Jones. This message was to bring more prominently before the world the uplifted Saviour, the sacrifice for the sins of the whole world. It presented justification through faith in the Surety; it invited the people to receive the righteousness of Christ, which is made manifest in obedience to all the commandments of "God. Many had lost sight of Jesus. They needed to have their eyes directed to His divine person, His merits, and His changeless love for the human family. All power is given into His hands, that He may dispense rich gifts unto men, imparting the priceless gift of His own righteousness to the helpless human agent. This is the message that God commanded to be given to the world. *It is the third angel's message, which is to be proclaimed with a loud voice, and attended with the outpouring of His Spirit in a large measure."* (10LtMs. Lt 57, 1895; *The Ellen G. White 1888 Materials,* p 1336.2; *Testimonies to Ministers,* p. 91, 92, emphasis added)

Later in the same letter, Mrs. White gave strong warning to the brethren:

> "I would speak in warning to those who have stood for years resisting light and cherishing the spirit of opposition. How long will you hate and despise the messengers of God's righteousness? God has given them His message. They bear the Word of the Lord. There is salvation for you, but only through the merits of Jesus Christ. The grace of the Holy Spirit has been offered you again and again. Light and power from on high has been shed abundantly in the midst of you. Here was evidence, that all might discern whom the Lord recognized as His servants. But there are those who despised the men and the message they bore. They have taunted them with being fanatics, extremists, and enthusiasts. Let me prophesy unto you: Unless you speedily humble your hearts before God, and confess your sins, which are many, you will, when it is too late, see that you have been fighting against God. Through the conviction of the Holy Spirit, no longer unto reformation and pardon, you will see that you have been fighting against God. Through the conviction of the Holy Spirit, no longer unto reformation and pardon, you will see that these men whom

> you have spoken against have been as signs in the world, as witnesses for God. Then you would give the whole world if you could redeem the past, and be just, zealous men, moved by the Spirit of God to lift your voice in solemn warning to the world; and like them, to be in principle firm as a rock. Your turning things upside down is known of the Lord. Go on a little longer as you have gone in rejection of the light from heaven, and you are lost. 'The man that shall be unclean, and shall not purify himself, that soul shall be cut off from among the congregation.'" [Numbers 19:20.] (*The Ellen G. White 1888 Materials,* p 1336-1343; *Testimonies to Ministers,* p. 92-97, emphasis added)

> "Several have written to me, inquiring if the message of justification by faith is the third angel's message, and I have answered, "It is the third angel's message, in verity." (*Advent Review and Sabbath Herald,* April 1, 1890; *Selected Messages,* Volume 1, p. 372.2).

> "The enemy of man and God is not willing that this truth should be clearly presented; for he knows that if the people receive it fully, his power will be broken. If he can control minds so that doubt and unbelief and darkness shall compose the experience of those who claim to be the children of God, he can overcome them with temptation." (*Advent Review and Sabbath Herald,* September 3, 1889, par.13)

> "I have had the question asked, 'What do you think of this light that these men are presenting?' Why, I have been presenting it to you for the last forty-five years—the matchless charms of Christ. This is what I have been trying to present before your minds. When Brother Waggoner brought out these ideas in Minneapolis, it was the first clear teaching on this subject from any human lips I had heard, excepting the conversations between myself and my husband. I have said to myself, It is because God has presented it to me in vision that I see it so clearly, and they cannot see it because they have never had it presented to them as I have. And when another presented it, every fiber of my heart said, Amen." (Ellen G. White, 6LtMs, Ms. 5, 1889, par 38)

I pray you know this part of our church history. If not I would strongly recommend that you read the books by Ron Duffield: *The Return of the Latter Rain and Wounded in the House of His Friends.* (Available from Amazon)

As I mentioned, Satan has two ditches for Christians: cheap grace and legalism, and he is happy to keep us in one of those two ditches. The harmony between the law and God's character revealed in the Gospel of Jesus Christ, which is "the power of God unto salvation," will keep you in balance on the straight and narrow road, away from those ditches.

Ellen White wrote extensively about the Most Precious Message of righteousness by faith. In fact, her writings on the subject are contained in four large volumes, which called *The 1888 Materials.* Over 137 years have passed since the 1888 General Conference in Minneapolis, and we are still on this sin-sick planet. The church acted as Israel of old at the border of the land which God had promised to give them. The Israelites did not believe in the power of God/the Gospel, to fulfill His promise. We as a church acted in the same way. We did not believe the Gospel. We did not take hold of the Power of God – the Gospel. Satan took advantage of this. Through his agencies he distorted the Gospel. And this resulted in the loss of the power of God. The false Gospel tightens the hands of the Holy Spirit. That is why we do not have the Latter Rain yet.

Today you can hear up to five different Gospels in Christian churches including the Adventist church, but there is only one True Gospel – The Everlasting Gospel that was first announced to Adam and Eve in Genesis 3:15, when God promised that the power of the serpent would be broken. And this true Gospel is the Power of God. The good news is, this Gospel will be restored and proclaimed, with or without us. And God gave us the privilege of restoring the Gospel.

When Jesus gave the "Great Commission" recorded in Matthew 28:18, He said that *"All authority has been given to Me in heaven and on earth...."* This established that He had the authority to give us that "ring" which was given to the prodigal, to represent Him and proclaim His Gospel to the entire world. By giving us the rich robe of His Righteousness, He provides for us to become fit representatives of the task of reflecting His undistorted character. Finally, He fits us with sandals so we are always ready to "go" proclaim the Gospel. He is anxiously waiting for us to take hold of the Power of God, so he can finish His work through these weak vessels and bring us into the Promised Land.

When the Israelites came to the borders of the Promised Land, they did not believe in the power of God to bring them in. Not accepting, embracing, and believing in the power of the Gospel is the same as what the Israelites of old did.

Friends, there is nothing wrong with our doctrines. They all are biblical. But if we are missing the Gospel, we are missing the power of God. Once we unite doctrines with the power of God, it makes every doctrine Christ-centered. Then we might have 100 baptisms where we have only 1 today. It will repeat the message of the three angels with the great power of the Revelation 18 angel that will enlighten the whole world with the glory of God.

Satan will take any advantage to distort the Gospel. Today we have many voices preaching many different Gospels. The Apostle Paul warned us of this. I was in a church when a man came up to me and asked if he could have lunch with me, and I agreed. He began telling me his story. He believed that the Gospel was the way the church supported his family and that is what kept them in the church. I said, "Friend, this is not the Gospel. It is the fruit of the Gospel." He was trying to prove to me that the social gospel is the Gospel. It isn't the Gospel. The Gospel is the power of God unto salvation, to everyone who believes.

I will repeat: Through his agents, Satan has distorted the Gospel, which has resulted in a loss of the power of God. The false gospel has tied the hands of the Holy Spirit, and that is why we still don't have the outpouring of the Holy Spirit in a large measure. But the true undistorted Gospel will be proclaimed, and I want to be part of it. What about you?

God gave us this privilege. He has given us the robe of Jesus' righteousness. He has given us the authority to represent him. He is giving us the readiness, and He is waiting for us to take hold of the power of God, the Gospel, so He can finish His work through these weak vessels and bring us into the Promised Land.

THE OLDER SON

Now let us turn our attention to the older son.

> "Now his older son was in the field. And as he came and drew near to the house, he heard music and dancing. So he called one of the servants and asked what these things meant. And he said to him, 'Your brother has come, and because he has received him safe and sound, your father has killed the fatted calf.' But he was angry and would not go in. Therefore his father came out and pleaded with him. So he answered and said to his father, 'Lo, these many years I have been serving you; I never transgressed your commandment at any time; and yet you never gave me a young goat, that I might make merry with my friends. But as soon as this son of yours came, who has devoured your livelihood with harlots, you killed the fatted calf for him.' And he said to him, 'Son, you are always with me, and all that I have is yours. It was right that we should make merry and be glad, for your brother was dead and is alive again, and was lost and is found.'" (Luke 15:25-32)

Why was the older brother angry and would not go in to celebrate? What is the underlying diagnosis of him? He did not care for his younger brother, did not have love for him, and he did not share in his father's pain for him. That is why he did not want to share in joy of his father. He did not want to welcome the lost! This "older brother syndrome" still exists in the church today. The older brother did not leave his father's house, as did the prodigal. In the scripture he refers to himself as a servant, and a servant expects and works for a reward. The father never treated either son as servants. As sons, each was entitled to the rich robe and the father's authority and sandals. Yet, the older son's comment suggests that he was acting like a son not out of love for the father and the family, but because he wanted what he hoped would be his reward.

As the prodigal brother came and the father received him, showering him with many gifts, wouldn't you suppose that the older brother feels he's been wronged?

In reality he is simply stating that if he were in his father's place, he wouldn't do it! He doesn't acknowledge his brother. "This son of yours" he said to his father.

The father replies:

> "Son, you are always with me, and all that I have is yours." (Luke 15:31) (cf. verse 12, the father "divided his wealth between them")

POINT NUMBER FIVE – ALL THAT IS MINE IS YOURS

I wish every Christian would hear and learn this. So many Christians are trying to earn and deserve the favor of God, and the gift from God. They don't realize that all that is the Father's is ours, and all includes everything! We are co-heirs with Christ. All that is His is ours. That includes His righteousness.

> "He that spared not his own Son, but delivered him up for us all, how shall he not with him also freely give us all things?" (Romans 8:32)

That "all" must mean *all*, which includes His Righteousness.

We must believe our Father's love and accept the gift. Salvation is a gift. You don't have to earn it. Honestly, you cannot earn it.

Let me share with you a radical Biblical statement that I heard from Pastor Bill Liversidge at one of his seminars: "Christianity is the only religion where you begin with perfection!" Any other way is paganism. Because other ways crept into Christian church from pagan religions; trying to be good to appease God, to deserve something from God, not realizing that while we (human race) were helpless, ungodly, sinners, even the enemies of God, He reconciled us to Himself through the death of His Son. (Romans 5:6-10)

The Scripture to back up that radical Biblical statement given by Bill Liversidge: *"For by one offering He has perfected forever [for all time] those who are being sanctified."* (Hebrews: 10:14) (Read also 1 Corinthians 1:30, followed by Colossians 2:10 so it will settle this in your mind.)

That one offering refers to the Cross of Jesus. Through the death of Jesus, God declared you righteous and He has perfected you forever while you are being sanctified. He is making you now into what He declared you to be. We cannot be saved without righteousness. We must have it to enter the courts of heaven, but we have none of our own. The Bible says our righteousness is like filthy garments. We are destitute of it, so God has imputed it to us, and is now imparting it to us. Both imputed and imparted righteousness is the righteousness of God. It is not you that produces righteousness. And the only way to have the Righteousness of God is by not resisting it. Receive it by Faith. Salvation is both an accomplished fact and an ongoing process. Both are gifts, let us not resist this precious gift that cost God so much to give it to us. .

"For God so loved the world" (human race, that means YOU dear reader, if you belong to human race),

"that He gave His only begotten Son, that whoever believes in Him" (that God was so generous to you)

"shall not perish, but have eternal everlasting life" (John 3:16). God emptied His treasury just for you!

Did the younger son earn the share of his father's estate? No. He received it by claiming it. What about the older brother, who was a son also? He reminded the Father that he stayed and worked, he was thinking and acting like a hireling. And what are those that are hired work for? Wages! Hirelings are not sons. They work for the reward. And I will repeat, this is while he had a rich robe, authority and sandals. He was trying to earn what was already his.

In the time of Jesus, this parable was told with a different ending that went like this:

The son came to his father and said, "Father, I wish you were dead. Give me the money. I want your money more than you."

The father sold the portion of the property and gave him the money. The son left and squandered it all and came back poor, sick, stinky, and dirty. He knocked on the father's door, and the father opened the door, he scanned his son from head to toe and said, "Son, you wished me to be dead? I am dead for you. Goodbye."

That was the end of story. That is how the understanding of the character of God had been distorted in the time of Jesus.

The question you must ask yourself, my Dear Reader, is: What is your picture of God? I can assure you that if you read this book to the end, it will reveal to you the beauty of His character, and you will not be able to resist falling deeply in love with God.

Jesus changed the end of this story to restore the picture of God, because He came to reveal His Father and His character, which is the Gospel. Do you like how Jesus changed the ending of the story? I am sure you do.

When He did that, what do you think the Pharisees felt? They were stirred up to jealousy. And so it is with self-righteous Christians today who think they can earn their reward from God. They are jealous when grace is given to the sinner. They become cold-hearted to the lost. They are critical toward the brethren, and an unforgiving spirit is exhibited. In this they misrepresent the Father. When a Christian exhibits this spirit, where does he place himself? He places himself in the place of a hireling, not the position of a son.

The scripture says that when the son heard the celebration, he was not willing to go in. So the Father comes to him and begins pleading with him.

Why? The Father wants to bring the older to the party. He wanted him to be a part of the celebration.

Why? The Father loved both sons. God loves both the younger prodigal and the older self-righteous sons. He wants both sons who were both lost in the Father's house, to discover the character of the Father, which is the Good News, which is the Gospel, the Power of God unto salvation to all who believe.

In both cases, the lost-ness occurred in the father's home. This is a parallel to the church today. We are losing over 85% of our young people to the world...I believe the solution to stop this trend is the Gospel — the revelation of the character of God. We will address reclaiming the lost in the second part of this book.

CONCLUSION

It is essential that we all understand the true character of God, otherwise we risk becoming lost in our Father's house which is the church, or we become prodigals and leave the church. Jesus summarized it:

"...he who has seen Me, has seen the Father." (John 14:9)
"I and My Father are one." (John 10:30)

Before Jesus went to the cross, He prayed to His Father in the presence of disciples saying,

"That the world may know that You have sent Me, and have loved them as You have loved Me." (John 17:23)

I would paraphrase it this way: "God the Father loves you no less than He loves His son Jesus Christ." Please hear it. And in John 15:9 Jesus said:

"As the Father loved Me, I also so have I loved you; abide in My love...."

Here you have it: God the Father loves you infinitely, and God the Son loves you infinitely. Then Jesus went to the cross and signed with His own blood what He said.

As He is hanging on a cross, Jesus was tempted three times: "If you are the Son of God, come down and save yourself." Could He have done it? Yes, He could. But could He, by coming down from the cross and saving Himself, save us also at the same time? The answer is "NO." (See Hebrews 9:22) He had to make a choice, and the choice that He made should speak loudly to every human being today. He never spoke these words, but His actions speak to you right now louder than any words saying, "I can come down and save myself, but I cannot same you and Me at the same time. So I choose to stay on the cross because I love you more than I love Myself." And then He died. For you!

What are you going to do with this Jesus? Even if you choose to reject His gift, it does not change the fact that He loves you and died for you. What is your response to Him?

This is your God, my friends. This is my God. This is the God we serve! And the Lord God, says:

"...You are Mine...." (Isaiah 43:1)
"...I have inscribed you on the palms of My hands...." (Isaiah 49:16)

And the Father says "all that is Mine is yours." That "all" means *all*. It includes His righteousness, both imputed and imparted to us. You see, imputed righteousness is justification. He justified or declared us righteous through the death of His Son. We can be confident that *"He who began a good work in you is faithful to complete it."* (Philippians 1:6) That means the imparted righteousness which is called sanctification, is His work also. *"I am the Lord who sanctifies you."* (Leviticus 20:8)

Let's read the statement below:

> "This robe, woven in the loom of heaven, has in it not one thread of human devising. Christ in His humanity wrought out a perfect character, and this character He offers to impart to us. 'All our righteousnesses [sic] are as filthy rags.' Isaiah 64:6. Everything that we of ourselves can do is defiled by sin. But...by His perfect obedience He has made it possible for every human being to obey God's commandments. When we submit ourselves to Christ the heart is united with His heart, the will is merged in His will, the mind becomes one with His mind, the thoughts are brought into captivity to Him; we live His life. This is what it means to be clothed with the garment of His righteousness. Then as the Lord looks upon us He sees, not the fig-leaf garment, not the nakedness and deformity of sin, but His own robe of righteousness, which is perfect obedience to the law of Jehovah." (*Christ's Object Lessons*, pp. 311-312)

Sanctification does not come about by human effort. It all comes through Christ's effort within those who allow Him to take control of their lives.

> "As in humility they submitted to the molding influence of the Holy Spirit, they received the fullness of the Godhead and were fashioned in the likeness of the Divine." (*Acts of the Apostles,* p.s 49, 50)

In Revelation 3:20 Jesus said: "...I am standing at the door and knock.... whoever will open, I will come in."

In Ephesians 3:16-19 the Apostle Paul is saying:

> "That He would grant you, according to the riches of His glory, to be strengthened with might through His Spirit in the inner man, that Christ may dwell in your hearts through faith; that you, being rooted and grounded in love, may be able to comprehend with all the saints what is the width and length and depth and height— to know the love of Christ which passes knowledge; that you may be filled with all the fullness of God."

It is the function of the Holy Spirit to bring the life of Christ into the believer. And with Christ you have the fullness of God! (Colossians 1:19) What moves the Holy Spirit to bring the life of Jesus into you? It is the believer's gratitude to God for His unconditional love unveiled on the Cross. That is why it is so crucial to come to the foot of the Cross every day and to consider and appreciate the tragedy of God, how much it cost Him to save you. The gratitude for the precious sacrifice of God is the invitation and open door for the Holy Spirit to come into the heart of the believer, and "Christ in you" is not attracted to sin. *"Christ in you the hope of glory."* (Colossians 1:27) That is the way to victory. *"Put on the Lord Jesus Christ and you will not fulfill the desires of the flesh."* (Romans 13:14)

My friends, whether you are a prodigal hearing this Good News, or you are lost in the Father's house, or you are considering leaving God and His church, God is calling you by revealing His character.

He is anxious to see the prodigal come to his senses. The Father is ready to run towards you. He wants to embrace you and kiss you. He wants to cover you with rich robe of His Righteousness and give you the authority to represent Him. You can come to Him just as you are, but He will never leave you the way He found you. If you are deciding right now that you want to come back to God, or perhaps it's your first time, find us through our website contact, www.CreativeMediaMinistries.org, which is also on the inner cover of this book. We will send to you *Bible Study Guides in the Light of the Gospel* that will help you to fall in deeper love with God. We will help you to locate a local church that will be safe for you to return to, where you can enjoy your relationship with Jesus and His people. By God's grace you will find a loving church family.

CHAPTER 3

WHAT MOVES JESUS

Jesus has had several busy days. The end of the fourth chapter of Mark contains the story of Jesus calming the stormy sea with the words "Peace, be still." Those words of Jesus still have power to quiet the storms in our lives today.

Once safely across the lake at their destination in the Gerasenes, Jesus heals a demon-possessed man by casting out the many demons that possessed him. As Jesus was leaving, this freed man begs Jesus that he might be with Him but Jesus tells him, "...Go home to your friends, and tell them what great things the Lord has done for you, and how He has had compassion on you." The man became an evangelist to the entire area of Decapolis. Jesus again crosses to the other side of the lake and is met by a great crowd which included a synagogue official named Jairus.

> "Now when Jesus had crossed over again by boat to the other side, a great multitude gathered to Him; and He was by the sea. And behold, one of the rulers of the synagogue came, Jairus by name. And when he saw Him, he fell at His feet and begged Him earnestly, saying, 'My little daughter lies at the point of death. Come and lay Your hands on her, that she may be healed, and she will live.' So Jesus went with him, and a great multitude followed Him and thronged Him." (Mark 5:21-24)

A ruler of the synagogue named Jairus came to Jesus. In spite of at least two long busy days and two boat trips, Jesus is willing to help the distraught father and goes with him immediately. Tucked into this encounter with Jairus, is a "story within a story". I call it a bread with sweet stuffing. You're going to enjoy it because it's filled with something really sweet between the slices of bread. Probably you have previously looked at this story, but now we are going to dig a little deeper for those tasty, sweet gems.

Jairus was a ruler of the synagogue. In the Hebrew culture, names always had meanings. The name Jairus has two meanings, the first is "Jehovah Enlightens." This implies that there is an object that is darkened and in need of light. The other meaning of the name Jairus is "God's presence is my authority." Both meanings are applicable to the story. Jairus begs Jesus to come heal his little daughter, who is at the point of death. Specifically, he asked Jesus to come lay hands on his daughter, and she would be healed. So Jesus went with him, and a great multitude followed them.

Let us look in the context of the story and see what the ruler did that moved Jesus to go with him.

1. He fell at Jesus' feet.
2. He recognized Christ's authority and humbled himself.
3. He had faith that Jesus can do what he is asking.
4. He begged him and asked for help.

By falling at Christ's feet he publicly demonstrated his humility which is never easy especially for a person with authority. His humble prostration also revealed his helplessness and his faith that Jesus had power to do what he could not do, heal his daughter. All these moved Jesus to go with him.

Let's focus on Jairus' emotional state. What do you suppose this ruler may have been feeling? Here is a man who loved his daughter deeply, and she was lying at the point of death. He was no doubt having feelings of

1. Fear of losing his child.
2. Desperation at having nothing left to help.
3. Panicking at the thought of losing his daughter.
4. Helplessness.
5. Needy and vulnerable; his levels of anxiety and anguish must have been extreme.
6. A lot of emotional pain.
7. Yet he came with a measure of faith and hope that Jesus could help.

All of these things moved a compassionate Savior to go with him. And Jesus is the same yesterday, today, and forever. (Hebrews 13:8) So what moves Jesus to go with you? I hope you are hearing this. All these things are what moves Jesus to go with each one of us today.

Even though there might be a momentary interruption on the way to meeting our need, we can have faith that Jesus will come to attend to our needs.

> "Now a certain woman had a flow of blood for twelve years, and had suffered many things from many physicians. She had

> spent all that she had and was no better, but rather grew worse. When she heard about Jesus, she came behind Him in the crowd and touched His garment; For she said, 'If only I may touch His clothes, I shall be made well.'" (Mark 5:25-28)

On the way to the ruler's house, a woman that had been very ill for many years interrupted the procession. The woman touched Jesus' garment seeking healing, and He perceived that power had gone out from Him, and He looked around to see who had done this. In fear and trembling she confessed to Him, and He told her to go in peace because her faith had made her well. Interruptions are not something unusual in our lives, even in the life of the Christian. You may imagine the anxiety of the ruler of the synagogue, who would rather have Jesus to attend his need first and not have this woman to interrupt this procession. But Jesus's action is telling him, "but this is my daughter too".

> "While He was still speaking, some came from the ruler of the synagogue's house who said, 'Your daughter is dead. Why trouble the Teacher any further?' As soon as Jesus heard the word that was spoken, He said to the ruler of the synagogue, 'Do not be afraid; only believe.'" (Mark 5:35-36)

The child of the ruler of the synagogue had died while he was walking with Jesus.

Today your children may be at the point of death or already dead spiritually while you walk with Jesus. What two things did Jesus want this ruler of the synagogue to have?

1. Do not be afraid.
2. Only believe.

Jairus and Jesus did not get there in time before the worst had happened. Imagine the horror and grief this father felt upon hearing this. Perhaps your children have been lost to the world. You may be walking with Jesus, and your children may be spiritually dead. Maybe you've lost your business or your job. Your security appears to be suddenly pulled out from under you, and you fear for your future. Do you believe that Jesus would tell you the same thing today? "Do not be afraid, only believe?" Isn't Jesus the same yesterday, today, and forever? If you believe this, your heart can begin to rejoice day after day.

POINT NUMBER ONE – DO NOT BE AFRAID, ONLY BELIEVE!

What caused the ruler to be afraid? The worst had happened, his daughter was dead.

Did anything else cause him to be afraid? Yes, losing faith and forgetting that Jesus was still with him. This will always result in fear. Often, our faith goes out the door when we find ourselves in this position. When that happens, fear creeps in along with bitterness. The father may have thought, "If only that woman hadn't come along and interrupted us, this wouldn't have happened." He may have feared being looked down upon by his peers for publicly seeking Jesus for help. In this overwhelming moment, Jairus may have forgotten that Jesus was with him. But Jesus promises never to leave us or forsake us. Jesus is still with us! That's why He said, "Only believe."

How is your faith today? Have you had moments where you feel that Jesus has forsaken you? Sadly some people leave Jesus when the trial hits. I believe this poor parent now pressed even closer to the Savior. The Bible says that those who endure to the end will be saved. How easy it is for us to forget Jesus is with us in our trial. This reminds me of the disciples on the boat, desperately trying to save themselves when they forgot that Jesus was on the boat with them. But Jesus promises that He is with us to the very end.

He promises,

> "When you pass through the waters, I will be with you; And through the rivers, they will not overflow you. When you walk through the fire, you shall not be burned, nor shall the flame scorch you." (Isaiah 43:2)

What happened to the three Hebrew boys who were thrown into the fiery furnace? It cannot get any hotter. Who went into the furnace with them? Jesus was there with them, and He is the same yesterday, today, and forever.

> "Those who are living upon the earth when the intercession of Christ shall cease in the sanctuary above, are to stand in the sight of a Holy God without a mediator." (Ellen G. White, *The Great Controversy*, p. 425, emphasis added)

Based on this quotation, many Seventh-day Adventists say with fear "but we won't have an intercessor/mediator in the sanctuary at the end of time, how will we stand?" When the investigative judgment is finished and the cases of all have been decided, believers will no longer need Jesus as mediator because the sealing work of the Holy Spirit has taken place and they will have stopped sinning. Savior and mediator are two distinct functions of Jesus. We will never cease to have Him as our Savior, but after the sealing and probation has closed, mediation will no longer be necessary.

"The Holy Spirit is the breath of spiritual life in the soul. The impartation of the Spirit is the impartation of the life of Christ. It imbues the receiver with the attributes of Christ." It is the function of the Holy Spirit to impart the life of Christ into us. (Ellen G. White, *The Desire of Ages*, p. 805)

When Christ is in us, we will never have fear. We will be bold, just as Jesus was bold. We can have the fullness of God in us!

"That He would grant you, according to the riches of His glory, to be strengthened with might through His Spirit in the inner man, that Christ may dwell in your hearts through faith; that you, being rooted and grounded in love, may be able to comprehend with all the saints what is the width and length and depth and height—to know the love of Christ which passes knowledge; that you may be filled with all the fullness of God." (Ephesians 3:16-19)

ALL THE FULLNESS OF GOD is available to us according to Ephesians 3:19! Jesus said, *"Behold I stand at the door and knock, if any one hears My voice and opens the door I WILL COME IN.."* (Revelation 3:20)

"Then He took the twelve aside and said to them, "Behold, we are going up to Jerusalem, and all things that are written by the prophets concerning the Son of Man will be accomplished. For He will be delivered to the Gentiles and will be mocked and insulted and spit upon. They will scourge Him and kill Him. And the third day He will rise again." (Luke 18:31-33)

Persecution in Jerusalem never kept Jesus from going there. Persecution should never hold us back on our way to the New Jerusalem. Jesus said, "Fear not, only believe." Never give up. When you walk with Jesus, you have no reason to be in fear. He promises that He will be with us, even to the very end. We must believe His Word. "Believe in His Word and you will be established." (2 Chronicles 20:20) Jesus could have left Jairus, this ruler of the synagogue because he was afraid and possibly losing his faith, but He stayed right there with him. The same compassionate God will do the same for us.

"And He permitted no one to follow Him except Peter, James, and John the brother of James. Then He came to the house of the ruler of the synagogue, and saw a tumult and those who wept and wailed loudly. When He came in, He said to them, 'Why make this commotion and weep? The child is not dead, but sleeping.' And they laughed Him to scorn. But when He had put them all out, He took the father and the mother of the child, and those who were with Him, and entered where the child was lying. Then

> He took the child by the hand, and said to her, 'Talitha, cumi!' which is translated, 'Little girl, I say to you, arise!' Immediately the girl arose and walked, for she was twelve years of age. And they were overcome with great amazement. But He commanded them strictly that no one should know it, and said that something should be given her to eat." (Mark 5:37-43)

Upon entering the house and hearing a commotion and weeping, He said, "The child is not dead but is asleep." This is the same thing He said when His friend, Lazarus, had died. He said, "Lazarus is sleeping." Was he dead? Yes, he was. Jesus reluctantly uses the word "dead." Jesus is not the originator of death. He is the originator of life. Death is our enemy, and praise God, Jesus will destroy it. The people did not believe that He was the Son of God. They did not believe in Him and what He could do, so they laughed at Him and scorned Him. Then Jesus put them all out of the house, and took the father and mother of the child, the disciples and entered where she was lying. He took her by the hand and said to her, "Little girl, I say to you, get up."

Why do you suppose Jesus would put all of the others out of the house? Who were these people? They were the unbelievers, the neighbors, the family members, and friends who laughed Him to scorn. He put all of them out because unbelievers cannot see the kingdom of God and His glory. It was the believers and the needy ones that were in the room. Dear friend, are you a believer? Are you needy? If your answer is "yes, I believe," you will see the kingdom of God and His glory.

So Jesus says to the little girl, "Arise." How does this statement illustrate the mission of Jesus? It is symbolic of raising a church. In the Bible, a woman is a symbol of the church. Girl then, is a symbol of a young, pure church. The story of the woman with a hemorrhage of blood for twelve years represents Israel with its sacrificial system. Mark mentions in verse forty-two that the girl was twelve years old. That means that this little daughter of Jairus that Jesus raised up, came into existence at about the same time the woman with the flow of blood became ill. God always had in mind a pure church. The sacrificial system in Israel of the Old Testament could not help in any way unless they came by faith to the reality of that system—Jesus Christ, the Lamb of God. They must take hold of His righteousness and be healed from their impurities. Up until this time, Israel was trying to boast in their self-righteousness and exclusiveness, not fully comprehending the meaning of the sacrificial system which pointed to Jesus – the ultimate sacrifice. It was the girl, the pure woman, who died. Jesus stopped the flow of blood in the woman (Israel—God's church of that time) and raised a pure woman to life! And Jairus means Jehovah enlightens.

Let's summarize this before we taste the sweet stuffing in this slice of bread.

Jesus is healing a woman/church from the issue of blood, which symbolically points to the sacrificial system that the Jews perverted into self-righteousness. They had lost the true meaning. In a healthy woman the monthly cycle represents preparation for the possibility of nurturing a new life. When conception fails to occur, the woman's cycle loses the nutrient-rich blood. The woman with 12 years of dysfunctional bleeding that never supported life is a fitting symbol of the Jewish distortion of the sacrificial system. They had turned God's beautiful faith-based ritual pointing to our dependence on Christ's sacrificial death, into a self-centered mindless bloody ritual that could never support the "new creation" that is totally dependent on Jesus. He heals the woman, and He raises up a pure woman who has died. Jairus' daughter, at 12 years old, is just beginning to mature into a woman capable of supporting life, which is a fitting symbol of the new church Jesus will soon be raising up.

God speaks to us through the sequence of events, and sometimes repeatedly if we do not see or hear it. Let's go back and look closer at the interruption that took place in Jairus' story. In God's wisdom, He allows these interruptions, and we are to not question His delay in attending to our needs.

> "Now a certain woman had a flow of blood for twelve years, and had suffered many things from many physicians. She had spent all that she had and was no better, but rather grew worse. When she heard about Jesus, she came behind Him in the crowd and touched His garment; for she said, 'If only I may touch His clothes, I shall be made well.'" (Mark 5:25-28)

POINT NUMBER TWO – IF ONLY I COULD TOUCH HIS GARMENT, I WOULD BE MADE WELL

The woman could not easily approach Jesus because the crowd was pressing in on Him. Most likely, she was in despair at the sight of the crowd. Since she was unclean, she was required to stay away from others so as not to contaminate them. There may be obstacles in your life that cause you to despair and keep you from approaching Jesus. It may be some sin that causes you to feel shame and filthiness, and you fear it will be exposed. Maybe you have done something so offensive to God that you keep Him at a distance. Please hear these words of the great apostle Paul once again, from Romans, chapter five, that while we were HELPLESS, while we were UNGODLY, filthy SINNERS, while we were ENEMIES of God, He reconciled us to Himself through the death of His Son, Jesus Christ.

God does not wait for us to be clean, good, righteous, or even a friend of His before we can come to Him. God made His way to sinners! Whoever you are, or wherever you are in your walk with Jesus, don't hesitate to approach Jesus. Come to Him as you are in faith. Take hold of the garments of His righteousness.

Jesus made His way through the crowd through the obstacles, towards this desperate woman. If you are desperate, Jesus will make His way to you through your obstacles. He came near where she was. Dear Reader, He is near to you wherever you are as He availed Himself to her, He is availing Himself to you.

As He came close to her, she saw her opportunity to touch His garments, and she reached out her hand and made connection by faith with Jesus, in whom all the fullness dwells, and she received what she lacked. She was healed!

POINT NUMBER THREE – IMMEDIATELY SHE WAS HEALED OF THE AFFLICTION

When she took hold of His garments, immediately the flow of blood dried up, and she felt in her body that she was healed. (verse 29) Dear friend, what about you? Did you take hold of His garment of righteousness so that you might get well, or have you not come to the end of your own resources yet? Jesus not only makes Himself available to you to touch His garments, but He gives you His garments to wear as well. It brings healing from sin! They may be a bit large on you when you first put them on. But if you will put on His righteous garments every day, you will grow into them. Can you believe this?

> "And Jesus, immediately knowing in Himself that power had gone out of Him, turned around in the crowd and said, 'Who touched My clothes?'" (Mark 5:30)

How could Jesus know that someone had touched Him differently than the careless jostling from others in the crowd? It was because power went out of Him. He knows the touch of faith, because in His government faith is always automatically rewarded. Immediately the power goes out of Him. If you took hold of Christ's garments of righteousness by faith, how can you be assured that power has gone out of Him to you? Of the same thing Abraham was assured. In the book of Romans, Paul says:

> "And not being weak in faith, he did not consider his own body, already dead (since he was about a hundred years old), and the deadness of Sarah's womb. He did not waver at the promise of God through unbelief, but was strengthened in faith, giving glory

> to God, and being fully convinced that what He had promised He was also able to perform. And therefore *"it was accounted to him for righteousness…."* Therefore, having been justified by faith, we have peace with God through our Lord Jesus Christ." (Romans 4:19-22; 5:1)

If you are experiencing the peace with God, it means that you are fully convinced that what He has promised, He is able also to perform. Then, God will reckon that belief as righteousness. This results in emotional, spiritual, physical, and mental healing, that means power has gone out from Him to you.

If you are praying for loved ones to receive God's peace, you can be certain God wants to give that to them if they are willing to believe. Do not stop praying for them to come into belief.

That touch of faith was different from all other touch. It drew power from the source—Jesus Christ. That power was the power of His life, which supplies all the need. She received from Jesus what she did not have. And by what means did she receive the power of His life? By faith! Dear friend, that power is available to us today! My prayer is that every Christian would realize that all heaven is geared and anxious to release its power on our behalf. Consider the following quotations from Ellen G. White in support of this:

> "The inexhaustible supplies of Heaven are at their command… in their human weakness they are enabled to do the deeds of Omnipotence." (*Gospel Workers,* p. 112)

> "The power of God awaits their demand and reception." (*Testimonies to Ministers,* p. 175)

> "The Spirit awaits our demand and reception." (*Christ's Object Lessons,* p. 121)

> "The whole heavenly treasure awaits our demand and reception." (*Testimonies to Ministers,* p. 510)

Can it be that we do not have it because we do not ask? Asking is a sign of dependence on God. "Ask, and it shall be given to you", (Matthew 7:7), and Jesus said, "Greater things than I will you do." (John 14:12)

So, while we are praying for our loved ones, for prodigals, we are to pray with faith, believing we are touching the source of life. Jesus is waiting for the invitation to heal those who are spiritually dying, and raise up those who are spiritually dead.

"Saving faith is a transaction by which those who receive Christ join themselves in covenant relation with God. Genuine faith is life. A living faith means an increase of vigor, a confounding trust, by which the soul becomes a conquering power." (*The Desire of Ages*, p. 347)

When Jesus had spoken, His disciples said to Him, "Look at the crowd pressing around you. How can you ask, 'Who touched Me?'" Why does Jesus want to bring attention, to put the spotlight on this woman?

Jesus always has a purpose, and He wanted to put the spotlight on her, to comment on her faith, for others to see what faith can do. Jesus wanted to speak a word of encouragement to her. The faith she displayed and the comfort she received from His word, would bring joy and encouragement not only to her, but to believers down through time, and even to us today. Jesus wanted to demonstrate that this was not just the physical act of touching His garment, but rather her faith that took hold of Divine power, which brought healing. It served as a rebuke to the Jews of His time who were focused on rituals and missed the reality.

The woman in the Bible is a symbol for church. When we, the church will take hold of the righteousness of Jesus by faith, this will move Jesus. He will bring the spotlight on us, the believers, His church, and all in darkness will see the light and come to the light. This is what He is waiting for. Jesus wants His church to be a shining light reflecting His love for the entire world. If the church experiences His blessings and healing, but "hides this light under a bushel" she is not fulfilling her function. If that continues, she will become more dysfunctional, and the Gospel message will be distorted.

The woman fell down before Jesus in fear and trembling and told Him the whole truth. Why would she be afraid and trembling before Jesus when He had just healed and restored her? Shouldn't she be jumping for joy?

In the Jewish culture, a woman with an issue of blood was considered unclean. An unclean person was not allowed to touch anyone or anything; otherwise, the person or the object she touched was considered unclean. She could not come to the temple in this state. Jesus referred to Himself as the temple when He said, "Destroy this temple, and in three days I will raise it up." He was referring to His body. By touching Jesus, her uncleanness was transferred to Him. You can understand why she was in fear and trembling. But Jesus came to tabernacle with humanity. He came to the pit where the sinner is. She had made many attempts to get well. It was costly and bankrupted her. Jesus' healing did not cost her anything. And she had nothing to pay with. Now trembling, she realized that she was cleansed of this infirmity, and her uncleanliness was transferred to Jesus, and that will cost Him so much.

Most of the time when we read the stories of Jesus' healings, it was Jesus touching the people. In this case, the woman touched Jesus' garments. This has deep meaning for the church today.

Once again, the woman is a symbol of the church. This woman recognized she was sick and needed healing. When the church is blind like Laodicea, she cannot recognize her need of healing, but Jesus advises her to obtain "eye salve", or spiritually enlightened sight, so she can realize her true condition. Once she does, the church as a body will recognize her need of the righteousness of Jesus, and she will reach out and take hold of His garments of righteousness. Instantly, virtue will go out of Jesus into the woman, and the church will be healed. Then God will put a spotlight on His church so that everyone that is in darkness may see it, and come to the light. Until we take hold of the righteousness of Jesus, we will not cross into the promised land.

There are fewer Christians in proportion to the world population today than there were one hundred years ago. I believe with all my heart that when we take hold of Christ's righteousness, we will see the work go as it did in the Apostles time, if not faster. In Colossians 1:23, Paul said that the Gospel *"...has been proclaimed to every creature under heaven."* That was approximately thirty years after Jesus' death and resurrection. The population of the then-known world was in the millions. Today there are more than eight billion people on our planet. I believe that once God's people take hold of Christ our Righteousness, the final work will go like wildfire even though God's people may not be many. I am excited about this message of Christ our Righteousness. We have no righteousness of our own, but He is making His righteousness available to us.

So the woman's uncleanness was transferred to Jesus,

> "And he looked around to see her who had done this thing. But the woman, fearing and trembling, knowing what had happened to her, came and fell down before Him and told Him the whole truth." (Mark 5:32, 33)

What was the whole truth? You will find it in verses 25-26 that have been quoted above.

POINT NUMBER FOUR – SHE CONFESSED THAT NOTHING HAD WORKED BEFORE

For twelve years she had tried everything. She spent every penny she had, and nothing worked. Spiritually speaking, the same thing is happening today. We have tried many different things that have crept into the church. Things like the "Social Gospel", "Love Reality" and the "One Project" and a number of others. Another group says the Holy Spirit is not a person. In the meantime we are holding on to legalism and Pharisaical spirit. We have tried the same things over and over and did not get better, but rather grew worse. I am saying this with pain in my heart and all the while we had the power of God—the Gospel, right in our hands. Don't buy into anything else. Those things have no power of God. Somehow we are resisting the Good News. Please take hold of the pure, unadulterated Gospel, Christ our Righteousness. Give it to our young people and we will stop losing them by the droves. Eighty-five percent of them left! If we had kept them in the church for the last forty-five years, we would have over ten million Seventh-day Adventists in the North American Division alone!

The woman confessed that nothing had worked. But when faith led her to take hold of Jesus' garments of righteousness, healing came immediately. This story is not recorded in the Bible by accident. Paul writes in the book of Romans,

> "For whatever things were written before were written for our learning, that we through the patience and comfort of the Scriptures might have hope." (Romans 15:4)

This story is for our learning and comfort. The touch of faith implies that a transaction is taking place. Jesus Christ came down to this earth and took humanity upon Himself and allowed Himself to be touched by sinners, by unclean people, in order that this transaction might take place in the life of the sinner. Nothing else will work.

> "And He said to her, 'Daughter, your faith has made you well. Go in peace, and be healed of your affliction.'" (Mark 5:34)

POINT NUMBER FIVE – BE HEALED OF YOUR AFFLICTION

What do you hear in these Words of Jesus? Jesus speaks as a Father to her: It was your faith that brought healing to you from Me. Nothing else brought healing to her—nothing at all. As for us as believers – nothing else will work! Jesus says: I am taking your uncleanness upon Myself. Now go in peace.

How can you make that personal to yourself? Jesus says to us, "Be healed of your affliction." His Word has creative power to accomplish what it says. Do you believe it? In the beginning God said, "Let the earth bring forth trees and grass. What happened? Immediately there were trees and grass upon the earth. His Word was sufficient to establish what it said. If the power in His word would be effective only for that moment of time, you would not see any beautiful trees and grass today. The Apostle Peter says, "But the Word of the Lord abides and endures forever." (1 Peter 1:25). It means that the power in God's Word abides and endures forever.

Even the Roman pagan centurion understood that when he said to Jesus, "Just say the word and my servant will be healed." (Luke 7:7, Matthew 8:8) The faith of centurion brought joy to Jesus. Let us also bring joy to our Lord by believing His Word. God's Word still has power today to do what it says, to recreate and restore us. In the Word of God there is power.

> "In every command and in every promise of the Word of God is the power, the very life of God, by which the command may be fulfilled and the promise realized." (*Christ's Object Lessons,* p. 38).

That power in the Word of God is the very life of God through which every command might be fulfilled, and every promise realized! Power and healing are in the Word! The Word is life-giving bread, and this bread contains a sweet stuffing or filling in every slice. That sweet stuffing (filling) is the Gospel, the power of God, the revelation of the character of God. It is GOOD NEWS to all.

Dear friend, unless we understand the Gospel, we will not experience the sweetness of God's Word (the Bread of Life) nor its power.

This beautiful message came to light in the Seventh-day Adventist Church when, in the fall of 1888, two men, E. J. Waggoner and A. T. Jones, who had been enlightened in their studies by the Holy Spirit, presented the message at the fall General Conference session. Ellen White was present at that session and so moved by it that she called it a "most precious message" that would enlighten the whole world with the glory of God, His character, as seen in Revelation 18:1. Later, she described it:

> The Lord in His great mercy sent a most precious message to His people through Elders Waggoner and Jones. This message was to bring more prominently before the world the uplifted Saviour, the sacrifice for the sins of the whole world. It presented justification through faith in the Surety; it invited the people to receive the righteousness of Christ, which is made manifest in obedience to all the commandments of God...This is the message that God commanded to be given to the world. It is the third angel's message, which is to be proclaimed with a loud voice, and attended with the outpouring of His Spirit in a large measure. (*Testimonies to Ministers and Gospel Workers,* p. 91-92)

It is important to recognize that the message of that time was pointing to the Righteousness of Jesus and His garments, not mine or yours. Nothing else will accomplish this.

Since then, over 137 years have passed. Have we experienced the Holy Spirit "in a large measure", (the Latter Rain) since that time? Is it possible that we, as a movement, acted like the Jews of old, when they came to the verge of the PROMISED land, and went back into the wilderness? They did not believe His Word, they did not believe in the power of God to bring them into the Promised Land. THEY DID NOT BELIEVE THE GOSPEL, THE POWER OF GOD – WE ACTED THE SAME WAY. That is why we are still here. We tried everything. We are like the woman in this story who (verse 26) *"had spent all that she had and was no better, but rather grew worse."* Again, we as a church have tried everything. You name it, we have tried it. Everything but the Gospel – the Power of God! Nothing has worked. And nothing else will work. The Lord is anxiously waiting for His people to take hold of His garments of Righteousness and count on His power.

> "... Had the purpose of God been carried out by His people in giving the message of mercy to the world, Christ would have come to the earth, and the saints would ere [before] this have received their welcome into the city of God. (*Union Conference Record (Australasian),* Oct. 15, 1898)

This means that the powerful Gospel message of Christ our righteousness entrusted to our church in 1888 had in it the power of God to finish the Gospel Commission by 1898!

> "Many who heard the first and second angels' messages thought they would live to see Christ coming in the clouds of heaven. Had all who claimed to believe the truth acted their part as wise virgins, the message would ere [before] this have been proclaimed to every nation, kindred, tongue, and people. But five were wise and five were foolish. The truth should have been proclaimed by the ten virgins, but only five had made the provision essential to join that company who walked in the light that had come to them. The third angel's message was needed. This proclamation was to be made. Many who went forth to meet the bridegroom under the messages of the first and second angels, refused the third angel's message, the last testing message to be given to the world." (Ellen G. White, *Letters and Manuscripts*—Volume 13 Ms 92a, 1898)

> "Several have written to me, inquiring if the message of justification by faith is the third angel's message, and I have answered, "It is the third angel's message, in verity." (*The Review and Herald,* April 1, 1890; *Selected Messages,* Volume 1, p. 372.2)

> A similar work will be accomplished when that other angel, represented in Revelation [18], gives his message. The first, second,

> and third angels' messages will be repeated. The call will be given to the church, "Come out of her, my people, that ye be not partakers of her sins, and that ye receive not of her plagues." (Ellen G. White, *Letters and Manuscripts*—Volume 13 Ms 92a, 1898)

Whether we are on board or not, this message of the righteousness of Jesus that we receive by faith will be proclaimed, and it will finish the work. When you begin to understand this message, you will be on fire. This message from God points to the righteousness of Jesus, not our righteousness, because we have none.

IN CONCLUSION

POINT NUMBER ONE – DO NOT FEAR, ONLY BELIEVE

If you are in fear today, remember the Words of Jesus in Matthew 28:20. *"I will never leave you, nor forsake you."* The Lord is still with you. He is always with you. "Always" means even up to now. If you are in fear of anything in your life, the Lord is with you. He is saying in His word 365 times "Fear not, do not be afraid" Why is it 365 times in the Bible? God doesn't want His people to be in fear even for one day, so He repeated it 365 times. If you want this kind of peace my friend, kneel right where you are, and ask Him to take away the fear. God doesn't want you to live in fear.

POINT NUMBER TWO – IF ONLY I COULD TOUCH HIS GARMENTS, I WILL BE MADE WELL

Jesus makes Himself available to you so that you may touch His garments and be healed from all impurity. He wants the transaction to take place in your life. *"God made Him who knew no sin to be sin for us that we might become the righteousness of God in Him."* (2 Corinthians 5:21) If you want to touch His garments of righteousness right now, Jesus is making Himself available to you. He welcomes you to touch His garments of righteousness right now.

POINT NUMBER THREE – IMMEDIATELY SHE WAS HEALED OF HER AFFLICTION

Have you touched Christ's garments of righteousness, or are you still depending on your own resources to get well? Nothing else has been working, and if you avoid that touch, nothing else will work. Only that touch of faith will bring the healing and the peace that you are seeking for. Jesus is waiting for us to reach out and to receive the transaction of power into our life that comes from Him, so that He can put the spotlight on us to be seen by a world in darkness, and they in turn also come to the light.

POINT NUMBER FOUR – SHE TOLD HIM THE WHOLE TRUTH

What was the whole truth? She confessed that nothing had worked before. None of her resources would do it. It was only that touch of faith in His garments of righteousness that brought her healing. We must admit this truth as well, if we want to be healed. Then we will experience genuine revival.

Through His sacrifice/death on the cross, He justified you – declared you righteous. Take it by faith. And now He is making you into what He declared you to be.

> "For by one offering He has perfected forever those who are being sanctified." (Hebrews 10:14)

> "But of Him you are in Christ Jesus, who became for us wisdom from God – and RIGHTEOUSNESS and SANCTIFICATION and REDEMPTION." (1 Corinthians 1:30, emphasis added)

He is our Righteousness and Sanctification. The work that He has begun in you HE is faithful to complete it. If this is your desire, dear friend, confess this to the Lord just now that nothing has worked, and by faith, touch the garment of righteousness of our loving Savior and be healed.

POINT NUMBER FIVE – GO IN PEACE AND BE HEALED OF YOUR AFFLICTION

The faith in Him will make it happen. Nothing else will work! He already took your uncleanness upon Himself. Be at peace. Jesus says to us, "Be healed of your affliction." His Word has power to accomplish what it says.

> "In every command and in every promise of the Word of God is the power, the very life of God, by which the command may be fulfilled and the promise realized." (*Christ's Object Lessons*, p. 38)

That power in the Word of God is the very life of God through which every command might be fulfilled, and every promise realized! Power and healing are in the Word! The Word is life-giving bread, and this bread contains a sweet stuffing (filling) in every slice. That sweet stuffing (filling) is the Gospel, the power of God, the revelation of the character of God. Feast yourself on His Word.

Loving Father,

I want to praise You and thank You for the beauty of Your Word and the power in Your Word that brings conviction to our hearts. Thank you for the precious Gift of Your Only Begotten Son that you did not spare. You emptied heaven for us wretched sinners. You expressed on the cross of

Jesus that You love us more than you love Yourself. We do not deserve any of this, yet You love us so much that You came down to the pits of hell that we are stuck in. You came to rescue us from this problem of sin. It is the enemy that has brought upon all of us our troubles and fear. We know that where You are, fear cannot exist. I claim Your promise for this dear Reader that is being convicted by Your Holy Spirit, that from this moment on and for the rest of his or her life, Jesus will live in his or her heart expelling all fear so it will never return. I pray give us all the faith to take hold of Your garments of righteousness, and for the anointing of the Holy Spirit upon us that will bring power of the very life of Jesus into us, and that we will not be attracted to sin. Give us victory in Jesus in every area of life where there is a need.

Father, we may have grown to a large body of believers in this world, but the world is growing at a faster pace than us. We understand that no matter what we try, just as with the woman with the issue of blood, we must confess this truth to You – nothing else will work. I pray on behalf of Your people that we will touch the garments of Jesus' Righteousness and put them on by faith every day until we have grown into them, and reflect Jesus fully so that the whole earth will be enlightened with Your glory. I ask that You will pour out Your Holy Spirit on us in abundance so that all who are in darkness will see the Light and come to it. We make ourselves available to You for that very purpose. Give us a continuous hunger and thirst to take hold of Christ's garments of Righteousness, by faith, believing that healing comes with them.

Thank you in advance for what You are about to do.

I pray in Jesus name. Amen!

CHAPTER 4

BE OF GOOD CHEER, YOUR SINS ARE FORGIVEN

Creative Media Ministries was founded by Pastor Bill Liversidge. Perhaps you've heard of him, or knew him and enjoyed him. I was privileged to be mentored by him. We spent a lot of time together, both in the United States and abroad. He trained groups of people to teach the Word and to preach the Word. We worked on a number of sermons together, to identify big points in passages of Scripture. This particular passage, Matthew 9 which we will discuss below, was developed at one of the seminars where he taught the class on preaching.

By the grace of God, doors opened for us to go to a number of different countries including the former Soviet Union, where he trained pastors from one of the SDA Church Unions. One of the countries that we visited was Armenia. This is the territory that I was born in. We had a series of meetings there, and when they were over, Pastor Bill wanted to visit Mount Ararat. Today Mount Ararat is in Turkey. The eastern part of modern Turkey is the ancestral homeland of the Armenians and was historically referred to as Western Armenia. It was renamed Eastern Anatolia by the Turkish government in the 1920s after the well-known genocide of Armenians in that region.

We came to the very border of Armenia at the foot of Mount Ararat. It is a very tall mountain, 5137 meters above sea level, (16,854 ft.). Half of it is covered with snow in the summertime. We entered a village. The road was just dirt, no pavement. There were homes on both sides of the road and in one of the backyards, we could see a family working in the garden. They saw us and motioned for us to come in. When we entered, they immediately set before us a table with fruits and drinks. After we partook of their hospitality they asked us who we were and where are we from? We told them we were missionaries to their country.

There was a young man there who had just come out of jail. His shirt was unbuttoned, and on his chest was a large tattoo of the cross. Did you know that Armenia is a Christian country? It was the first nation to adopt Christianity as its official state religion, 12 years before it was adopted by Rome. The young man asked, "Can you tell me what happens to a person when he dies?" I was about to answer that question when Pastor Bill stepped ahead of me and said to the young man, "We will come tomorrow at this time. You have your Bible ready, and we will have our Bibles with us, and we'll see what the Word of God says." When we left, Pastor Bill shared a biblical principle with me that I have never forgotten. He said, "Grant, never share biblical truths with anybody without first opening God's Word, because it will not be your word that will bring conviction to the heart of a person, but the Word of God."

We came back the next day with our Bibles. This family had gathered at a table and had their Bible open on the table. As Pastor Bill led them through the scriptures that teach what happens when a person dies, the young man broke into tears. He asked why his priest had never shared this biblical truth with him? You see, when he was at a tender age as a child, his mother had died. And the priest told him that God took his mama to heaven. At a time when this kid needed his mama the most! Can you imagine what kind of picture of God was formed in the mind of this child and carried into his adulthood?

The following year we were invited by Armenian Mission to come back with series of meetings. And while we were there Bill and I wanted to visit that family at the foot of the Mt. of Ararat. We arrived there and knocked on their gate. Grandmother opened it and hugged us with tears. She told us her grandson had been killed by a truck as he was waiting for the bus on the rainy night. She said that he often remembered us with gratitude and expressed a desire to find us so he can learn more about God.

When we came back from that first mission trip, I ran across a statement in the book *Acts of the Apostles* p. 520 that says, "The Word of God is the truth and the channel through which God manifests His Spirit and power."

With this in mind, open your Bibles with me to the gospel of Matthew chapter 9. This chapter is the story of forgiveness, healing, and restoration. You may need forgiveness today. You may be in need of healing. You may be in need of restoration. Whatever your need is, God is offering to meet that need through His word. As you open your Bible, please bow your head and ask God to reveal more of His truth. Ask for the Holy Spirit to lead and guide you, and open your heart and mind to receive a deeper understanding of God's character that you might be drawn to Him, so the enemy will not lead you into stumbling. Pray that your heart will be softened towards God.

> "So He got into a boat, crossed over, and came to His own city." (Matthew 9:1)

POINT NUMBER ONE – JESUS CAME TO HIS OWN

In my mind's eye I see a bigger picture of the ministry of Jesus. Not only did He get into the boat and cross over, but He actually crossed over and came to His own.

Let me try to explain what I just said.

God is love. From the very beginning there is a river of love that flows from God the Father towards the Son, and from the Son towards the Father. God created man and placed him into this river of love. Man became an object of God's love. But the enemy kidnapped that object of God's love by injecting sin into the human race. We became slaves to sin. No longer were we able to produce righteousness or holiness. If your child was kidnapped, how would you take this?

Seeing the condition of the object of His love, God came to rescue us. In order to do this He had to take upon Himself human flesh to be qualified to represent us. He laid aside His divinity and clothed Himself with humanity. We could actually say that He did cross over, and came to His own to restore his own. He could not live with the thought of seeing the object of His love enslaved by sin forever, so He came to save us from sin.

Matthew 1:21 gives us a biblical definition of salvation. An angel appeared to Joseph in a dream to reassure him that the child Mary had conceived was from the Holy Spirit. He tells Joseph,

> "And she will bring forth a Son, and you shall call His name JESUS, for He will save His people from their sins." (Matthew 1:21)

This is the first time in the New Testament that salvation is spoken of. This scripture sets the meaning for the word "salvation" to the entire book. Salvation does not mean getting to heaven and living there forever. That is the result of salvation. The Biblical meaning of salvation is deliverance from sin.

The Bible speaks of salvation in three tenses. In one place you can read:

"We have been saved" (Ephesians 2:5, 8)

The other places would say:

"We are being saved" (1 Corinthians 1:18)

And yet the other places would say:

"We will be saved" (Romans 5:10)

Which one is correct? And because everything in the Bible is correct (simply because "The Word is Truth"), how can we explain these three tenses of salvation?

The only way you can explain this is through the understanding of the Hebrew Sanctuary. Through the Sanctuary God gave the model and plan of how He saves humanity from the sin problem. This teaching was present and known by the Children of Israel (first movement that God had raised, and it went into apostasy). It was present in the early Christian church (the second movement God raised, and it went into apostasy as well). In 1844, according to prophecies in the books of Daniel and Revelation, God raised the third and final movement. Through this movement, He restored the Sanctuary message which has the complete plan of salvation. This movement was called the Advent movement which became the Seventh-day Adventist Church.

Let us see now how these three tenses/phases of salvation fit into each compartment of the Sanctuary model.

We have been saved—past tense. We have been saved from the guilt and punishment of sin by the death of Christ/the Lamb of God. This happened when Jesus, the Lamb of God, was crucified on the Cross. This is modeled in the courtyard of the sanctuary at the altar of burnt offering, where the lamb was sacrificed. HE HAS DONE THIS; it is an accomplished historical fact. Why was the altar of burnt offering in the very center of the courtyard of the sanctuary? It pointed to the Cross of Jesus as the central event in the history of this earth. That is why date references call it BC (Before Christ) and AD (After Divinity). Our earth is the courtyard of the heavenly Sanctuary. No wonder God is telling to Moses to build the Sanctuary according to the model that He showed him.

We are being saved—present continuous tense. We are being saved from the power and slavery to sin in our lives. This is reference to the ministry of Jesus in the Holy Place. How is it modeled in the Holy Place of the sanctuary? Through three articles of furniture, symbolically speaking here, Jesus is feeding us with His Word, giving us the Holy Spirit, and interceding for us. HE IS DOING THIS.

We will be saved—future tense. We will be saved from the presence of sin in our lives. This is modeled in the Most Holy Place of the Sanctuary. HE WILL DO THIS.

With such a High priest as Jesus Who is alive and well now, how difficult is it to be saved?

You can find an excellent book on our website (https://www.CreativeMediaMinistries.org) called *The Sanctuary: God's Show and Tell.* I highly recommend it to you. It reveals the beauty of the entire plan of salvation, so you can share this with others.

With this background, we can return to the interaction between Jesus and the paralytic in Matthew 9.

> "And behold, they brought to Him a paralytic lying on a bed. And Jesus, seeing their faith, said to the paralytic, 'Son, be of good cheer; your sins are forgiven you.'" (Matthew 9:2)

POINT NUMBER TWO – BE OF GOOD CHEER; YOUR SINS ARE FORGIVEN YOU

Who does this paralytic represent? He represents you and me. He represents the entire human race. Notice that Jesus calls the man "son" (child in the original which includes daughters also). We are not only His own, Jesus calls us sons and daughters.

Sin has crippled and paralyzed the whole human race and brought death. The paralytic was brought into the presence of Jesus. Jesus says, *"The one who comes to Me, I will by no means cast out."* (John 6:37).

Then Jesus says to the paralytic, "Son, be of good cheer; your sins are forgiven you." The scripture tells us, the man's friends brought him by faith. Every time a person comes to Jesus by faith, something happens. If you are reading this Bible story with faith right now, something will happen. Do you believe it?

The faith of the friends is a big factor in this story. Do you have loved ones or friends that you wish would come to God? Perhaps you have a son or daughter who has been wandering from God for years, and you think they are hopeless. Sin paralyzed them and they are no longer able to bring themselves to God, and now you have given up all hope. My friends don't ever give up on them, no matter what sin has done to them. Bring them on hands of prayer with your heart full of faith into the presence of Jesus. Never give up, even on someone you think is a hopeless one. Man's impossibility is God's opportunity.

In the Gospel of Mark, we find a little addition to the story.

> "Immediately many gathered together, so that there was no longer room to receive them, not even near the door. And He preached the word to them. Then they came to Him, bringing a paralytic

who was carried by four men. And when they could not come near Him because of the crowd, they uncovered the roof where He was. And when they had broken through, they let down the bed on which the paralytic was lying." (Mark 2:2-4)

The scripture tells us the paralytic was brought to the house where Jesus was, and there was no room, not even at the door. Often, there are those who are seeking Jesus that prevent the lost from seeing or approaching Jesus. It is still happening today. But praise God for the friends who have faith. The story did not end at the door through which they could not bring their paralyzed friend into the presence of Jesus. Genuine faith always finds a way. It never gives up, it will never be turned down. Genuine faith always seeks for the benefit of others and it will always break through, just as these believing friends in this story broke through the roof.

What must the people in the packed house with no elbow room have thought, when someone was breaking through the roof while they were listening to the words of Jesus? Everyone begins to gaze up. They see cracks in the ceiling and pieces of clay falling down. Pretty soon they see the sky and people walking on the roof. As the hole grows larger, a bed drops down through the ceiling. Wouldn't you think this was a bit crazy? If that kind of thing were to happen now we'd probably call the police. These friends were so determined to bring their friend into the presence of Jesus, they were willing to be ridiculed and pay the price. Do you have these kinds of friends? Are you that kind of friend to someone? I am sure these kinds of encounters were the most satisfying for Jesus, because people came to Him by strong faith.

As the paralytic, helplessly lying on his bed, is being lowered into the room, he hasn't seen Jesus yet. He sees the hands of his friends holding tightly to the ropes that were attached to his bed. He sees their faces shining in anticipation of what is about to take place. This boosts the faith of the paralytic man. If your faith isn't strong enough to bring your loved ones into the presence of Jesus, I encourage you to get more hands. *"For where two or three are gathered together in My name, I am in the midst of them."* (Matthew 18:20) *"And the one who comes to Me, I will never cast out."* (John 6:37)

How is your faith today? Have you given up on those for whom you have been praying for years? Nothing has happened, so you quit. Have you forgotten the precious promises in God's Word? My friends, God cannot lie. One of my favorites is Isaiah 49:25.

"But thus says the LORD: 'Even the captives of the mighty shall be [not might be] taken away, and the prey of the terrible be delivered; for I will contend with him who contends with you, and I will save your children.'"

Jesus wants to teach us through this story to never give up in seeking Him and bringing to Him on the hands of prayer our friends and loved ones and our children who have strayed from the Lord.

So looking at the paralytic, catching his pleading eyes Jesus said to him:*"Son, be of good cheer; your sins are forgiven you."*

Just like that! The paralytic did not have to become "good" before he was restored. He realized his need and was brought to Jesus just as he was, and he was restored. It is the same for us. When we recognize our condition, our need for Jesus, and we come to Him as we are, we are justified, declared righteous. If we come to Jesus every day, acknowledging our sinfulness, our wretchedness, and our inability to save ourselves, He will make us into what He has declared us to be. This is sanctification. This is the message of the sanctuary. In every compartment, it is Jesus who does the work. It is God's plan for saving the human race from sin. If it were possible for me to save myself from sin, then Jesus need not have come. This amazing work of God awakens in us gratitude that leads to obedience.

Here is how it works: Come to the foot of the Cross every day, and meditate on how much it cost Him to save you. This will awaken love and gratitude to Jesus in your heart every day. The more you love Him, the more you will hate sin for what it has done to Jesus. That is practical sanctification. Instead of trying to fight sin, learn to love Jesus more and you will hate sin. Sin will become abhorrent to you. The love for Jesus will keep you from sinning. And what will awaken that love in you is the coming to the Cross every day. And according to 1 Corinthians 1:18, the Cross of Jesus *"is foolishness to those who are perishing, but to us who are being saved it is the Power of God."* Romans 1:16 says that *"the Gospel of Christ is the Power of God to salvation for everyone who believes…."* That means that the Cross is the Gospel. That is how you can be empowered every day! If you want actual personal practical experience in coming to the Cross, read Bill Liversidge's book *Victory in Jesus.*

So my dear reader, you may come to Jesus as you are, but He will never leave you the way He found you.

Today Jesus is looking at each one of us, feeling our pain—emotional, physical, and relational—whatever the pain may be that our choices, decisions, mistakes, and sins may have brought upon us. With compassion, He says, "My son, my daughter, be of good cheer; your sins are forgiven you." But Hebrews 9:22 tells us that there is no forgiveness of sin without the shedding of blood. By saying to the paralytic, to you and to me "Your sins are forgiven you," Jesus is looking to His cross, where our sin, our guilt, our shame, our judgment, and even our second death would be lifted from us and placed upon Him who did not deserve it, and that would kill Him. Why would He go through such an agony?

I remember my teacher in primary class, and I still remember her name. She would say to me, "Grant, never forget that repetition is the mother of learning." When Pastor Liversidge was teaching and mentoring people he would say, "Remember to reinforce the points by repeating them. That's what they will remember." You have heard it from me before, and I am going to reinforce this again. The agony that the Godhead suffered for sinners was extremely costly. God did not do this for good people, but sinners, which we all are. In the words of Jesus Himself, *"For God so loved the world* [the human race] *that He gave His only begotten Son, that whosoever believes in Him should not perish but have eternal life,"* He didn't say whoever is good. God made it very easy. "*Whoever* believes in Him should not perish but have eternal life." This is the love of God. I'm repeating this to you so you will remember, so that the devil will never steal it from you.

In John 17:23, Jesus is praying to His Father, saying, *"That they may know that You love them as You love Me."* He is praying in the presence of His disciples. He is saying to them, as He does to us today, "God the Father loves you no less than He loves Jesus." This motivates me to respond to His love. In John 15:9, Jesus said, *"As the Father has loved Me, so have I loved you."* In other words, you are loved by the Father, and you are loved by the Son. God the Father and God the Son love us infinitely, and then Jesus went to the cross and signed that pledge of God's love on the cross with His blood.

While hanging on the cross He was tempted three times: *"If you are the Son of God, come down and save Yourself."* But He could not come down from the cross and save you and me at the same time. He had to make a choice, and the choice He made should speak loudly to every human heart today. His action speaks louder than any words. Hear what His action, His choice, to stay on the cross tells you dear reader:

> "Whoever you are, whatever country you are from, it does not matter to Me. Whatever color of skin you have, it does not matter to Me, whatever you have done in the past, it does not matter to Me. I am making a choice to stay on the cross because I love you more than I love Myself."

That's who God is. This is the undistorted picture of God, which is the Good News for the human race.

It is this message of God's love for the human race that turns the hearts of rebellious people to their Maker. With this Good News the disciples turned the world upside down. God is waiting with longing desire for Christians to bring the message of God's compelling love with such a force that HE could have one hundred baptisms where we have only one.

With His heart overflowing with compassion and love for you, Jesus says to you today, "Son, daughter, be of good cheer, your sins are forgiven you." Will you embrace His forgiveness? Or are you still struggling to forgive yourself for the things that you have done in the past? You may say, "Grant, you have no idea what I have done in the past." You've been carrying this guilt for years now. You might forget about it for a while and even have a little happiness. But then Satan reminds you, and you're broken down again. So you live an unhappy life, carrying the wretchedness of guilt through your whole life. God wants to take that from you. If you are in that condition, then you are in unbelief because Jesus has already told you your sins are forgiven. *"No sin can be committed by man for which the satisfaction has not been met on Calvary."* (*Selected Messages*, Vol. 1, p. 303). *"...The blood of Jesus Christ, His Son cleanses us from all sin."* (1 John 1:7) Whatever guilt you may have in your life, my dear friend, let it go and receive His forgiveness. God wants you to be free today from that wretchedness of guilt that you carry, so you may be free to grow into Christ.

Perhaps the problem is that you cannot forgive someone else in your life. Perhaps they have offended you so deeply that even the mention of their name makes your blood boil in your veins. Maybe it is your son or daughter whom you've raised in a Christian environment and then sent them away to college, and there or then they have gone astray. In your heart you have resentment and pain. It's difficult to forgive their choice. You've invested so much in them, and then they turn away, and with no gratitude for all that you have done for them, they make their choice to go their own way. Jesus is asking us to extend forgiveness to everyone, including those who have hurt us the most. To whom is much forgiven is to forgive much.

The Apostle Paul tells us in 2 Corinthians 2:10-11,

> "Now whom you forgive anything, I also forgive. For if indeed I have forgiven anything, I have forgiven that one for your sakes in the presence of Christ, lest Satan should take advantage of us; for we are not ignorant of his devices."

Christ is inviting us to forgive everyone in our lives so that Satan will not take advantage of us because we are aware of his schemes. Plain and simple, if you are still harboring un-forgiveness in your heart this verse tells me that you have already been taken advantage of by Satan. Let it go my friend.

Jesus said, "Blessed are the peacemakers." Do you notice that the word "blessed" is in the past tense? What blessings do you have if you forgive someone who has offended or hurt you? You may gain back a friend, a child, or a loved one. You will live longer. It's been proven by medical science that when we harbor un-forgiveness, retaining it in our minds and our hearts, it creates inflammation in our bodies and can eventually cause cancer. It attacks the weakest organs. When you forgive, God is glorified. Forgiveness opens the door for the fullness of the Holy Spirit to come into your life. God is holy and God is love, and whatever is done that is motivated by love, it is holiness to God.

What if you cannot bring yourself to love the person enough to forgive them? You know you need to do that, you want to even if it is for selfish reasons, but you are just as paralyzed as the man let down through the roof. What do you do?

God understands your problem. The formula is still the same: come to Him. Jesus said, *"With men it is impossible, but not with God; for with God all things are possible."* (Mark 10:27) If you realize that you do not have forgiveness in you, God can fix even that. It shows that He is digging deeper into your subconscious mind and He wants to cleanse you of sin you do not even realize is there. Let Him do that work. Ask Him to give you the mind of Christ. Every time God reveals something that blocks you from complete submission, give Him permission to come into your mind, ask Him to give you the attitude you need to get past the block. He will be delighted that you are willing to work out your salvation with fear and trembling by giving Him permission to come into your mind.

> "Righteousness is holiness, likeness to God, and "God is love." (1 John 4:16). It is conformity to the law of God, for "all Thy commandments are righteousness" (Psalm 119:172), and "love is the fulfilling of the law" (Romans 13:10). Righteousness is love, and love is the light and the life of God. The righteousness of God is embodied in Christ. We receive righteousness by receiving Him. Not by painful struggles, or wearisome toil, not by gift or sacrifice, is righteousness obtained; but it is freely given to every soul who hungers and thirsts to receive it." (*Thoughts from the Mount of Blessing* p..18)

We now return to the story of the paralytic.

What condition was the paralytic in when he heard the words, *"Your sins are forgiven you"*? The condition of the paralytic is the condition of the entire human race. Paul describes in Romans 5:6-10 that while we were *"without strength"*, (helpless), while we were *"ungodly,"* and while we were *"sinners"* and *"enemies"* of God, God reconciled us to Himself through the death of His son. He did not wait for us to be godly, or good, or strong, or righteous, or to be His friends. He did this while we were in those conditions.

During the time of COVID, many churches around the country were closed down. People began to order a book written by Pastor Bill Liversidge called *Overcoming Through Jesus.* In one of the churches in Oregon, they used the book to start small Bible study groups in their homes, and revival began to take place. When the churches reopened, the people came back to church and shared their testimonies about the revival they had experienced. The members were inspired by their testimonies to study the book. One hundred and thirty people signed up for a study group. The whole church experienced revival. It was the impact the book was having on the lives of those who were hearing the Gospel message.

During that time when the church had reopened, a young man came to visit his parents, who were members of this church and the study group. He had left the Lord and the church twelve years before. He was living in California and had gotten involved in drugs. He decided to join his parents on the Sabbath that the members from the home study group were sharing their testimonies. He was moved as he heard the testimonies, especially that of his father, of how the message in the book *Overcoming Through Jesus* had impacted their lives.

When he returned to his parent's home, he found the book on his father's desk. He picked it up and began reading it. He told me he couldn't put it down, and he finished the entire book before he returned to California. He purchased twenty-five copies of the book and gave a book to each of his drug-using friends. Sad to say, many of them were from Adventist homes. A few months later, he called me and told me that he was free from drugs, and that he wants to go into ministry.

I had to ask myself what had happened here? He was raised in a Christian home. He went to church and church school. He knew all of the biblical teachings, yet he walked away from it all. What brought him back? Read that book *Overcoming Through Jesus,* and you will understand for yourself. Your prodigals need this book. They need to hear the simplicity of the Gospel presented in a practical way that they have not heard before. They will see the undistorted picture of God through this book. Your youth in your church need to read this book. When they hear the Gospel, it will safeguard them from the enemy's attempts to wrestle them out of the hands of the Lord, and away from their family and the church. ASI Magazine recently published an article about this book which resulted in many Christian academies and Andrews University obtained this book for all their students.

We again return to the story of the paralytic.

> "And at once some of the scribes said within themselves, 'This Man blasphemes!' But Jesus, knowing their thoughts, said, 'Why do you think evil in your hearts?'" (Matthew 9:3-4)

Again, Mark adds something more.

> "But some of the scribes were sitting there and reasoning in their hearts, 'Why does this Man speak blasphemies like this? Who can forgive sins but God alone?'" (Mark 2:6-7)

Jesus perceived their thoughts. They should have realized that the Son of Man was the Son of God and they were standing in the presence of their Maker.

And what Jesus calls evil here? Thinking that God cannot forgive sins – Jesus calls evil. Jesus said to them:

> "For which is easier, to say, 'Your sins are forgiven you,' or to say, 'Arise and walk'? But that you may know that the Son of Man has authority on earth to forgive sins"—then He said to the paralytic, 'Arise, take up your bed, and go to your house.'" (Matthew 9:5-6)

POINT NUMBER THREE – ARISE FROM BEING PARALYZED BY SIN, FROM BEING DEAD IN SIN INTO A NEWNESS OF LIFE!

Jesus is speaking not only to the paralytic but to every human being who is affected by sin. Arise from being dead in sin, from being paralyzed by sin into newness of life. Do you believe that Jesus can raise you from the dead? If you do, can you also believe that Jesus can give you victory over sin? Jesus not only can forgive your sins, He can heal you from sin.

It was by the Word of Jesus Christ the Creator, that the world was created. His Word still has power to create and to restore. He is the same yesterday, today, and forever. He is the Word. How much time are we spending in the Word, the truth, and the channel through which God manifests His Spirit and power?

If we want to have the Spirit of God and the power of God manifested in our lives, we need to hear the Word and act upon it. The moment we do, we can have the assurance that the Holy Spirit is in us.

> "For it is God which works in you both to will and to do for His good pleasure." (Philippians 2:13)

> "The impartation of the Holy Spirit is the impartation of the life of Christ." (*Desire of Ages* p. 805).

When you hear the Word of God, the moment you act upon it, the Holy Spirit is in you, and He brings the very life of Christ into you. Christ in you through the Holy Spirit, is not attracted to sin. That is how we have victory over sin. We cannot do this ourselves; it is Christ in us, the hope of glory. This is how simple God made it. Even children can understand. Hear the Word and act upon it. That is our department; the rest is God's department. Leave it to Him.

> "Wherever His word is obeyed, [acted upon] with a sincere heart, there Christ abides" *(Desire of Ages* p. 442).

Dear reader, are you hearing this? We can rise above sin and have a victorious Christian life. The Word of God is the truth and the channel through which God manifests His Spirit and power. It's not Oxford, Harvard or Stanford Universities, or even Loma Linda or Andrews Universities. It is the study of the Scriptures that awakens, ennobles and develops the faculties of the human mind to its highest potential. It will guard us from deception.

The time is coming when we will need this as never before. The reason why so many Christians are powerless is because they do not spend daily time in the Word of God and do not act upon the Word of God.

> "No other study will so ennoble every thought, feeling, and aspiration as the study of the Scriptures." (*Testimonies to the Church,* Vol. 5, p. 24).

> "No other book is so potent to elevate the thoughts, to give vigor to the faculties, as the broad, ennobling truths of the Bible. If God's word were studied as it should be, men would have a breadth of mind, a nobility of character, and a stability of purpose rarely seen in these times." (*Steps to Christ,* p. 90)

Remember, when the Pharisees sent officers to arrest Jesus, they came back without Him, and they were asked, *"Why have you not brought Him?"* They answered, *"No man ever spoke like this Man!"* (John 7:45-46) No man lived like this Man either, because Jesus Christ lived according to the scriptures, and His words and deeds were filled with power, and that very power is available to us today.

> "The power of God awaits their demand and reception." *(Desire of Ages* p. 672)

> "In their human weakness, they are enabled to do the deeds of Omnipotence." (*Gospel Workers,* p. 112)

We have the inexhaustible supplies of heaven at our command.

"The whole heavenly treasure awaits our demand and reception" (*Testimonies to Ministers*, p. 510)

What a generous God we have.

"In every command and in every promise of the Word of God is the power, the very life of God, by which the command may be fulfilled and the promise realized. He who by faith receives [acts upon] the Word is receiving the very life and character of God." (*Christ's Object Lessons*, p. 38)

Are you trying to obtain a character that will fit you for heaven? Then hear the Word and act upon it. It's that simple. Don't find a shortcut way around it. We must spend time in the Word of God and receive it, believe it, and prove that you believe it by acting upon it. The determining factor whether you believe His Word or not is this: If you truly believe it, you will act upon it, doing what It says out of gratitude for Who God is and what He has done for you. If not, you will be doing what the Word of God says out fear of punishment or out of desire for reward.

When you act upon the Word of God by faith, two things will happen:

"And he arose and departed to his house. Now when the multitudes saw it, they marveled and glorified God who had given such power to men." (Matthew 9:7-8)

POINT NUMBER FOUR – GOD IS GLORIFIED WHO HAD GIVEN SUCH POWER TO MEN

The onlookers could hardly believe what had just happened. Jesus spoke the Word, the paralytic acted upon it, and he got up and went to his house. It is by acting upon the Word of God that he was restored. So it is with us; it is by acting upon the Word of God that we are restored from the damages of sin. Do you realize that when an individual acts upon the Word of God, multitudes will be glorifying God? No matter where you are, you are enough. We don't need to be many. When this man acted upon the Word, they saw a restored life. Restoration happened through the Word of God. I have experienced this in my own life through the Word of God. At age 28, after six years of illness, doctors gave me one year to live, they gave up on me. For the first time in my life, someone gave me a Bible and as I was reading the Word of God, I began to believe there is a God. As I began to act on the health principles in the Word of God, my health was restored. The Word of God is the truth and the channel through which God manifests His Spirit and power.

What else was it that they saw? They saw a restored life, and they glorified God, who had given such power to men. The word "men" in this passage is plural. God restored one man, and the Bible tells us that God gave such power to "men" and "women." Why?

God through Jesus, the Word that became flesh, gives power and authority to both men and women to have victory over sin. The Apostle Paul said, *"Sin shall not have dominion over you…."* (Romans 6:14) if you let Jesus, the Word of God, abide in you. When you do this you are allowing His victorious life to be exhibited in you which glorifies God.

In Revelation 3:20, Jesus is standing at the door and knocking. He says, *"Whoever hears My voice and opens the door, I will come in.."* The Good News in this verse is that Jesus Christ already lived in human flesh. Divinity, dwelling in humanity, conquered sin in the flesh. The reason He is knocking every day at the door of our hearts is because He wants to come in and repeat the same experience in our lives. Are we allowing Him to come in? And if we do, is He coming in as a visitor or as a resident? That will make all the difference, my friends. If you want to put a stop to the yo-yo experience, make Him a resident.

When Jesus spoke and healed the paralytic, the pen of inspiration tells what took place:

> "The healing of the body was an evidence of the power that had renewed the heart….The paralytic found in Christ healing for both the soul and the body. The spiritual healing was followed by physical restoration. This lesson should not be overlooked. There are today thousands suffering from physical diseases, who, like the paralytic, are longing for the message, 'Your sins are forgiven'. The burden sin, with its unrest and unsatisfied desires, is the foundation of their maladies. They can find no relief until they come to the Healer of the soul. The peace which He alone can give, would impart vigor to the mind, and health to the body…. Physical disease, however malignant and deep-seated, was healed by the power of Christ; but the disease of the soul took a firmer hold upon those who closed their eyes against the light. Leprosy and palsy were not so terrible as bigotry and unbelief." (*Desire of Ages*, p. 270, 271)

In summary four points came out of this story:

POINT NUMBER ONE – JESUS CAME TO HIS OWN

Jesus came to His own. You are not alone in this struggle. He said, *"I am with you always, even unto the end of the world."* (Matthew 28:20) Jesus came to forgive, heal, and restore His own. You are His own precious possession. Even when you were a helpless, ungodly, sinner and even the enemy of God, He reconciled you to Himself through the death of His Son.

I don't know if I should whisper or shout this next thing to you so that you will embrace it and keep it in your heart for the rest of your life.

- You are LOVED!
- You ARE Loved!!
- YOU are loved!!!

It doesn't matter whether you feel it or not. It doesn't have anything to do with your feelings. It has all to do with what took place on the cross of Jesus two thousand years ago, where God the Father and God the Son expressed to every human being from the cross, "I love you more than I love Myself."

You are loved, my friends. You are loved!

POINT NUMBER TWO – BE OF GOOD CHEER; YOUR SINS ARE FORGIVEN YOU

It is possible that friends of this paralytic were thinking "Why is He focused on forgiveness while healing is needed?" Then Jesus shows that there is a healing power in forgiveness. Did you embrace His forgiveness? Or are you living with that wretched guilt that weighs on you like a heavy stone on your shoulders? People see it in your unhappy face. It makes your life hard, and it's killing you. God wants to roll that guilt away from you today. He wants you to be set free from that wretchedness of guilt.

Perhaps you haven't been able to forgive someone in your life. Maybe someone has offended you, and you are carrying an unforgiving spirit, anger, and resentment towards them. That's not good for your physical or spiritual health. Forgive them before the sun goes down so that you can have the fullness of the Holy Spirit in you without any hindrance. Visit them. Call them. Write them a letter. Send them a text. Seek reconciliation. Maybe it wasn't your fault that the relationship is broken. They may never come to you and ask for forgiveness. Make that first step, my friends. Don't worry about how they will respond. And if you have offended someone – ask forgiveness. Clear the way for the Holy Spirit to flow into you freely, and let God worry about the other person. But you do what the Lord requires of you.

POINT NUMBER THREE – ARISE FROM BEING PARALYZED BY SIN INTO NEWNESS OF LIFE

It may be that you have some sin in your life that keeps you paralyzed. You may have something in your life that is not pleasing to God. You've tried overcoming it time after time and you keep failing. And you live with that, given up on victory. You say to yourself, "God knows that I am just a human. He still loves me. I can live this way." Friend, God does not want you to live in sin. He will never take the seed of sin back to heaven. He is offering victory to you today. Are you willing to receive it? He's inviting you to hear His word and act upon it. He will take care of the rest. He wants to produce a people who will fully reflect Jesus so that He can put the Holy Spirit upon them in such measure that the whole world will be enlightened with the glory of God. Do you want to be part of that?

"Whatever may be our inherited or cultivated tendencies to wrong (sin), we can overcome through the power that He is ready to impart." (*Ministry of Healing*, p.175, 176)

POINT NUMBER FOUR – GOD IS GLORIFIED WHO HAD GIVEN SUCH POWER TO MEN

If it is your desire to glorify God, you will want to commit yourself to hearing the Word daily and acting upon it. When you do this, the Holy Spirit will come in and bring the very life of Jesus into you. It is Christ in you that is not attracted to sin. He is the solution to the sin problem, and God will be glorified. The promises of Revelation are to him who overcomes. And the key to become overcomer is Jesus in you, the hope of glory. For with Him in you all things are possible. Jesus is knocking at the door of your heart right now...

My prayer, Dear Reader is:

Dear Father, we want to praise You and thank You for Your unconditional love for the human race, the object of Your love. Our hearts are moved as we are discovering the undistorted picture of the Creator, the loving, caring Father. Forgive us, Lord, if in the past we haven't comprehended who You really are. Forgive us if our actions might have offended someone, maybe even our children. I pray for the reader, whatever their past may have been, that they will hear Your Words, "My son, My daughter, be of good cheer; your sins are forgiven." And if Satan brings that wretched memory and guilt back to them, encouraged them to say, "Get behind me, Satan, in the name of Jesus." I pray that the readers will find joy and freedom to grow in Christ, rejoicing in Jesus, free from the wretchedness of guilt. Deliver them from guilt.

I pray in the name of Jesus for those who have a broken relationship. We all have experienced broken relationships in our lives. Give us the grace to seek reconciliation even if we are not at fault. Open the way for the Holy Spirit to fill us with His fullness that we may glorify Your Name. I ask that the Holy Spirit will go ahead of us, and touch the hearts of those individuals to be receptive and responsive to this reconciliation so that

Satan will be pushed back, Your banner will be moved forward and the heavens will be rejoicing as Your Name is glorified.

Dear Father, if the reader identifies with the call to rise up from the paralysis of sin into newness of life, I pray You will give them the desire to open their heart's door to receive Jesus. Give them grace as they hear the Word of God that they might understand that the key to victory is in believing and acting upon the Word. And that when they do, may the Holy Spirit bring into their life the very life of Christ who is not attracted to sin, thus allowing Him to have victory in their lives and conquering every besetting sin for the glory of Your Name.

I pray in Jesus name. Amen!

CHAPTER 5

YOUNG MAN, I SAY TO YOU "ARISE"

Chapter seven of the book of Luke begins with the story of the healing of a centurion's slave in Capernaum. Capernaum was a quaint fishing village located on the northern shore of the Sea of Galilee. It had a peaceful, consoling nature about It and was Jesus' base during His ministry. The next few verses have several points for us.

> "Now it happened, the day after, that He went into a city called Nain; and many of His disciples went with Him, and a large crowd. And when He came near the gate of the city, behold, a dead man was being carried out, the only son of his mother; and she was a widow. And a large crowd from the city was with her. When the Lord saw her, He had compassion on her and said to her, 'Do not weep.' Then He came and touched the open coffin, and those who carried him stood still. And He said, 'Young man, I say to you, arise.' And he who was dead sat up and began to speak. And He presented him to his mother. Then fear came upon all, and they glorified God, saying, 'A great prophet has risen among us'; and 'God has visited His people.' And this report about Him went throughout all Judea and all the surrounding region." (Luke 7:11-17)

Nain was a small city built on a hill and located in lower Galilee about 20 miles from Capernaum. Names in Hebrew culture had meanings, and Nain means pleasant place.

Many of His disciples went with Him and a large crowd followed Him. The word about Jesus spread all over Galilee. Everywhere Jesus went, the lives of people were changed. As He passed through the towns and villages, He was like a vital current diffusing life and joy wherever He went. People brought their sick and afflicted to Him for healing and Jesus was healing them all. As a result a large crowd followed Him, and this was a happy crowd. And if we are the followers of Jesus, we must be a happy crowd too!

The presence of Jesus was changing the lives of people and the entire villages. "Jesus Christ is the same yesterday, today and forever." Hebrews 13:8. Jesus is still changing lives today. I've experienced that in my own life.

I was raised an atheist. The Word of God came into my life, and it changed my life. The Word of God is Jesus Himself.

> "In the beginning was the Word, and the Word was with God, and the Word was God.... And the Word became flesh and dwelt among us, and we beheld His glory, the glory as of the only begotten of the Father, full of grace and truth." (John 1:1; 14)

The presence of Jesus is a life-changing presence.

POINT NUMBER ONE – THE PRESENCE OF JESUS IS A LIFE CHANGING PRESENCE

If you choose to live in His presence, it will change your life and the lives of those around you.

> "And when He came near the gate of the city, behold, a dead man was being carried out, the only son of his mother; and she was a widow. And a large crowd from the city was with her." (Luke 7:12)

When Jesus approached the city gate, a dead man was being carried out. He was the only son of a widow, and she had a large crowd with her. Imagine Jesus approaching the gate of the city at the same time this full procession is coming out of the gate of the city. Do you think this encounter was by accident? I want you to take note of this.

POINT NUMBER TWO – NOTHING EVER HAPPENED BY ACCIDENT IN THE LIFE OF JESUS! AND IF JESUS IS IN YOU – NOTHING WILL EVER HAPPEN BY ACCIDENT IN YOUR LIFE!

So a large procession of people who were very sad was coming out of the city gate carrying a dead body just as Jesus, the life Giver, was coming into the gate with a large happy crowd following Him. It was not by accident that the two crowds met at the gate. The happy crowd with Jesus had a purpose. They were happy because they have come to know Jesus, and they would influence the unhappy crowd. That is also our purpose in our world that is such an unhappy place today. The mournful crowd was changed and glorified God.

These two big crowds met at the gate of the city of Nain. Jesus was tired as He had just traveled twenty miles on foot on dusty and stony roads to get here in this precise moment. In spite of His tiredness, His priority was to rescue humanity, to free them from the captivity to sin, distress, disease, and death, whatever it may be. He is still in that business today Jesus has not changed. He is the same yesterday, today, and forever.

The funeral procession was making its way to the burial site with slow and sad steps. In front of the procession they carried a dead body. Mourners filled the air with their cries. All the people of the city gathered to show their respect for the deceased and sympathy to his mother, a bereaved widow. It was a site that awakens sympathy.

Why is the narrative of the funeral procession so detailed?

"The only son of his mother, and she was a widow." (Luke 7:12) It reveals that he had no father, and she had no husband. In those times to lose the father and the husband was to lose a provider, to lose security. This poor widow lost her husband and her son. Besides the tragedy of loss and grief, her future was one of insecurity and poverty without any hope.

The Apostle James defines pure religion:

> "Pure and undefiled religion before God and the Father is this: to visit orphans and widows in their trouble, and to keep oneself unspotted from the world." (James 1:27)

Pure religion is introducing the fatherless to their Heavenly Father. Many in the world are fatherless today. That is why our ministry is the ministry of reconciliation.

> "Now all things are of God, who has reconciled us to Himself through Jesus Christ, and has given us the ministry of reconciliation, that is, that God was in Christ reconciling the world to Himself, not imputing their trespasses to them, and has committed to us the word of reconciliation. Therefore we are ambassadors for Christ, as though God were pleading through us: we implore you on Christ's behalf, be reconciled to God." (2 Corinthians 5:18-20)

Jesus is engaged in the ministry in which He wants to engage us, His ministry of reconciliation. He said *"...He who has seen Me has seen the Father...."* (John 14:9) Jesus was revealing the Father and His character. The Father was ministering through Jesus Christ. And Jesus Christ is ministering through us to reveal the Father and His character to the world.

POINT NUMBER THREE – THE MINISTRY WE ARE PART OF IS JESUS'S CHRIST MINISTRY THROUGH US, RECONCILING PEOPLE TO GOD AND INTRODUCING THE FATHERLESS TO THEIR HEAVENLY FATHER

> "When the Lord saw her, He had compassion on her and said to her, 'Do not weep.'" (Luke 7:13)

POINT NUMBER FOUR – THE LORD HAS COMPASSION

After the loss of her husband, her son had been her sole provider. This was a sight that awakened compassion in the heart of Jesus, and he said to her, "Do not weep." And He might have thought of His own mother, knowing that the sorrow of losing a son will also pierce her heart. I praise God that He has feelings and He never changes. I am intrigued by the incredible depth of identity that Jesus has with suffering humanity! Aren't you glad that Jesus has compassion when you are going through trials? I've been through trials in my life and have experienced the compassion of God so many times. He is so faithful.

My wife and I became Seventh-day Adventist Christians after coming to the United States. We had been communicating the precious light of the Gospel to everyone we knew in Russia and Armenia, but no one would open their hearts to receive it. In 2003, together with our friend, Pastor Michael, one of the conference presidents in Russia at that time, we organized an evangelism series in the country of Armenia where my parents were resided. The funds had been raised, the advertising was done, and everything was prepared. I had my airline ticket, and I was anxious to see my parents whom I hadn't seen for ten years. They had been invited to the meetings, and I was looking forward to these series. Ten days before my flight to Armenia, I got a call from my brother, who told me my father had an accident and died shortly after. Do you think that I didn't ask God why? Not only did I ask, but I argued with Him. I was shouting at God, "Couldn't you hold him for ten days till I come and have these meetings?" What a big shot I was in my own eyes. I later repented.

As I was waiting for my flight, I meditated on the character of God. Words that described God and His character were coming into my mind. He is almighty, all-powerful, omnipresent, and omniscient. Then one word came into my mind like a neon light, a word that I had heard only once in my life and was given the meaning of it. This word settled my grief and disappointment. The word was omni-pathic. I tried looking it up in a dictionary but it was not there. It is actually a combination of two words, "omni" meaning in all ways and in all places, and for those of you who are in the medical field, "pathic" meaning feeling all. They told me omni-pathic means God is feeling all. God is feeling all we feel. That satisfied all my questions.

I flew to Armenia and we proceeded with the meetings. A number of my relatives were present. When the meetings came to an end and a call was made, my mother was the first person to take her stand for Jesus and ask for baptism, and my sister followed. This was one of the happiest days in my life. God feels our pain. He will never allow us to suffer more than we can bear. "In all their afflictions He was afflicted." (Isaiah 63:9) He will always give us relief and comfort. Sometimes it takes tragedy or trial to move people into belief, but why wait?

I felt His compassion, and I left the destiny of my dad in the hands of God because I could trust Him.

Based on the following Scriptures:

> "Jesus Christ is the same yesterday, today and forever." (Hebrews 13:8),
>
> "I AM with you always." (Matthew 28:20)
>
> "Where two or three are gathered in My name, I AM in their midst." (Matthew 18:20)

Today we all can have the assurance that Jesus is with us at this moment and has compassion for all.

> "And when the Lord saw the widow He had compassion on her." (Luke 7:13)

The widow, following the coffin, was deeply grieved and her eyes were filled with tears, that she didn't even notice the presence of Jesus. In her sorrow she did not notice the One who had come to change her sorrow into joy. How often when we experience sorrow, or are burdened with our problems, we too fail to notice and trust the One who has come to take our burdens and grief, to comfort and encourage us, and to change our sorrow into joy. He is the One who promised that He will never leave us or forsake us. Are you feeling sorrowful or burdened today? Jesus has compassion on you, and He comes to you to turn your sorrow into joy.

Jesus came to the side of the widow and gently told her, "Do not weep." Only Jesus can say these words in a situation like this, because He is the only one that can change a situation like this. If you are at the point of weeping this moment, in fear, hurting and the trial is intense, Jesus is beside you, and He has compassion on you. He's gently saying to you, "Do not weep." Jesus is able to turn your sorrow into joy.

> "Then He came and touched the open coffin, and those who carried him stood still. And He said, 'Young man, I say to you, arise.'" (Luke 7:14)

In order to stop the procession, Jesus had to touch the coffin.

POINT NUMBER FIVE – JESUS CAME AND TOUCHED THE COFFIN

Have you ever seen people touching a coffin? Why would people touch a coffin? Jewish law considers the person who touches a coffin or a dead body, to be unclean. They remained unclean until they went through the ceremony of cleansing. What shocked people is the willingness of Jesus to take upon Himself the defilement. Jesus had a motive.

I was six years old the first time I saw someone touching a coffin. I watched my grandmother touching the coffin of her son, who was my uncle.

My grandmother had raised four children, and this was her youngest son. He was born in 1942. War broke out between USSR and Nazi Germany in 1941, during the Second World War. My grandfather was drafted in 1941 to fight against Nazi Germany, and was killed in 1942. My uncle, who never saw his father, was like the last gift that was left for my grandmother. Now at the age of twenty-five and engaged to be married, the boy tragically died. I watched my grandmother, who was in love with her late husband, fall on her son's casket weeping and wailing.

As I was studying this passage, those memories flooded back into my mind. Why did my grandmother touch the coffin? She touched it because she loved the person in the coffin. The reason and motive why Jesus touched the coffin is because He loves the human race, and if you are part of the human race, I have news for you: you are loved so very much by Jesus. In Jewish culture, as we just mentioned, you were defiling yourself by touching the coffin. What He did by touching the open coffin was unthinkable. In the Jewish culture, you were defiling yourself by touching a coffin or the dead. But to Jesus even the contact with the dead could not bring defilement. Jesus came to touch the dead and to impart life. And He is still in the same business today.

Jesus did not follow traditions that were standing in the way of the truth. Tradition said, "Do not eat with sinners. He ate with sinners. Do not touch coffins or the dead. Do not speak to a woman in a public place. Do not touch a leper. Jesus did it all. Jesus spent His entire ministry touching the unclean, not just sanitized sinners. If Jesus is in you, He will not only touch the clean things but the unclean as well. In other words, you will not only associate with the members of the church, but you will also come close to sinners who are living in sin and need salvation because it will be Jesus in you touching them and associating with them.

Jesus came and touched the coffin. When he did, the men who were carrying the coffin came to a sudden standstill.

When most of the churches were closed at the pandemic time I was invited to preach at one of the Spanish churches in Riverside, California. I presented this very message. When the service was over pastor asked me to shake hands with people coming out of the sanctuary. I noticed a young man in the sanctuary waiting for everyone to leave.

Then he came up to me, strongly squeezing my hand he said, "Pastor, this was to be my last day in the church, I came to say goodbye to God and to church". Then he burst into tears and said: "Thank you for coming today! I will never leave God, and I will never leave His church!"

Whoever you are, dear reader, as you are reading this chapter today, and you may be spiritually dead and in the coffin, or you may be dying spiritually, you are about walk away from God and to leave His church, to be buried away spiritually.

PLEASE *KNOW* THAT JESUS IS BY YOUR SIDE RIGHT NOW TO STOP THAT PROCESSION!

Those who carried the coffin stood still. They were shocked by Jesus' interference. They were intent on getting the dead man to his grave. Now they were not only going to see the compassion of Jesus revealed, but also the power of God. The wailing ceased. Angels are watching... With clarity and authority, the words were spoken, "Young man, I say to you, arise!"

POINT NUMBER SIX – YOUNG MAN, I SAY TO YOU, ARISE!

How many young people need to hear these words today?

The dead man in the coffin represents the human race, men and women, young and old. That voice of Jesus pierced the ears of the dead. Sin is so subtle it stings, and you don't even realize that you are dying spiritually. If this is you in that coffin of spiritual deadness, Jesus wants to touch your coffin right now, and He says to you "Arise"! Dear friend, His Word can raise you up from any deadness in sin. His Word has power to accomplish what it says. *"...The word of God, which also works effectively in you who believe."* (1Th 2:13)

> "And he who was dead sat up and began to speak. And He presented him to his mother." (Luke 7:15)

Now Jesus takes him by the hand and helps him up out of the coffin and gives him back to his mother. Just moments before, the mother of this young man was weeping. Now the mother and the son cling to each other in long and joyous embrace! Praise God! Can you picture this? This was a real event. This grieving mother receives her son back to life. Jesus wants to raise your spiritually dead children by the hand and give them back to you. And if you are spiritually dead, He wants to take you by the hand and lift you up out of your coffin of spiritual deadness. What a long and joyous embrace there is when the spiritual life of a wayward child is restored and the dead are risen!

If you have loved ones that you have lost to a physical death, and they are in the grave, I have good news for you. There will be a long and joyous embrace in your future.

> "For the Lord Himself will descend from heaven with a shout, with the voice of an archangel, and with the trumpet of God. And the dead in Christ will rise first. Then we who are alive and remain shall be caught up together with them in the clouds to meet the Lord in the air. And thus we shall always be with the Lord." (1 Thessalonians 4:16-17).

Dear friend, I cannot wait for that day. It is coming, and we are to hasten it. If you have children and grandchildren that have lost their way, there will be a long and joyous embrace in your future as well.

> "But thus says the LORD: 'Even the captives of the mighty shall be taken away, And the prey of the terrible be delivered; For I will contend with him who contends with you, And I will save your children.'" (Isaiah 49:25)

> Thus says the LORD: "'Refrain your voice from weeping, And your eyes from tears; For your work shall be rewarded,' says the LORD, And they shall come back from the land of the enemy. 'There is hope in your future,' says the LORD, 'That *your* children shall come back to their own border.'" (Jeremiah 31:16-17)

These promises along with many others are yours. The promises of God are the words of God. In the beginning God spoke the Word, and it stood fast. This tells me there is power in the Word of God to accomplish what it says. How is your faith today?

The funeral procession returned to the city of Nain as a triumphant procession praising God! And Nain means a pleasant place. This is a story, in a nutshell, of God restoring the human race to the paradise of God, that pleasant place. And it is by touching a dead man. Please notice that the dead could not go back to that pleasant place, he had to be resurrected.

What was Jesus actually doing by touching the dead?

By touching the coffin Jesus Christ was symbolically committing Himself to go forward to the cross, to become sin for us, to change places with the dead man so we can all be reconciled to God so He can bring us home. There is no reason for this young man to remain dead and in the coffin, because Jesus Christ will take his death and be in the coffin. And there is no reason for you and for me to remain dead in sin.

> "... God was in Christ reconciling the world to Himself...For He made Him who knew no sin to be sin for us, that we might become the righteousness of God in Him." (2 Corinthians 5:9, 21)

Note, it is not God who is reconciled to us. It is God who reconciled the world to Himself. Jesus is not trying to gain the favor of God towards us. Just the fact that God sent Jesus shows the favor of God towards us.

> "Glory to God in the highest, and on earth peace, good will toward men!" (Luke 2:14)

Through the touching of the coffin Jesus was saying to the Father, "I am committed to go forward to the cross to take the sin, guilt, shame, judgment, and the second death of the human race upon Myself." There is no reason for you or me to be afraid of the judgment or the second death. (Revelation 20:14)

> "Most assuredly, I say to you, 'He who hears My word and believes in Him who sent Me has everlasting life, and shall not come into judgment, but has passed from death into life.'" (John 5:24)

In other words, "I guarantee this. Whoever hears My Word and believes in Him who sent Me HAS eternal life." Eternal life is not a future reward; in Jesus, it is a present reality!

The trial process in any court involves investigation, verdict and condemnation. The word "judgment" in John 5:24 (Greek *krisis*) means a verdict of condemnation. I believe that God will judge every person in a fair and thorough investigation, which determines who has or has not chosen to believe and accept what Jesus has done for him or her. Only those who refuse to believe and thereby reject the incredible Gift of Jesus are condemned. So "coming into judgment" is only a bad thing if you reject Jesus. Since your condemnation has already fallen on Jesus when He died on the cross, it is good news for a believer to come into an investigative judgment. But condemnation (Greek *krisis*) is not in the believer's future, since the investigative judgment establishes that he or she has accepted Jesus, Who took our judgment on Himself. Christian believers must be the happiest people on this planet!

Every encounter that Jesus had from His birth to His death is powerful and meaningful. No one but the Father and Christ knew what really took place in the raising of this young man from death. While we were ungodly, helpless, sinners and enemies of God, He reconciled us to Himself through the death of His son. Jesus took the place of sinful humanity, taking upon Himself what we deserved. Why would He go through so much agony in order to save wretched sinners like you and me?

There are two answers:

FIRST: Jesus went through such agony on the cross because humanity has a sin problem. Many are still playing with sin today. Many have forgotten that sin put Jesus on the cross. This was the mentality of the antediluvian people. They heard the message. Many believed the message. But they told themselves that they could still enjoy the pleasures of sin a little longer, and then jump on board at the last minute. Sadly, when the boat sailed, they weren't on it. Don't harden your heart when you hear the voice of the Holy Spirit.

Let me give you a radical definition of sin. Sin is blatant mutiny against God, and either the sin or the presence of God must die in our lives. If sin rules in my life, the Spirit of God in me will be grieved away. If God rules in my life, sin will no longer control my thoughts and actions.

The culmination of sin was the crucifixion of Jesus Christ. And what was true in the history of Jesus on this earth will be true in your history and mine, that is, sin will crucify the life of Jesus in us.

SECOND: God is love. His love is unconditional, self-emptying and self-sacrificing. "For God so loved the world" (human race, and if you belong to human race – you are loved!) "that He gave His only begotten Son, that whoever believes in Him should not perish but have everlasting life." (John 3:16) Let me remind you of this love:

Jesus was praying to His Father in the presence of disciples and He said:

> ".. that the world" (human beings) "may know...that You have loved them as you have loved Me." (John 17:23)

He is simply saying that God the Father loves you dear reader, not less than He loves Jesus Christ!

Jesus also said:

> "As the Father loved Me, I also have loved you; abide in My love." (John 15:9)

Here is what we have: God the Father loves us infinitely, Jesus loves us infinitely. Then Jesus went to the cross and He signed this with His own blood. As He was hanging on the cross, He was tempted three times,

> "If you are the Son of God, come down from the cross and save Yourself." (Matthew 27: 39-44 and other places)

Jesus could come down and save Himself, He had power to do so. But He could not come down from the cross, save you and me at the same time.

> "...without shedding of blood there is no remission." (Hebrews 9:22)

Jesus had to make a choice. And the choice that He made to stay on the cross speaks loudly and profoundly to every human heart today. I call it the last words of Jesus from the cross. He never uttered these words, but His action speaks louder than any words. As I was meditating on the cross of Jesus and studying the cross, God spoke to my heart and to my mind. Once I have heard this I was not the same person. It broke me into tears and I still remember that moment, where I was and all the circumstances. I could not stop my tears. May the Lord through His Spirit touch you now as you continue to read and discover the last words of Jesus from the cross through His action of remaining on the cross.

I invite you to use your sanctified imagination and come with me to the foot of the cross, back into that moment two thousand years ago. You are standing not far from the foot of the cross. You watched Jesus being nailed to the cross after scourging, which left Him with deep and bleeding wounds. You saw how He was crowned with thorns, which is the symbol of curse – second death. You saw the cross with Jesus being plunged into the hole in the ground, it shook His nailed body... And as you are watching Him on the cross, Jesus lifts up His head and looks at you with His friendly eyes, and you know that He wants to speak to you. As you keep watching Him, Jesus lifts up His body on the nailed hands, He takes His last breath and He speaks to you His last words. Have you ever wondered what the last words of Jesus would of been to you if you would be there? I have heard them. It changed me. And the Lord wants you to hear them.

Don't get me wrong. Jesus never uttered them, but it is His action of staying on the cross instead of saving Himself speaks.

Here they are. Jesus is saying to you from the cross through His action:

"Whoever you are, whatever country you are from—it does not matter. Whatever color of skin you have—it does not matter. Whatever you have done in the past—it does not matter. I can come down and save Myself, but I cannot save Me and you at the same time. I choose to stay on the cross because I love you more than I love Myself." And he died so He can save you. That is who your God is.

Dear friend, if you had been offended by or had a bad experience associated with any religion in your past, please give God another chance to love you. If you come to understand the beauty of God's character and His love for you, you will discover such a beautiful balance between the law and the gospel, like a needle and thread.

The apostle Paul writes:

> "Looking unto Jesus, the author and finisher of our faith, who for the joy that was set before Him endured the cross, despising the shame, and sat down at the right hand of the throne of God." (Hebrews12: 2)

The joy of Jesus was to restore us to eternity and to righteousness. The cross of Jesus was to be abandoned by His father. So the joy of Jesus is to restore us to eternity and to righteousness which was so much greater than the prospect of being abandoned by His Father. Whenever you make a mistake, don't run away from Jesus to clean yourself up. You will never be able to do it. Come to Him as you are, and He will cleanse you. Just as a little baby is tenderly fed, bathed and nurtured by its caring parents, Jesus will do the same. God is not out there to chase you down to punish you. He's chasing you to save you because He loves you more than He loves Himself. Please, let this picture be imprinted in your mind, and don't let Satan put any other picture in your mind. You are loved. Period! Whatever good work Jesus begins in you, He is so faithful to complete the work. (Philippians 1:6)

In conclusion, the story of raising the Widow of Nain's son gives six big points.

POINT ONE – THE PRESENCE OF JESUS IS A LIFE CHANGING PRESENCE

If you choose to live in His presence, it will change your life and the lives of those around you.

POINT TWO – NOTHING EVER HAPPENED BY ACCIDENT IN THE LIFE OF JESUS!

And if Jesus is in you, nothing will ever happen by accident in your life!

POINT THREE – JESUS MINISTERS THROUGH BELIEVERS, WE ARE PART OF HIS MINISTRY

The ministry we are part of is Jesus Christ's ministry through us, reconciling people to God and introducing the fatherless to their heavenly Father.

POINT FOUR – THE LORD HAS COMPASSION

If you are in sorrow today, going through trials, pain emotional, physical, relational—the Lord has compassion on you, to comfort you, and He wants to change your sorrow into joy. He is a compassionate, gentle Shepherd. He can bind your wounds so gently and heal every wound. And He is the Almighty God of the universe.

Jesus is asking you, "Would you like Me to be your Father and love you with an everlasting love; the love you may be lacking in your home situation. Would you like Me to be your friend from now on to eternity? I will never leave you nor forsake you." Answer Him at this moment.

POINT FIVE – JESUS CAME AND TOUCHED THE COFFIN

Dear reader, if you are dying spiritually, or may be dead in sin, Jesus wants to touch your coffin and raise you up. If you want to be raised up from the spiritual deadness, then insert your name in verse 14 of this story and hear the words of Jesus:

POINT SIX – MY SON, DAUGHTER, I SAY TO YOU, ARISE!

His word has power to accomplish this very thing. He wants you to be in the triumphant living procession of the redeemed.

Dear friend, just let Him touch you, right here and now.

Loving, compassionate Father, I pray that You will come close to this child of Yours and change the sorrow and pain into joy. You're the same yesterday, today, and forever. Your mission has never changed. For those who may be going through various trials in their lives, give them an intimate sense of Your presence with them. Put Your hand around their shoulders. Comfort them, hug them.

For those who may have turned cold towards You because of sin in their life, touch their coffin and raise them up. Change the procession of Your people: from funeral procession to a triumphant procession, from the life of sin to the life of victory, from mournful funeral procession of death to a vibrant living procession of joy and peace. We are the sheep of Your pasture. Feed us with the Bread of Heaven and sustain a spiritual life in us.

I pray in Jesus name. Amen!

CHAPTER 6

WASH ALL OF ME!

The Communion service is misrepresented today by Christianity, both Catholics and Protestants. One group claims that they are above Christ and they can command Christ to enter into the bread. No one, no matter what position you hold, is above Christ. No one can command Christ. Another group serves leavened bread and fermented juice, which are meant to be symbols of Christ's body and blood. Fermentation and leaven are symbols of sin. By serving these at the communion, they are stating that Jesus and His life was sinful. Both practices are a form of blasphemy. The devil has brought every possible form of deception into Christian churches. And it is even creeping into the Seventh-day Adventist church.

I invite you to see the deeper meaning of the communion service.

> "Now before the Feast of the Passover, when Jesus knew that His hour had come that He should depart from this world to the Father, having loved His own who were in the world, He loved them to the end. And supper being ended, the devil having already put into the heart of Judas Iscariot, Simon's son, to betray Him, Jesus, knowing that the Father had given all things into His hands, and that He had come from God and was going to God, rose from supper and laid aside His garments, took a towel and girded Himself." (John 13:1-4)

The hour mentioned in verse one refers to the hour of redemption. It is pointing to His cross, and Jesus loved His own to the end, knowing well that they will forsake Him in His hour of trial. How would Jesus know that His hour had come? Passover is coming. He is the main part of the Passover. He knows that He is coming to His end. He is the Lamb of God!

In addition, He was guided by the Holy Spirit. All four Gospel writers witness this fact. (Matthew 4:1, Mark 1:12, Luke 4:1, John 1:32, 33). To what conclusion can this fact bring us? If Jesus is in you, you have the same privilege of being guided by the Holy Spirit, and you will never live in uncertainty.

Let us make a list of what Jesus knew from the John 13:1-4 verses:

1. That His hour has come.
2. That He would be departing from this world to return to the Father.
3. That the devil put it into the heart of Judas to betray Him.
4. That the Father had given all things into His hand.
5. That He had come from God and was returning to God.
6. That His own would forsake Him.

Jesus knew each of these things, including that they would all forsake Him, yet He loved them to the end.

This means that even if a person leaves Jesus, He still loves him. But it also means that when a person leaves Jesus Christ, that person never discovered the true Gospel, which is the revelation of undistorted character of God. After hearing the genuine Gospel, if a person still rejects God, Whose character is nothing but love and goodness, he runs the risk of committing the unpardonable sin. It is the goodness of God that leads sinners to repentance. It is my prayer that through the p.s of this book the character of God will be revealed to the prodigals in such a clear way that they will run into the loving arms of God and nothing will ever take them out of His hand.

> "Jesus, knowing that the Father had given all things into His hands, and that He had come from God and was going to God, rose from supper and laid aside His garments, took a towel and girded Himself." (John 13:3, 4)

The towel was different than the towels we use today. The servants would take a very long piece of cloth and wrap around their waist, leaving an extended piece that would hang over their hand to serve their master. So the picture we have is Jesus, the King of the universe, standing without His garments and wrapped in a towel as a servant ready to serve. In Matthew 20:28 Jesus says, *"Just as the Son of Man did not come to be served, but to serve, and to give His life as a ransom for many."* Jesus' whole life was unselfish service. Now He is repeating His teaching to impress it upon the hearts of His disciples forever.

This is the last act of Jesus with the twelve disciples and it is as a servant! His character is the complete opposite of the devil, whose desire is always to be elevated.

> "Let this mind be in you which was also in Christ Jesus, who, being in the form of God, did not consider it robbery to be

> equal with God, but made Himself of no reputation, taking the form of a bond-servant, and coming in the likeness of men." (Philippians 2:5-7).

Who is Jesus serving? He is serving the selfish, unconverted, deserting disciples who had been taught and nurtured by Him for three and a half years, and even the betrayer Judas. The King laid aside His garments and His prestige. Is it possible for us to put aside everything that blocks and prevents us from lifting Jesus up and serving one another? It is possible if we "let this mind" of Jesus be in us. With Jesus in us, it is possible to love the unlovable because He is the lover of souls. He came to die for ungodly, helpless, sinners and enemies of God. In laying aside His garments, He is demonstrating that He put away His Divine privileges by coming to this earth to rescue us from the pit of sin. But now He is about to take a further step by making Himself of no reputation in taking the form of a bond servant.

A bondservant was a Jewish slave who, out of poverty, sold himself into slavery to another Jewish man for a period of time. The custom was that he would be a slave for six years, and on the seventh year, he would go free. If he came as a single man, at the end of six years he would go free as a single man. If he came with his family, at the end of six years he would go free with his family. But if he came as a single man and the master gave him a wife, and he has gotten children by her, he could go free, but his wife and children had to remain with the master. The servant loves his family, and he loves his master who gave him a wife, and he decides to remain in his master's house. Then a ritual was performed where the master would lead the servant to a wooden doorpost of the house where his ear would be pierced leaving the blood as a reminder of his lifelong commitment to his master and his own family. The servant is now a "pierced" man. (*cf.* Exodus 21:5,6; Deuteronomy 15:16,17)

Christ took the form of a bond servant and became a pierced man.

What implication is there for the followers of Jesus? The members of every church who profess to know Christ and are called to be a part of His household are also called to serve one another. That is what the kingdom of God is all about. If you love God, you will love your neighbor. Anyone that says He loves God but does not love his neighbor is deceiving himself. Have we laid aside the external tokens of our prestige to be devoted to His service?

> "After that, He poured water into a basin and began to wash the disciples' feet, and to wipe them with the towel with which He was girded." (John 13:5)

Imagine this picture!

These are the actions of Jesus.

1. Jesus got up—this was His initiative.
2. He laid aside His garments—this was His intention.
3. He took the towel— this was His determination.
4. He girded Himself with the servant's towel
5. He poured the water into the basin
6. He washed the dirt and filth off the feet of His disciples.
7. He wiped their feet dry with the towel He was wearing.

These are the actions of service, and the disciples stubbornly sat watching, missing the blessed opportunity to wash the feet of Jesus. Would you like to wash the feet of Jesus? What an honor that would be. Do you realize that we are missing the opportunity to wash the feet of Jesus by not participating in the communion service? Because Jesus said, "Inasmuch as you did it to one of the least of these My brethren, you did it to Me." (Matthew 25:40, NKJV) And if you have not done this unto My little ones, you have not done this unto Me, right?

In order to wash the feet of His disciples, Jesus had to untie the dirty sandals of the disciples. This was the lowest task for the servant to do. (*cf.* John 1:27). They had come in from walking on the dusty roads. In one basin and with one towel, Jesus washed and wiped twelve pairs of feet. What do you think the condition of the towel would be after wiping twelve pair of feet? Dirty! Jesus had just transferred all that dirt and filth from them onto the towel wrapped around His body.

In the Jewish system, sinners were to bring their sacrifice to the temple, and after tying it securely, they were to place their hands on its head while silently confessing their sins to God. At that point their sins were symbolically transferred to the sacrifice, which was then killed by the sinner. The priest caught the blood in a bowl for transfer of the confessed sins into the sanctuary where they provided a record of confessed and forgiven sins. That record remained in the sanctuary until the Day of Atonement which provided an annual cleansing of the sanctuary itself. As each disciple looked down on the head of Jesus as He washed their feet, did they think to confess their sins silently to God while the filth of sin was being transferred to the body of the Sin Bearer?

Whose dirt was on the towel? It is noteworthy that the sins of all the disciples, even those of Judas were transferred to Jesus during this process. When Judas deliberately chose to reject the pardon so graciously provided, his cowardly act of suicide occurred when "there no longer remains a sacrifice for sins." (Hebrew 10:26)

Are you seeing what Jesus was trying to communicate to the disciples and to us as He was girded with the dirty towel? The dirt from the feet of the disciples was transferred to the towel that Jesus was wearing! It demonstrates the transfer of their (and our) sin, guilt, shame, judgment, and condemnation onto Jesus from the disciples. Dear friend, you are Jesus' disciple today.

Jesus was so different from the aloof and clean Pharisees. He was always dealing with and was accustomed to touching the dirty things like sinners, coffins, lepers, and dead people, because He was in a redemptive, restoring, cleansing and saving business.

This Passover meal and communion service took place just before Christ was to go to the cross. The innocent One was about to die for the sins of the whole world. He intentionally, willingly and deliberately allowed the sins of the whole world to be transferred onto Him.

There is a beautiful prophecy in Zechariah. What Jesus was about to do fulfills this prophecy.

> "'For behold, the stone that I have laid before Joshua: upon the stone are seven eyes. Behold, I will engrave its inscription,' says the LORD of hosts, 'and I will remove the iniquity of that land in one day.'" (Zechariah 3:9)

> "For He [God] made Him [Jesus] who knew no sin to be sin for us, that we might become the righteousness of God in Him." (2 Corinthians 5:21)

Jesus was about to remove the iniquity of this land when He went to the cross, and the sins of the whole world were laid upon Him. When that was complete:

> "He said 'Father, into Your hands I commit My spirit.' And having said this, He breathed His last." (Luke 23:46)

In this one act, every human being was redeemed. The price was paid. Since most of the people in our world do not know this, God has entrusted His believers to let the world know about this precious message.

Unfortunately, many of those who believe, do not understand that God is now anxious to make those believing, forgiven and justified sinners into what He declared them to be at the cross.

Salvation means to be saved from sin. Salvation does not mean making it to heaven and to live there forever. That is the result of salvation. The Bible says,

> "And she will bring forth a Son, and you shall call His name Jesus, for He will save His people from their sins." (Matthew 1:21)

This is how the penalty for sin (the second death, Revelation 20:14) was satisfied on behalf of the entire world. ("God so loved the *world*"). Christ's death on the Cross paid the human race's punishment and removed our guilt. In the typology of the Old Testament Sanctuary, this takes place in the courtyard where the altar of burnt offering symbolizes that the redemptive reach of the cross reached backward before the cross and forward after. The Cross stands as a separation between life and death on the only planet that rebelled against God.

If it had not been that Christ was given for man's redemption, death would have ended all for Adam and the human race in Eden on the very day he had "eaten thereof."

> "God's only begotten Son volunteered to take the sin of man upon Himself, and to make atonement for the fallen race. There could have been no pardon for sin had this atonement not been made. Had God pardoned Adam's sin without an atonement, sin would have been immortalized, and would have been perpetuated with a boldness that would have been without restraint" (Ellen G. White, *Advent Review and Sabbath Herald*, April 23, 1901; 1SDABC p. 1082)

But, after the Cross, Christ's work of reconciling the world to Himself had just begun. Reconciliation is more than satisfying the judgment of death. Now that Christ, as our High Priest, had obtained His own spilled blood, the human race must be told the Good News of the Cross, and given the opportunity to decide if they will accept it as applying to themselves individually. What was man going to do with the additional probation the Cross afforded?

Let us now return to the Upper Room with Jesus. So by wearing the dirty towel Jesus was symbolically telling His followers that it was all their sins, their guilt, their shame, their judgment, and even their second death that would fall on Him at the cross. What a generous God we have, lifting all of this from us in one predicted moment two thousand years ago.

Why would He do this? I will repeat the 60 seconds Gospel to you now so you can remember it and share with everyone:

Why would Jesus go through this agony? Because:

> "God so loved the world that He gave His only begotten Son, that whoever believes in Him should not perish but have everlasting life." (John 3:16)

Let us see the depths of God's love. In John 17:23, Jesus was praying to His Father in the presence of His disciples. He said,

> "Father, that they may know that You love them, as You love Me."

Let me paraphrase this and bring it home. Jesus is actually saying that God the Father loves you no less than He loves His Son, Jesus Christ. Let that sink in. In addition to that, Jesus says,

> "Just as the Father has loved Me, I also have loved you."
> (John 15:9)

There you have it. God the Father loves you infinitely, and God the Son loves you infinitely. Then Jesus went to the cross, and there He signed it with His own blood.

While He hung on the cross, He was tempted three times to come down from the cross and save Himself if indeed He was the Son of God. (Matthew 27:40 "those passing by"; Luke 23:35, the "rulers"; and verse 37 the "soldiers") Could He have done it? Absolutely! But could He, by coming down from the cross, save us at the same time? No. He had to make a choice. He chose to stay on the cross to save humanity, and that action of Jesus should speak loudly to every human heart, including you, and me. Every time you look at the cross from now on, you should hear these Words of Jesus demonstrated through His actions: "Whoever you are, whatever country you come from, whatever color of skin you have, no matter what you've done in the past, it doesn't matter to Me. I could come down and save Myself, but I can't save Myself and save you at the same time, so I choose to stay on the cross BECAUSE I LOVE YOU MORE THAN I LOVE MYSELF."

That is who God is, dear friend. That is what people in the world need to hear. This is what our young people must hear continually, so nothing will take them out of His hand. Instead of saying, "Johnny, if you will be good, God will take you to heaven," we must instill in the hearts of our young people that they are loved by the Creator of the universe and that He loves them more than He loves Himself. Then you don't need to worry. Do your part to instill the Everlasting Gospel in them, and trust God. Train up a child in the way of the Everlasting Gospel which is the Power of God, and the child will not depart from The Way.

When Jesus was washing the feet of His disciples and wiping them with the towel He was wearing, He was symbolically transferring the sin of His disciples upon Himself. You are His disciples! It is the same for Christ's disciples today when we participate in the communion service. How grateful we should be that He has transferred the judgment of God that is due us upon Himself. Jesus died our death so we could live His holy life.

> "Then He came to Simon Peter. And Peter said to Him, 'Lord, are You washing my feet?' Jesus answered and said to him, 'What I am doing you do not understand now, but you will know after this.' Peter said to Him, 'You shall never wash my feet!' Jesus answered him, 'If I do not wash you, you have no part with Me.'" (John 13:6-8).

Why is Peter so offended? He expected Jesus to be the king, and kings and rulers do not serve. Peter was expecting to have an elevated position. Remember, the disciples had come to Jesus inquiring about who would be the greatest in the Kingdom. (Matthew 18:1) Jesus is crushing Peter's expectations. Jesus said, "My kingdom is not of this world." (John 18:36) As followers of Jesus, we are not to be served, but to serve. Even after walking with Christ for three and a half years and witnessing all of the miracles, Peter still had no idea that he was rejecting the greatest love this world would ever know, displayed in the atoning sacrifice for him.

And today Christ is present on this earth through His church, His disciples. Let's return to Scripture:

> "You call Me Teacher and Lord, and you say well, for so I am. If I then, your Lord and Teacher, have washed your feet, you also ought to wash one another's feet. For I have given you an example, that you should do just as I have done to you." (John 13:13-15) "Do this in remembrance of Me." (Luke 22:19)

Based on this understanding of this beautiful ritual, Seventh-day Adventists Christians believe that Jesus wants His followers to prayerfully and humbly participate in the Lord's Supper including the foot washing ritual, to remember the meaning of what Christ did for us. Yet, many Christians avoid church on communion day or do not participate in the service. There is a verse that has been taken out of context, which I believe has deceived some people. Let us take a look at this verse in its context:

> "For I received from the Lord that which I also delivered to you: that the Lord Jesus, on the same night in which He was betrayed took bread; and when He had given thanks, He broke it and said, "Take, eat; this is My body which is broken for you; do this in remembrance of Me." In the same manner He also took the cup after supper, saying, "This cup is the new covenant in My blood. This do, as often as you drink it, in remembrance of Me." For as often as you eat this bread and drink this cup, you proclaim the Lord's death till He comes. Therefore whoever eats this bread or drinks this cup of the Lord in an unworthy manner will be guilty of the body and the blood of the Lord." (1 Corinthians 11:23-27)

How do we proclaim the Lord's death by eating and drinking? By remembering, understanding, and being mindful of its meaning, we are to be filled with gratitude to Christ. This gives us zeal to witness and proclaim the Lord's death till He comes.

Verse twenty-seven is where many people get hung up. They say, "I have sinned this week. I have acted foolishly. I am not worthy to participate." My friends, that is exactly why you need to come and partake of it! Were the disciples perfect when they were at the communion service with Christ? No. Just the day before, they were arguing about who would be the greatest, and pride is the greatest sin.

The issue of "worthiness" to participate in the Passover was resolved by God when men who had been defiled asked for permission:

> "...And Moses said to them, 'Stand still, that I may hear what the Lord will command concerning you.' Then the Lord spoke to Moses, saying, 'Speak to the children of Israel, saying: 'If anyone of you or your posterity is unclean because of a body, or is far away on a journey, he may still keep the Lord's Passover.''' (Numbers 9:6-10)

When we take a Bible verse out of context, we can make it say anything we want. Let me give you an example. In one Scripture verse it says, "...and he went away and hanged himself." (Matthew 27:5) In another Scripture verse it says, "Go and do likewise." (Luke 10:37) This is out of context, and we should not do that.

> "But let a man [person] examine himself, and so LET HIM EAT of that bread and DRINK of that cup. For the one who eats and drinks in an unworthy manner eats and drinks judgment to himself, not discerning the Lord's body." (1 Corinthians 11:28-29, emphasis added)

Eating at the Lord supper in unworthy manner simply means not being mindful of its meaning! Not discerning the Lord's body, His sacrifice. Not being mindful of the meaning of what it represents. You see at the Lord's supper they gave themselves over to gluttony! In case you are not aware—The Passover meal was a solemn meal that was an actual feast, where every dish had meaning. Even the sequence of the dishes served was pointing to the plan of salvation.

> "For this reason many are weak and sick among you, and many sleep [died]. For if we would judge ourselves, we would not be judged. But when we are judged, we are chastened by the Lord, that we may not be condemned with the world. Therefore, my

brethren, when you come together to eat, wait for one another. But if anyone is hungry, let him eat at home, lest you come together for judgment…." (1 Corinthians 11:30-34)

As you see, verse 27 taken in context, it becomes clear that this passage is a discourse on gluttony and the abuse of the Lord's Supper. The Apostle Paul is addressing this issue where people were prioritizing the desire of the flesh, the stomach, and not discerning or being mindful of the meaning of the Lord's Supper and His flesh and blood. They weren't remembering what the Lord had done for them when they partook of the Lord's Supper and participated in the foot washing. It is a very meaningful service in Christianity. Many don't understand the depths of the service. I pray that you will now understand it in its entirety.

WHAT IS THE SYMBOLIC MEANING OF THE FOOT WASHING?

When we wash each other's feet, we are to remember the love and atonement of Jesus for us. "Do this in remembrance of Me". I have removed your dirt, and I do it continuously." I wish we could do this every month, not just once a quarter. If someone has sinned against you, try to work with them to resolve the issue, then wash that person's feet. When Mary of Bethany anointed Jesus' feet with perfume, He said,

> "For this reason I say to you, her sins, which are many, have been forgiven, for she loved much; but the one who is forgiven little, loves little." (Luke 7:47)

When the goodness of God is revealed through you, it will lead that sinner to repentance, and their sins will be washed away. Instead of leaving a congregation because you are offended, wash each other's feet. If no one has been offended, wash each other's feet even so. The symbolism is that Jesus is washing away your sins using the hand of another person. We are His hands. We are His body. Are you seeing it? We accumulate sin as we walk through life day by day, and we come to have our sins washed away. If we don't come, we rob the Lord from washing us and washing others. Then, instead of leaving that congregation /the body of Christ, people would want to be part of it.

WHAT IS THE SYMBOLIC MEANING OF THE CUP?

In ancient Jewish custom, marriages were arranged by the Father of the groom. Before the negotiations were completed the Father and the groom to be went to the bride's house for a small ceremony. The groom would take the cup of wine, drink from that cup of wine (unfermented grape juice) and give it to the bride. By taking and drinking it, the bride indicated her acceptance and willingness to be married to the groom.

When she did this, engagements were considered binding, and the bride now belongs to the groom. The wedding did not take place immediately as the groom was expected to return to his home for an undetermined length of time to "prepare a place for her". When he has finished those preparations, he comes unannounced to claim her as his bride. The bride was expected to continually remain ready, since the exact time of his return was unknown.

Do you see the symbolism here? When you partake of the wine in the communion service, it signifies that you accept that you belong to Christ. He says, "You are Mine now." He is coming back to take you to the home that He is preparing for you. Isn't that beautiful? We don't want to miss this.

When Israel was about to go into battle, the commander would ask if there was any man present that was engaged to get married. Those men would be sent home. (Deuteronomy 20:7). Why? It pointed to the coming of Jesus, the groom, for His bride. It is certain! Nothing in the Bible is by accident. The wisdom of God placed it there. When you partake of that cup, Jesus is saying, "This is the blood of my Covenant. Now you belong to Me and I will come back and take you home. Do this in remembrance of Me that you belong to Me." This is the cup of blessing. (1 Corinthians 10:16)

WHAT IS THE SYMBOLIC MEANING OF THE BREAD?

The bread is the symbol of Christ's body. When Christ took the bread and broke it into pieces there was enough to give it to every member of the body of Christ and this demonstrated that everyone would have his own piece. If you were to take all of those pieces back, and put them together as they originally were, there would be one loaf of bread.

> "...when we eat the bread we break, isn't that sharing in the body of Christ? By sharing in the same loaf of bread, we become one body, even though there are many of us." (1 Corinthians 10:16-17)

Each one of us is a vital part of the body of Christ. If we refuse to partake of the communion service, we exclude ourselves from the body of Christ. It's just that simple. Jesus commanded His disciples, *"Love one another as I have loved you."* (John 15:12) Their unity and love for each other was to be the defining mark of His disciples. Many fail to understand the depths of the foot washing and the Lord's Supper that Jesus instituted. Even Peter didn't understand. I praise God that there is hope for you and me!

> "Then He came to Simon Peter. And Peter said to Him, 'Lord, are You washing my feet?' Jesus answered and said to him, 'What I

am doing you do not understand now, but you will know after this.' Peter said to Him, 'You shall never wash my feet!' Jesus answered him, 'If I do not wash you, you have no part with Me.' Simon Peter said to Him, 'Lord, not my feet only, but also my hands and my head!' Jesus said to him, 'He who is bathed needs only to wash his feet, but is completely clean; and you are clean, but not all of you.' For He knew who would betray Him; therefore He said, 'You are not all clean.'" (John 13:6-11)

When Jesus said to Peter, *"If I do not wash you, you have no part with Me,"* He was saying, If your sins are not transferred onto Me, you have no part with Me. Please don't miss this. Come take part in the communion service no matter what it may cost you. Let us partake of this beautiful service and not reject the atoning death of Jesus on our behalf!

Jesus said, "Do this in remembrance of Me." Where else is the word "remember" found in the Bible? It's found in the fourth commandment, where God said, "Remember the Sabbath day." God is aware that humans are forgetful, so He reminds us of what He wants us to remember. He wants us to remember His Sabbath and the ceremony that commemorates His cleansing sacrifice for us. And when we as Christians forget what the Lord said we should "Remember" we are in danger to end up in apostasy. History often repeats itself.

Please take this seriously, my friends. The communion service is a very important service that Christ instituted. In the foot washing, there is a transaction that transfers our sin to Jesus and that refers to the cross.

"For He [God] made Him who knew no sin to be sin for us, that we might become the righteousness of God in Him." (2 Corinthians 5:21)

Jesus is taking our dirt and giving us His purity. There is no life apart from the death of Jesus. He died our death and then rose again so that His life could be imparted to us through the Holy Spirit.

"That He would grant you, according to the riches of His glory, to be strengthened with might through His Spirit in the inner man, that Christ may dwell in your hearts through faith; that you, being rooted and grounded in love, may be able to comprehend with all the saints what is the width and length and depth and height – to know the love of Christ which passes knowledge; that you may be filled with all the fullness of God." (Ephesians 3:16-19)

We can be filled with all of the fullness of God! Think of it. We can be partakers of the divine nature. Christ in us is the hope of glory. And it is Christ in you that will be in unity with Christ in me. Just stop for a minute and think deeper about this.

This is the way to be in unity with Him and each other, Christ in us. This is what God is anxiously waiting for. If you truly follow the communion service and understand the meaning of it, it will bring us into unity. That is what it is designed for. Jesus is anxiously waiting to see this unity among His people because it is only through the united body of believers that the fullness of God can be revealed to the world.

When Jesus said, *"Do this in remembrance of Me,"* it was meant to remind us about His redemptive sacrifice for us and the power He has provided for us. In essence, He is saying:

You confirm that you are Mine when you drink from the cup.

You proclaim it when you eat the bread.

Your sins are transferred onto Me when you wash each other's feet.

As believers of Christ, we are His body. We are His hands. Every member accumulates sin and dirt as we walk through life. This is a reminder to us that He who has begun a good work in us is faithful to complete it, (*cf.* Philippians 1:6) because we cannot cleanse or wash ourselves from sin any more than the leper could cleanse himself from his leprosy. But Jesus can and will if we will let Him.

The only other reference to the "upper room" in the New Testament is found in Acts 1:13-14. After Jesus ascended to heaven, the disciples went to the upper room where they were staying, but now Jesus was not there in person. They remembered the last supper, and they washed each other's feet and were reconciled with one another. What was the result? They were with one mind, they had unity! They were ready for the outpouring of the promise of the Holy Spirit.

One more time let's return to the story. Jesus told Peter,

> "...What I am doing you do not realize right now, but you will know after this." (John 13:7)

They were now ready to begin understanding Jesus' plan for them. Jesus wanted them to turn the world upside down with the Gospel News. The big reason why the disciples turned the world upside down was because they understood this very thing.

When Christ went to the cross, and had risen from the grave—they now understood what He was telling them and what He had just done. Jesus commanded His disciples not to leave Jerusalem but to wait for what the Father had promised. Jerusalem is the symbol of the church, God's people today. It was there in Jerusalem, not outside of it, that the disciples came into unity through the Spirit of God and were in one accord. This resulted in the baptism of the Holy Spirit. Then, according to the apostle Paul in Colossians 1:23 which was written in AD 62, the whole world had heard the Gospel.

This is very thing that God has done through them. He wants to do through us now. We've been here too long. God is anxious to finish His work through us. WILL WE LET HIM? Our answer will be the determining factor for wise and foolish virgins. If your answer is yes, there is one thing that precedes it.

> "Peter said to Him, 'You shall never wash my feet!' Jesus answered him, 'If I do not wash you, you have no part with Me.' Simon Peter said to Him, 'Lord, not my feet only, but also my hands and my head.'" (John 13:8, 9) In other words, "Wash all of me!"

In Revelation 3, Jesus describes the condition of the church in our day, we are Laodicean, "lukewarm." We think we have plenty of time before Jesus returns for His bridal church, so we fail to hunger and thirst for righteousness. That is why very few people today are allowing God to wash all of them. Signs of the soon return of Jesus are clearer than ever before! Do you wonder why we are where we are today? Why don't we have the abundance of the Holy Spirit? The Seventh-day Adventist movement has existed for over one hundred and sixty years. This was not God's design for us to be here that long.

Are you willing to give God permission to wash all of you, from all unforgiveness and resentment towards others, from the cherished sin and pride in your life, so He can bring such a unity into the church that will result in the outpouring of the Holy Spirit, and make church safe for sinners to come. You will not have to go after them, God will bring them in. And every man and woman in your city who is seeking for the knowledge and the grace of God will see it in this body of Jesus Christ and they will flock to your church. This is why the church exists.

Before He can do this, He needs to see unity in His body. This must take place first before He will bring somebody else here. They are too precious for Him to lose. Dear friend, are you willing to give God permission to wash you entirely?

Dear Father, I pray on behalf of Your people, including myself, that You would forgive our humanity and our weakness. Forgive us for our un-forgiveness towards each other and anything offensive that we have done to You. I pray that You will bring healing to the body of Your believers around the world through the clear understanding of Your character, so that such a unity will take place that it will open the door like a green light for heaven to send the Latter Rain, so that You might finish Your work and the earth will be lightened with the glory of God.

As You have been so gentle in my own life, I trust Father in Your gentleness and care as You wash us completely.

I pray in Jesus name. Amen!

CHAPTER 7

THE PURPOSE OF TRIALS

In both the Old and the New Testaments, the lives of people were changed through the Word of God. Through the Word, the sick were healed and the dead were raised. The Word of God is the same yesterday, today and forever. It is still able to do these things today. Do you believe it? If you do, you will see the evidence of it as we go through this story. I have a great expectation that there will be healing and resurrection, not by my words, but by the Word of God. God's Word is the only thing that can heal and raise the dead. You may be in need of spiritual resurrection today, or you may need healing. As we look into Chapter 11 of the Gospel of John, the story of the death and resurrection of Lazarus, I pray that through this passage of the Scripture God will grant that resurrection and healing will be taking place in some of our lives.

In the Gospel of John, chapter 10:30-31, Jesus was almost stoned for telling the people that He was one with the Father. In verse 39, they tried to seize Him, but He escaped their grasp. So He went beyond the Jordan River to the place where John was first baptizing, about two day's journey, and he stayed there.

> "Now a certain man was sick, Lazarus of Bethany, the town of Mary and her sister Martha. It was that Mary who anointed the Lord with fragrant oil and wiped his feet with her hair, whose brother Lazarus was sick. Therefore the sisters sent to Him saying, 'Lord, behold, he whom You love is sick'. When Jesus heard that, He said, 'This sickness is not unto death, but for the glory of God, that the Son of God might be glorified through it.' Now Jesus loved Martha and her sister and Lazarus. So, when He had heard that he was sick, He stayed two more days in the place where He was. Then after this He said to the disciples, 'Let us go to Judea again.'" (John 11:1-7)

During the time of Moses and Joshua, the Jews were slow to believe the Word of God, so God performed miracles. Now Jesus was about to cross the Jordan River to go back to Jerusalem to perform the greatest miracle of all so that His people would believe that He is who He said He is. He wanted them to believe that He is the One who created life and He is the One who can restore it. Are we any different from the Jews of old? Do we have to see the miracles to believe God's Word? If we believe God's Word, we will see the miracles.

The story of Lazarus takes place in Bethany. The word Bethany means the house of figs. It was located two miles from Jerusalem in the countryside.

Lazarus, Martha and Mary lived in Bethany. The names in the Bible always have meaning. Lazarus comes from Eleazar, meaning God is Helper. Mary comes from the Miriam, meaning rebellious. Martha means mistress, a woman in a position of authority or control.

Their home was the place where Jesus so often found rest. It was in Bethany that Jesus lodged after the cleansing of the temple. It was from Bethany that Jesus sent two of his disciples to bring a colt on which He entered Jerusalem, and then went back to Bethany with His disciples. It was in Bethany, in the house of Simon the leper, that Mary poured expensive perfume on the head of Jesus anointing Him for burial. In the same place where Jesus was anointed for burial, He raised a person from the dead, symbolically demonstrating that He was about to change places with sinful humanity, and take upon Himself what we deserve and to give us His life. He was willing to allow beings He created to crucify Him. He did this as the second Adam, so humanity in Him and through Him could actually participate in the second death which is the penalty for sin, because we are so dear to Him. By doing this He provided a probationary life for every human being in order that they hear the Gospel and respond to it. What kind of life did He provide for us? Many would say "eternal life." Potentially, the life Jesus provided is eternal, but He will not impose that on people without their informed decision to accept it. Also, we should remember that eternal life is the life of victory which fits us for heaven. Jesus will even provide that for us in the process we call sanctification, where He gives us His victorious life that He worked out in the "likeness of sinful flesh."

It was also in the area near Bethany that Jesus blessed His disciples then ascended up to heaven. Bethany was a meaningful and important place for Jesus. That should tell us that every spiritual leader needs a Bethany place in their lives.

We will focus on several points in this story. They are bold and strong points since they come from the Word of God. It is my prayer that these bold and strong points will bring conviction to all of us.

When Jesus heard that His beloved friend, Lazarus, had fallen seriously ill, He knew that this would be a trial for all of them. Then He makes an interesting statement.

> "This sickness is not unto death, but for the glory of God, that the Son of Man may be glorified through it." (John 11:4)

POINT NUMBER ONE – THE PURPOSE OF TRIALS IS TO GLORIFY GOD!

The trial here is sickness, very serious sickness that ultimately resulted in death (see vs. 14)

> "Therefore the sisters sent to Him, saying, 'Lord, behold, he whom You love is sick.' Now Jesus loved Martha and her sister and Lazarus." (John 11: 3-5)

Please notice, this trial happened to very close friends of Jesus. And, if you are a friend of Jesus, you might have some trials in your life.

For those of you who are sick, in fear or having trials right now, notice the development of this story in the Bible.

> "So, when He heard that he was sick, He stayed two more days in the place where He was." (verse 6)

Jesus lingered two more days in the place He was staying. Why wouldn't Jesus go immediately?

Are you going through a trial today, through your "Bethany experience", and are wondering where Jesus is? Jesus always has a plan for every life, and His plan/His ways are higher than ours. You see, Jesus did not rush to Bethany, He was not impulsive. He wasn't led by His feelings, but by the Holy Spirit. Jesus knows that this sickness, this trial in the life of his friends will glorify God. How is God glorified through our trials?

> "My brethren, count it all joy when you fall into various trials, knowing that the testing of your faith produces patience. But let patience have its perfect work, that you may be perfect and complete, lacking nothing." (James 1:3, 4)

What does it mean to be perfect and complete, lacking nothing? It means to be spiritually mature. Trials are designed to mature us. You don't have to feel joy in the heat of your trial, but you can consider it joy because you know that trials lead to maturity as we grow into His likeness. Mature people reflect God's character. That is how God is glorified. Every circumstance in our life is allowed by God. Nothing happens by accident. Everything can bring glory to God. Bringing glory to God depends not on the strength of the trial, but on our attitude toward the trial that glorifies God. "..*consider it* all joy..." Trials are for our benefit.

> "To all who are reaching out to feel the guiding hand of God, the moment of greatest discouragement, is the time when divine help is nearest. They will look back with thankfulness upon the darkest part of their way. 'The Lord knows how to deliver the godly.' 2 Peter 2:9. From every temptation and every trial He will bring them forth with firmer faith and a richer experience." (*Desire of Ages*, p. 528)

Dear reader, are you going through a trial right now? Are you benefiting from it? What is your attitude towards it? Are you praising God for the opportunity to mature and grow up into Jesus Christ, and glorify God?

"Then many of the Jews who had come to Mary, and had seen the things Jesus did, believed in Him." (John 11:45; see also John 12:10-11) On account of Lazarus, many believed in Jesus. Can the same be said of us, and lead many to Jesus as well? Can God trust us with the trial so we can glorify God?

Let this thought encourage you. When we understand these things, we can learn to live by faith and not by feeling. We will look back upon the darkest parts of our journey with thankfulness. You can trust the Lord. He knows how to deliver the godly from every temptation and every trial, and He will bring you out of it with firmer faith and a richer experience in your walk with God. If you are a believer, nothing will ever happen by accident in your life.

> "If you are reproached for the name of Christ, blessed are you, for the Spirit of glory and of God rests upon you. On their part He is blasphemed, but on your part He is glorified... Yet if anyone suffers as a Christian, let him not be ashamed, but let him glorify God in this matter." (1 Peter 4:14, 16)

Worry and Fear

Jesus said to the disciples, "Let us go to Judea again." (John 11:7) Jesus is fearless, bold and courageous.

> "The disciples said to Him, 'Rabbi, lately the Jews sought to stone You, and are You going there again?'" (John 11:8).

The disciples were frightened and reluctant to return to Jerusalem. It had only been a short time since they had been there, and the Jews had intended to stone Him. Yet Jesus knew He had a mission, and He was fearless, bold and courageous.

Notice that it was Thomas who said to his fellow disciples, *"Let us also go, that we may die with Him."* (John 11:16)

They were with Jesus, following Him for a long time and yet they were afraid. We can follow Jesus for years and end up in fear. Perhaps fear of acting upon God's Word, or fear of standing for what is right, or telling the truth. We all fall into these traps from time to time, and we need deliverance from it. Human fear causes us to say and do things that may not be to the glory of God.

> "Jesus answered, 'Are there not twelve hours in the day? If anyone walks in the day, he does not stumble, because he sees the light of this world. But if one walks in the night, he stumbles, because the light is not in him.'" (John 11:9-10)

POINT NUMBER TWO – GOD'S CHILDREN AVOID BEING IN DARKNESS AND STUMBLING BECAUSE THEY HAVE THE LIGHT WHICH IS JESUS HIMSELF IN THEM

The day associates with the light. The disciples were failing to walk in the light that Jesus gave them in verse four, when He stated that what had happened to Lazarus was "for the glory of God."

Believers do not have to worry and be afraid. You can have courage and boldness to act fearlessly. If the disciples would have believed and walked in the light Jesus gave them in verse four, they would have courage, boldness, fearlessness and peace. The reason we often do not have these attributes is that we do not walk in the Light. For the disciples the light was the Spoken Word of Jesus. For us today it is the Written Word of God. God is always glorified when we walk in His Light.

Look very carefully at verse 10, *"If one walks in the night, he stumbles, because the light is not in him."*

Night is associated with darkness. If there is darkness in your life and you are stumbling, it is because the light is not IN you. Jesus declared that He is the Light of this world. If Jesus is in you, no matter how dark this world may be, you will not stumble because *it is Jesus in you* that does not stumble.

If you know that you are stumbling and you are in the night or darkness, or if you are in fear regarding your life, your health, or your future, do this my friend. Invite Jesus, the Light to come in and He will keep you from stumbling. There will be no fear, only total peace. Just as physical light dispels the darkness, the Word of God expels fear. It is "the light unto our path." Christ Himself is the Light, and He is love. It is important that Jesus is in our lives every moment, not just five minutes in the morning. We need to feed ourselves with the Word every day and to pray every moment of our life, especially at times like this.

God's children avoid being in darkness, fear and stumbling because Jesus, the Light, is in them. When you have Jesus in you, you can be as fearless, bold and courageous as Jesus. He is saying to each one of us in Revelation 3:20, "Behold, I stand at the door and knock. If anyone hears My voice and opens the door, I will come in to him...." Don't you want to open the door of your heart for Jesus right now?

CHRIST IN YOU THE HOPE OF GLORY

> "... and after that He said to them, 'Our friend Lazarus has sleeps, but I go that I may awaken him up'. Then the disciples said, 'Lord, if he sleeps he will get well.' However, Jesus spoke of his death, but they thought that He was speaking about taking rest in sleep. Then Jesus said to them plainly, 'Lazarus is dead. And I am glad for your sakes that I was not there, that you may believe. Nevertheless let us go to him.'" (John 11:11-15)

> "So when Jesus came, He found that he had already been in the tomb four days. Now Bethany was near Jerusalem, about two miles away. And many of the Jews had joined the women around Martha and Mary, to comfort them concerning their brother. Then Martha, as soon as she heard that Jesus was coming, went and met Him, but Mary was sitting in the house. Then Martha said to Jesus, 'Lord, if You had been here, my brother would not have died.'" (John 11:17-21)

Jesus has now come to Bethany. Martha believed in healing. She believed that Jesus could heal her brother. Most likely she had witnessed His healing power in the past. *"But even now I know that whatever You ask of God, God will give You."* (John 11:22) We should realize that when Jesus resides in our hearts and minds, He in you will ask of God and God will give Him. No wonder we are told that we will be healing the sick and raising the dead, through His power!

She displayed strong faith. In other words, she is telling Jesus she believes that nothing is impossible with Him.

> "Jesus said to her, 'Your brother will rise again.'" (verse 23)

His voice must have sounded very promising, He is about to do something about this tragedy.

> "Martha said to Him, 'I know that he will rise again in the resurrection at the last day.'" (verse 24)

Martha shifts from faith to head knowledge. Martha boldly declared her confidence in the doctrine of resurrection. She knows when and the details. Sounds like good Bible believing follower of Christ. She says this in the presence of the Resurrection Himself. She equated the resurrection with the end of time.

I know, she said, he will rise again. *But not now!*

She is giving a little Bible study on the doctrine of the resurrection to Jesus. She shared her doctrinal correctness with the Life Giver. So often we get hung up on a doctrine that we are missing Jesus in it. How often we do the same thing as Martha. I know many people that believe Jesus can perform a miracle, but do not believe that it can happen in their life. We believe it can happen to someone else, but not to us, or we are pushing into the future what God is willing to do for us now. God is willing to do this for you right now. According to your faith, it will be done unto you, if you ask according to His will. Faith is like a muscle. We must exercise it. Faith is hearing the Word of God and acting upon it. Doing what the Word of God says is the best exercise of faith.

Martha had the doctrine of the resurrection correct. She is sharing it with the Life Giver Himself.

> "Jesus said to her, 'I am the resurrection and the life. He who believes in Me, though he may die, he shall live. And whoever lives and believes in Me will never die. Do you believe this?'" (John 11:25-26)

POINT NUMBER THREE – I AM THE RESURRECTION AND THE LIFE!

Are you ready for a radical Biblical statement?

The resurrection is not just an event. It is the person of Jesus Christ. Jesus said it Himself in verse 25: *"I am the resurrection and the life."* The apostle John says:

> "The life was manifested, and we have seen, and bear witness, and declare to you that eternal life which was with the Father and was manifested to us." (1 John 1:2)

> "And this is the testimony: that God has given us eternal life, and this life is in His Son. He who has the Son has the life; he who does not have the Son of God does not have the life." (1 John 5:11-12)

The only way we are entitled to "the life" is by virtue of our position *In Christ* when He went to the Cross and thereby shared with us His satisfaction of judgment, the second death. At His death with us in Him, the entire human race stood justified, and could receive the gift of the Holy Spirit. It is the indwelling Spirit that makes possible the transforming process that changes our minds from being conformed to the world.

Intimacy with Jesus through Spirit-guided study of scripture and prayer is how we *"let this mind be in you which was in Christ Jesus"* (Philippians 2:5) that will bring eternal life into the human soul. Jesus Christ is the life. He is eternal life, Christ in you *is* the hope of glory.

Friend, do you realize you were placed in Jesus from the foundation of the world, and if you accept your position in Jesus, He is eager to abide in you? Do you realize that by your position in Christ, you have eternal life if you choose to accept it? Jesus wishes that none should perish, and they need not perish because of the Lamb slain from the foundation of the world, but Jesus will not force eternal life on anyone. You have it, you do not have to earn it, but you do have to accept it. Jesus stands at the door and knocks. To those that open the door to Him, He says, "I will come in." Jesus is willing! Will you let Him in?

We may be able to prove biblical truth and all of the teachings of the Bible, and yet not knowing Jesus personally, not having Him abiding in our heart results in losing your *eternal* life.

In the eighteenth century a black boatman was taking a professor across a wide river. The boatman never had an opportunity to get an education and piloting the boat was his only source of income. As they were coming to the middle of the river, the professor asked him, "Do you know anything about mathematics?" The boatman said, "No, I don't know anything about mathematics." The professor said, "You just lost one third of your life not knowing anything about mathematics." As he kept rowing, the professor asked him another question." Do you know anything about astronomy?" The boatman said, "No, I don't know anything about astronomy," and he kept on rowing. The professor said, "Man, you just lost two thirds of your life not knowing anything about astronomy and mathematics." At that time, a large wave hit the boat on the side and flipped the boat over throwing both of them into the river. The boatman cried out to the professor, "Do you know anything about swimming." Gasping for air, the professor shouted, "No, I don't know anything about swimming." The boatman shouted back to the professor, "You just lost all of your life not knowing anything about swimming."

Dear friend, we may have all the education, we may know all our Biblical teachings, but if we don't have Jesus, we are losing all of our life.

Don't get me wrong. Education is important, knowledge is important, doctrines are important. But they can not save us. It is Jesus who saves us. Christ in us is the hope of glory. (Colossians 1:27) It is the life of Christ in you that will save you.

> Jesus said, "I am the resurrection and the life. He who believes in Me, though he may die, he shall live. And whoever lives and believes in Me shall never die. Do you believe this?" (John 11:25-26)

POINT NUMBER FOUR – YOU WILL NEVER DIE IF YOU ARE TRUSTING IN THE ATONING DEATH OF JESUS

In verse twenty five, Jesus is referring to the first death which is a sleep. In verse twenty six, He is referring to the second death, or eternal death. The disciples died the first death, but they will never taste of the second death because they have eternal life in Jesus. Neither will we if we are trusting in the atoning death of Jesus Christ.

> "Most assuredly, I say to you, he who hears My Word, and believes in Him who sent Me has everlasting life, and shall not come into judgment, but has passed from death into life." (John 5:24)

Eternal life is not a future reward. Eternal life is a present reality, and for those who have eternal life, they will not come into judgment but *have passed* (past tense) from death into life. If you are fearful of judgment and the second death, I have good news for you. The second death and the judgment is no longer in your future because your second death and your judgment has been lifted up from you and placed on Jesus at the cross. Jesus was willing to lose His own existence in order to save you and me from that judgment and from the second death.

The Jews equated the death on the cross with hanging on a tree. To them, hanging on a tree meant the curse of God, the second death, or eternal death. "Christ redeemed us from the curse of the Law, having become a curse for us—for it is written: 'Cursed is everyone who hangs on a tree.'" (Deuteronomy 21:22-23; Galatians 3:13) Christ became a curse for us. The high priest at the time of Jesus belonged to the party of the Sadducees. They did not believe in the resurrection. Jesus challenged their belief by raising people from the dead and claiming that He also would rise in three days. The Sadducees became His most bitter enemies. They are the ones that stirred up the crowd to crucify Jesus. He submitted to it, "even to the death of the cross," (Philippians 2:8) because eternal death was the penalty for sin. The Sadducees and others in the crowd cried for crucifixion because they wanted Jesus to experience eternal death. They believed the text in Deuteronomy 21 meant that God would not resurrect someone who was "hanged on a tree". Jesus loved us so much that He was willing to submit to crucifixion death. When humanity was joined to divinity, Christ as the second Adam (1 Corinthians 15:22) could take all of humanity in Him to die the second death (the legacy the first Adam gave us), "even so in Christ shall all be made alive" by God's creative power.

Christ took your second death and your condemnation and judgment upon Himself. It is no longer in your future. Thorns and thistles symbolize the curse that was pronounced on our planet. (See Genesis 3:17-18) That curse, Jesus took upon Himself when the crown of thorns was placed on His head, and later He was nailed to the cross.

Jesus could have come down from the cross and saved Himself, but He couldn't save Himself and save us at the same time. The choice that He made should speak loudly to us, and bring us to tears. His choice and His action to stay on the cross instead of saving Himself tells us "I love you more than I love Myself." Paraphrasing John 17:23, God the Father loves you no less that He loves Jesus Christ. God the Father loves you infinitely, and God the Son loves you infinitely, and Jesus signed that with His blood on the cross.

The big question for you dear reader – What are you going to do with this Jesus?

In Jesus we have our death, our resurrection and the life.

If you have Jesus – you have it all! You already died.

If you have Jesus – you have the resurrection.

If you have Jesus – you have eternal life.

YOU CAN HAVE VICTORY IN JESUS!

God wants to remake us into His likeness. Jesus is coming and time is running very short. There is no more time to waste. Things are changing very quickly and it will never be the same. It's time for us to get serious about Jesus. In Jesus you died and were resurrected, and you have eternal life. If you have Jesus, you have everything.

God placed the resolution of the sin problem on Jesus Christ, not on you or me. And God accepted Jesus' death as yours and mine. What a liberating thing it is that we may freely grow up in Jesus. Here is another radical, biblical statement for you:

Christianity is the only religion where you begin with perfection.

"For by one offering He has perfected forever those who are being sanctified." (Hebrews 10:14) You have been perfected forever through the death and

righteousness of Jesus. He justified you, declared you righteous, while you are in the process of being sanctified which is being made into what He declared you to be! That is the Good News!

Any religion where you have to try to earn your perfection, your way to heaven, and your acceptance with God is a pagan, works-based religion. Any religion that says you have to do your best and God will do the rest is also coming from pagan religion. Even when we are trying to do the things of God because we fear to be lost or for the desire of reward, it is not the right motive to serve God. That is what pagans were doing. Unfortunately these ideas crept into Christianity. The Gospel was distorted. There is no genuine, Godly power in a distorted gospel.

God accepted Jesus, His life and death as mine and yours. And now God makes Christ's righteous life available to you and me. He offers us Christ's victorious life. Let us take hold of it!

We are to focus not to be resurrected, but to have the Resurrection and the Life in us, that is Jesus Christ.

Jesus wants to dwell in us. He wants to take up residence in us. He wants to be intimate with us. He wants to save us from sin. Salvation according to Matthew 1:21 means to be saved from sin. If you will let Him in, you will have peace and victory. There is no sin either inherited or cultivated that cannot be overcome. With men it is impossible, but all things are possible with God. It is Christ in you that is not attracted to sin. "Greater is He who is in you then he who is in the world." Jesus is righteous and holy. It is impossible to sin in His presence. When He comes in, you will experience righteousness and holiness.

I want to remind you again the verse from Revelation 3:20 *"I am standing at the door and knock....whoever will open (the door of their heart), I WILL come in...."* This is the condition of the Laodicean church – Jesus is on the outside of the door. Are we letting Him to come in? And if we do, is He allowed to come as a visitor or as a resident? Here is the solution for the Revival!

Martha said to Him, *"I know that he will rise again in the resurrection at the last day."* (verse 24) Martha knows the doctrine about resurrection, but still does not know Jesus as the Resurrection and the Life!

And just like Martha, we know the doctrine of resurrection but do we know Jesus as the resurrection and the life? We may be sitting in the churches for a long time listening to the Word of God, learning all the teachings and the doctrines, even serving God, but not knowing the resurrection Himself – Jesus. Only Jesus can bring eternal life, joy and resurrection from our spiritual deadness, so we may have peace in our souls that surpasses understanding. It is Jesus that brings all of these in. And we can glorify God even in the midst of trials.

TO BE READY FOR THE COMING OF JESUS

> "Then Jesus, again groaning in Himself, came to the tomb. It was a cave, and a stone lay against it." (John 11:38)

Look at the striking similarity of the tomb of Lazarus with the tomb of Jesus! Everything here speaks about Jesus changing places with Lazarus, who represents the human race that Jesus loves so much!

> "Jesus said, 'Take away the stone.' Martha, the sister of him who was dead, said to Him, 'Lord, by this time there is a stench, for he has been dead four days.'" (John 11:39)

Dear Reader, is there stone in YOUR life that keeps YOU dead in sin?

Hear the words of Jesus: TAKE AWAY THE STONE!

POINT NUMBER FIVE – TAKE AWAY THE STONE!

Some might be worried that if the stone will be taken away, it may cause a big stink. But unless the stone is taken away there will be no evidence of resurrection.

> "Jesus said to her, 'Did I not say to you that if you would believe you would see the glory of God?'" (John 11:40)

Have you seen the glory of God?

Every time someone is raised from the dead, God is glorified. Every time someone acts upon the Word of God by faith, person is raised from being dead spiritually into a newness of life and God is glorified.

I have seen the glory of God in the life of a young man named Edwin:

One day the Lord brought a young man from Iran into my life. He came to this country with his parents when he was a teenager. He received his education and became very successful in this country. By the age of forty he was financially set for life and ready to retire. But he had two problems. He couldn't forgive people who offended him, and he had developed a malignant brain tumor.

It was during this time that I met Edwin. I made an appointment to meet him at his home. When I arrived and rang the doorbell, no one answered, even though we just spoke on the phone 30 minutes before. The Holy Spirit prompted me to wait, which is not like me to do. After ten minutes his father came to the door. He apologized and explained that his son just had a seizure. He took me to his room, where I sat down next to him and opened my Bible and lifted up the cross of Jesus to him. That's where the power of God is. Within minutes Edwin broke down into tears. He had fallen in love with Jesus in a way that no other teaching could accomplish.

Eventually my wife and I studied biblical doctrines in the light of the Gospel with Edwin, and he embraced all of them. During one of our studies Edwin told us about his dream he saw before we met. In his dream he was in the pit of mire and dirty. And many of his friends and his enemies were there. He was trying to get out of this mire and dirt, but these people were preventing him to do so. With tremendous straggles he was able to get out of this pit and wanted to be cleansed. And he woke up. He said, "I could not understand this dream at first. But as we studied the Bible and I came to know God, now I understand the meaning of it. God wants me to forgive all people in my life and be out of this pit, to be clean from it."

He forgave all those who offended him. He took away the stone so to say. Edwin found so much joy and peace in the Lord. He was anxiously waiting for our next meeting to dive again into the Word of God. What is hindering us from it?

Within couple of months Edwin expressed that He wanted to be baptized, but because of his physical condition and unpredictable seizures, dizziness and drowsiness he could not get into the baptistery.

Then his condition declined. On my last visit to the hospital, I found women in the hallway outside his door and the room was filled with men. I knew instantly what had happened. His father laid his head on my shoulder and began to weep. He said he had pleaded with God that he would heal his son, and he was devastated that God hadn't answered his prayer. As I stood beside his bed, I reflected on how not that long ago he was a strong man. Every time we finished studying with him, he would squeeze us with his strong arms and whisper, "I love you guys so much," because of what he was learning from the Bible. Friends, you will be loved by those you share the Gospel.

Edwin's older brother who was in the room, knelt down at his bed across from me and began to kiss the body of his younger brother. He told me he used to be afraid of dead people, but he was no longer afraid.

At that moment, the Holy Spirit took over. God wanted to communicate something to him, and the words came flowing out of my mouth. I said, "Ramin, let me tell you what your younger brother told me as I was studying the Bible with him. He said, 'If I were to choose between living a long life and not know what I have come to know about God, or be faced with the life-threatening condition that I am in, I would choose this condition that led me to know the beauty of God's love.'"

Friends, we need to value the knowledge of the truth as much as this young man did. The older brother was shocked! He stood up from his knees, looked straight into my eyes and said, "Grant, I want you to speak at my brother's memorial service." Now I was shocked because I did not expect this from these people who were from a Muslim country.

And he added, I want to have a shortcut to this knowledge.

We made our church available to them. The day of the service, about three hundred and fifty people filled the sanctuary to overflowing. They were from all parts of the US. These people had been the cream of Iran, elites who had fled the country after the revolution. Edwin's father was a member of the Olympic team of Iran.

There were Muslims, Jews, Buddhists, Protestants, and Catholics. Men and women, all dressed in black. As I stood before them, I shared with them that Edwin had discovered something so precious to him that it was his dream to share it with every family member and all of his relatives and friends. I said to them, "Because Edwin can no longer speak to you, I will be his mouthpiece." There was such a silence that you could hear the pin drop. For nearly thirty minutes I lifted up the cross of Jesus, revealing the love of God for them. As I walked out of the sanctuary, people were coming up to me with tears in their eyes, shaking my hand and asking me where they could find Seventh-day Adventist churches in their hometowns.

God was glorified in the life of Edwin at the end of his life and even after he died.

Dear friends, we have a most precious message to share with a world that is groping in darkness. Things are changing rapidly in our world. We have no idea what may take place in the year ahead of us. God wants to use us to reach those who have never heard of nor discovered the fullness of the Gospel and the loving character of God and compassionate Father.

When you begin to walk with Jesus, you are no longer dead in sin, but alive unto God. And God reveals to us those stones in our lives that still keep us partially dead. Jesus is speaking through His Word to us now – Take away the stone!

Even if the stone that is preventing you from experiencing spiritual fullness is as heavy as the one covering the entrance of Lazarus' tomb, God knows how to remove it.

"Then they took away the stone...... And Jesus lifted up His eyes and said, 'Father, I thank You that You have heard Me. And I know that You always hear Me, but because of the people who are standing by I said this, that they may believe that You sent Me.' Now when He had said these things, He cried with a loud voice, 'Lazarus, come out!'" (John 11:41, 43)

POINT NUMBER SIX – COME FORTH!

Come forth from being dead in sin into a newness of life!

There was no reason for Lazarus to remain dead, because Jesus was about to exchange his death in the tomb through the offering of His own life!

And there is no reason for you and for me to remain enslaved to sin, because Jesus condemned and conquered sin in the flesh and He is offering His victorious life to you and to me.

"And he who had died came out bound hand and foot with grave clothes, and his face was wrapped with a cloth. Jesus said to them, 'Unbind him, and let him go.'" (John 11:44)

POINT NUMBER SEVEN – UNBIND HIM AND LET HIM GO!

In order to say "Come out" to Lazarus, who represents all of humanity, Jesus had to make a commitment to go to the cross.

In order to say "Unbind him", Jesus had to commit Himself to live the life of victory over sin. Therefore, He can make His overcoming life, the righteousness He accomplished in our flesh that was weakened by sin for 4000 years, available to us. Are we taking hold of His life?

Dear reader, if you are reading this now and you are bound by grave clothes of sin, just as Lazarus was, and you may be dead in sin, just as Lazarus was dead in the grave, *there is hope for you.*

Change the name of Lazarus in this passage to your name and hear the words of Jesus:

"Take away the stone!" "____________________Come forth!"

Yield to His Word! And He will command to unbind you and let you go. His Word has power in itself to do what it says. His Word has "all" authority. (*cf.* Matthew 28:18)

Do you realize that if Jesus did not say the name of Lazarus when He called him out of the grave, all the graves would be opened and all the dead would have been risen! There is power in the Word that Jesus is speaking personally to you right now.

> "In every command and in every promise of the word of God is the power, the very life of God, by which the command may be fulfilled and the promise realized. He who by faith receives the word of God [acting upon it, which is proof of the faith] is receiving the very life and the character of God." (*Christ's Object Lessons*, p. 38).

Please read this statement again, thoughtfully.

So when Jesus speaks – something happens. And as His Words are sounding again in your hearing today – something must and will happen!

Do you believe it? Then take His Word personally today. Jesus, Who was willing to lose His own existence to save you, is calling your name saying:

"Take away the stone!" "Come forth!" And He is waiting to add "Unbind him and let him go".

All His biddings are also enabling's. When God raises us from the dead, He also commands to unbind us and free us from sin that entangled us.

Allow the power of His Word to be active in your life. It will be active if you choose to believe it, and the proof that you believe is acting upon the Word of God. And all will see the glory of God in your life, and many will believe in God, just like what happened with Lazarus.

> "Therefore many of the Jews who came to Mary, and saw what He had done, believed in Him." (John 11:45)

Dear friend, Jesus came into our world to save us from our sin, not in our sin. God wants to save each one of us, and He will, unless we resist and continue to cling to sin. He will not take the seed of sin back to heaven.

IN CONCLUSION – SEVEN POINTS HAVE COME OUT IN THIS STORY

1. THE PURPOSE OF TRIALS IS TO GLORIFY GOD.

If you are going through a trial today and not benefiting from it, and you are not praising God for the opportunity to grow, mature and glorify God, ask God right now to change your attitude towards the trials, to consider them as joy. Your trials will come to an end much faster, and you will endure them with grace, which will result in bringing glory to God's name.

2. GOD'S PEOPLE AVOID STUMBLING, AND BEING IN DARKNESS AND FEAR, BECAUSE THEY HAVE THE LIGHT IN THEM.

If there is a fear and darkness in your life, and you are stumbling, why don't you ask the Light to come in? And having the Light – Christ in you, you will not be in fear and stumbling. Christ in you will keep you from it. The Light is willing to come in. Are we willing to let the Light in?

3. INTIMACY WITH JESUS IS WHAT BRINGS ETERNAL LIFE INTO THE HUMAN SOUL.

If you know your Bible from cover to cover but you do not have an intimate relationship with Jesus, and you are not experiencing resurrection power in your life, Jesus wants to come in. He will never force Himself in. One of the saddest verses in the Bible is when Jesus said to five virgins "Depart from Me, I never knew you." (Matthew 25:12) The word "knew" first time appeared in Genesis 4:1. "Adam knew Eve his wife…" It suggests intimacy. And the first usage of the word in the Bible sets up the meaning of it through the whole Bible. So Jesus is saying here "We never been intimate". My friend, open the door of your heart and invite Him to come in. He wants to be intimate with you. He will bring peace and joy into your life.

4. YOU WILL NEVER DIE IF YOU TRUST IN CHRIST'S ATONING DEATH.

If you've never allowed God to love you fully and completely, you were afraid of the judgment and the second death, perhaps now you are seeing glimpses of God's love for you. Ask Him to help you believe that He loves you more than He loves Himself. You may end up in the fire at times, but He always keeps His eye on you. He will never take His eye off of you for a split second. You are like precious silver to Him, and He doesn't want any of the silver to be destroyed. Open your heart and surrender to Him, and allow Him to love you!

5. TAKE AWAY THE STONE!

There is no reason for any of us to remain spiritually dead in sin. If there is a stone in your life that keeps you dead and in sin, it must be taken away. Ask Him to take the stone away. It is much too heavy for you. He will remove the obstacle and the Holy Spirit will flow freely into your life. Unless the stone is taken away there will be no evidence of resurrection.

6. COME FORTH!

Jesus is calling His children to come out from being dead in sin into a newness of life! Change the name of Lazarus in this passage to your name and hear Him calling you out from the life of sin.

7. UNBIND HIM AND LET HIM GO!

Jesus commanded to unbind us from grave clothes. He wants to cover us with His Righteous robe. And when you put it on, at first it may be large on you. But if you put it on every day, you will grow into it.

Dear Father in heaven, I pray that your people will reflect Jesus Christ fully, and being united and like-minded, your commission will be finished in no time, so that Jesus can come and put an end to sin, lawlessness, and wickedness on this planet. We thank you Lord that you have begun a good work in us, and that you are faithful to complete what you've begun in us. We know that you will not relent until you finish the work. Help us to submit to your working in this world that we might find peace in you.

I pray in Jesus name. Amen!

CHAPTER 8

THE 60 SECOND GOSPEL

Recently I heard an evangelist giving a class at a camp meeting on how to witness to people God brings to us as we live our daily lives. He suggested that with most encounters, we only have about one or two minutes to keep their attention. He urged that Christians need to carry a variety of literature with them since people are so different.

It occurred to me that we could become a walking library, and that is difficult for most people. I made a suggestion that might be better to teach Christians to pack the Gospel into 60 Seconds that would appeal to everyone.

Keep in mind that the Gospel, to put it simply, is the revelation of the character of God, which was distorted by the enemy of all that is good.

THE 60 SECOND GOSPEL – EVERY HUMAN BEING NEEDS IT

In John 3:16 Jesus said:

> "For God so loved the world, that He gave His only begotten Son, that whosoever believes in Him will not perish but have everlasting life."

Let me spell out that love of God for you.

In John 17:23, Jesus was praying to His Father in the presence of His disciples. He said, "...Father, that they may know that you love them, as you love Me."

Let me paraphrase this and bring it home. What is Jesus actually saying? He is saying that God the Father loves you no less than He loves His Son, Jesus Christ. Let that sink in.

And in John 15:9 Jesus said:

"Just as the Father has loved Me, I also have loved you." (John 15:9)

There you have it. God the Father loves you infinitely, and God the Son loves you infinitely. Then Jesus went to the cross, and there He signed it with His own blood.

While He hung on the cross, He was tempted three times to come down from the cross if He was the Son of God, and save Himself. (Matthew 27:39-44; Luke 23:35 & 37) Could He have done it? Absolutely! But could He, by coming down from the cross and saving Himself, save us at the same time? The answer is – no, He could not save us at the same time. He had to make a choice. And that choice was to stay on the cross, to save mankind, you my Dear Reader and me.

This must speak loudly to every human heart as something very profound. I call it the last words of Jesus from the cross. He never uttered them, but His actions speak louder than any words. And here is my paraphrase of what His actions tell you and every human being:

"Whoever you are, whatever country you come from, does not matter. Regardless of the color of your skin, no matter what you have done in the past, it does not matter. I can come down from the cross and save Myself, but I cannot save you and Me at the same time. I choose to stay on the cross because I love you more than I love Myself."

And He died....

Dear Friend, that's who your God, your Creator is. This is the undistorted picture of God.

And YOU ARE LOVED!

Again: For God so loved *YOU* that He gave His only begotten Son that if *YOU* believe in Him *YOU* will not perish but have everlasting life. Don't let Satan deceive you by distorting God's character of love for you that you choose not to believe in Him. Don't let Satan deceive you with his lies.

At this point you can offer to the person 1 of 3 things:

1. Offer to pray for any concerns the person has.

2. Ask them if they would like to know more about the things that God through Jesus has done for humanity. Invite them to join a Bible study group so their knowledge of God will deepen, so they can have real joy and peace, no matter their circumstances. "We have a Bible study group here in town, you are welcome to join".

3. You can give them literature which they most likely will read. "Creative Media Ministries" website has small tracts that are perfect for these encounters.

And, if the Holy Spirit impresses you, be bold enough to make a call for commitment:

> "What are you going to do with this Jesus? Do you want to accept and invite Someone who loves you that much into your life as your Lord and Savior to settle the storms of your life?"

When you pray with the person, invite him/her to repeat what you pray, line by line, because that person may have never prayed in his/her life and does not know how.

As I was about to leave at the end of this class on Evangelism, someone laid his hand on my shoulder. I turned around and this man introduced himself as a Ministerial Director of that Conference, and asked if I would repeat this 60 Seconds Gospel for him to videotape it, so he can share it with his pastoral team. He did record it.

After him another woman came and introduced her care giver to whom she is trying to witness for some time and he is resisting it. She wanted me to talk with him. This man was from Iraq and he said that he believes in the Creator but does believe that Jesus is the Son of God. All I said to him "whatever your belief is and whatever turn your life may take, you should know this. The time will come that you will need this, and I shared 60 seconds Gospel, and ended with the fact that the Creator loves you that much." The next day I was coming for the evening meetings at the main auditorium and heard my name called. I turned around and there was this woman who was very excited and wanted to share with me the fact that today her care giver, man from Iraq, stood up in the morning meetings and made a public statement: "I accept Jesus Christ as my Lord and Saviour"

Let me share with you a few more responses to this 60 seconds Gospel:

THE PORTLAND AIRPORT

I arrived to airport in Portland Oregon and made my way to the car rental location so I could get to the church for meetings that evening. The church was about 70 miles away. As I got my reservation and came to get the car, a young man in his late twenties met me and escorted me to row that had economy and mid-size cars to choose from. I chose the car and this young man, his name was John, asked me, "What brought you to Portland?" I answered, "I was invited to conduct Revival series in one of the churches nearby." He said to me, "Oh, I am a Christian too." And

I asked him to share with me something about Jesus. The only thing he could say is that Jesus died for him. Then I offered to give him 60 Seconds Gospel and assured him that it will deepen his love for Jesus.

In 60 seconds John was standing there with tears coming down his cheeks. He said to me: "Grant, you will not drive this car. I am going to give you an upgrade." He brought me to the luxury car section and pointed to a Mercedes Benz 350. I said no, I will not drive this car to the church. They will think I am a wasteful servant, misusing the Lord's resources. He then offered a BMW convertible, and my answer was still "NO". Then he proceeded to a large Chevy Suburban.. Finally after being tired of my rejections of his luxury car offers, he brought me to the Volvo SUV and said, "no matter what your answer is – you will drive this car.."

On another flight to Portland I overheard a conversation a couple rows back and it sounded like one of them was Adventist. As we were coming off the plane, I approached him, and sure enough, he was one of the teaching professors at Andrews University. He needed to rent a car in Portland so he could drive to Walla Walla for meetings. We both went to car rental location and were using the same rental company. When John saw me, he immediately proceeded to give me a free upgrade. I asked him if he could first take care of my colleague, he was happy to do it. This professor had an economy car reserved, but drove from airport in an SUV, not understanding what was happening. And this all taking place as a result of sharing the 60 Seconds Gospel.

ANOTHER AIRPORT STORY

When I arrived at one of the airports on West coast, and was escorted to the midsize car area, the young man asked me "what brought me to their town"? I replied, "I am here to provide a Revival series for one of the churches in town." He said "I was raised as Christian but no longer am. I consider myself a gnostic". I said to him: "let me share with you in 60 seconds what you missed in Christianity and it may change your standing. In 60 seconds that young man replied to me: "I must reconsider my belief and where I stand. I never heard anything like this."

IN THE COUNTRY OF GEORGIA

A number of years ago when Bill Liversidge was alive, we were invited to different countries to conduct meetings, mainly to equip and educate pastors. One of them was Georgia, a small country that borders Armenia, Russia, and Turkey. When the meetings were over, their young pastor took us for site seeing in the capitol of Georgia, Tbilisi. One of the places was the center of their Christian religion – their own "Vatican" where they have their own pope. It was a magnificent old church structure.

Inside was laid out with black marble, very high ceilings. Everywhere you look there are lighted candles and pictures of the saints, very similar as in orthodox churches. In one of the corners, I noticed a crucifix, and a young woman standing there at the foot of the cross. The Holy Spirit led me to approach her, and I asked a question: "Do you know what actually took place then at the cross 2000 years ago?" She said "I do not know much about it". I shared the 60 Seconds Gospel with her right there. This young woman began to weep. Her friends, students that came with her drew near and began to ask what had made her cry?

As I was sharing the Gospel again with half a dozen of young people, the young local pastor who was giving us a tour tried to pull me away from them saying, "it is illegal in Georgia to share faith if you are not an Orthodox Christian." I said to him, "go and ask Pastor Bill to come, I need help here". The pastor found Pastor Bill and began to plead with him to stop me. While Bill was still talking with the local pastor, Bill noticed a high ranking priest with angry face marching directly towards me. Bill said to our young pastor – we must pray right now.

While he was praying to get me out of trouble, Pastor Bill watched the priest. Suddenly the priest stopped, made a 90 degree turn and went away. We were able to go outside to the courtyard of the church and exchange contact information with this group of students. We also connected them with the SDA Georgian Mission and signed them up for the English class that was taught there by one of our teachers, where they also offered Bible Study.

Again it is not Grant or you who will be making any kind of impact on the people, but the Gospel of Jesus, for it is the Power of God unto salvation to all who believe. And we need to present it in simple and short time to awaken in people the gratitude to God and hunger to know more.

60 SECONDS GOSPEL IN THE UBER

After finishing a series of meetings in his church in Indiana, the head elder, Carlos, who was also a part time Uber driver gave me a ride to the airport. He said, "I have a regular client that I pick up every morning. Would you mind if we pick her up and drop her off at her work place on the way to airport? Her father was a pastor, and her husband, who recently passed away, was also a pastor. I am trying to witness to her, maybe you can help me."

Early in the morning Elder Carlos came to pick me up. He moved the front passenger seat forward all the way and asked me to sit in the back seat behind him. As we arrived to the apartment complex, this woman came out, Carlos graciously opened the back passenger door for her and she sat in the back. She greeted Carlos, and began to talk. I was sitting quietly and waiting for when the Lord would open the door for conversation. When this woman, her name was Cynthia, said to Carlos that she had "a morning manna", (meaning the Word of God) the Lord spoke to my mind, 'This is your time'.

Here is how our conversation went:

I asked her, "did you get enough manna?"

Now she looked at me for the first time. "What do you mean?" she replied.

"I meant what I said. Did you get enough morning manna?" was my reply to her.

"Oh, I could use some more" she said.

I said it will take 60 seconds, and then I unfolded the 60 Seconds Gospel to her. I could see appreciation in her eyes as she exclaimed, "I never heard anything like this!" (And she was a wife of the pastor).

Then I pushed the door further and ask if she would like to have more of the manna. To which she replied that we have time till our destination. And I gave her 5 minutes Gospel. And I believe we must be equipped to share the Gospel in a given time, 1 min, or 2, 3 or 5 or more. It is the understanding and appreciation of the Gospel, the revelation of undistorted character of God that equips us to share. This is how we become the priesthood of all believers. No other way.

As you can imagine, the 5 Minute Gospel goes a little deeper. This is what I shared with Cynthia in the Uber:

THE 5 MINUTE GOSPEL

When Jesus was on the cross, He cried, *"My God, My God, why have you forsaken me?"* (Matthew 27:46; *cf.* Psalm 22:1)

Do you know what the Father did? According to these two texts, the Father looked down at Jesus on the cross, laid all our iniquity on Him and then He turned His face away from Jesus and let Him die!

> "And the LORD has laid on Him the iniquity of us all." (Isaiah 53:6)
>
> "But your iniquities have separated you from your God; And your sins have hidden His face from you, So that He will not hear." (Isaiah 59:2)

Why would the Father do this? I will answer this question. But in order for you to appreciate the answer, we need to answer another question first, a seminary level question. WHEN ADAM SINNED, WHERE WERE WE? This verse helps to answer that question:

> "Even Levi, who receives tithes, paid tithes through Abraham, so to speak, for he was still in the loins of his forefather when Melchizedek met him." (Hebrews 7:9-10)

This is the concept of biblical oneness and corporate solidarity. Once you understand this concept, you're going to see it all through the Bible, and you will appreciate the Gospel on a deeper level. Even though Levi wasn't born yet, he was genetically in Abraham's loins, the Bible is telling us that when Abraham paid tithes to Melchizedek, Levi did it also, even thought he was not yet born.

Here is the same concept in a simple form:

God created all men in one man, Adam. The devil ruined all men in one man, Adam. God redeemed all men in one man, Jesus Christ. This is the same concept of Biblical oneness, or Biblical solidarity. "For as in Adam all die, so also in Christ all shall be made alive." (1 Corinthians 15:22.)

Now, to apply the principle in these two verses, when Adam sinned, where were we? We were in Adam, in his loins, in his seed, just like Levi was still in the loins of Abraham when he paid tithes to Melchizedek. Whatever happened to Adam, happened to us *in him*. In one man the devil ruined the whole human race, but God had a plan. That plan was the Lamb slain from the foundation of the world. My friend, before God created this world, before sin entered the human race, God had a plan to save us!

Hallelujah, praise God! What a God we have.

And when the fullness of time came, God sent His Son in the likeness of human flesh. Jesus Christ became the second Adam.

The Bible tells us that God put us in Christ.

> "But it is due to Him that you are in Christ Jesus, who became to us wisdom from God, and righteousness and sanctification, and redemption." (1 Corinthians 1:30)

The book of Ephesians is full of these statements. Jesus lived a sinless life. Both Adams (the first in Eden and the second , Jesus) are under every aspect of the same law. That is whatever happened to the first Adam because we were in him happened to us. And whatever happened to the second Adam because God put us in Him, now He considers that it happened to us. Have you ever heard the statement, "righteousness by faith?"

The apostle Paul tells us in Colossians 2:10 that *in Him* we are complete.

Then God took the whole human race in the flesh of Jesus Christ and brought it to the cross to meet the justice of the law. All mankind was represented in the humanity of Christ that died on the cross.

When He was on the cross He cried out, *"My God, My God, why have You forsaken Me?"* The Father turned His face away from Jesus and let Him die. Why did the Father turn His face from Jesus? What did the Father see on the cross that made Him turn His face from Jesus? Whom did the Father see on the cross?

He saw you. He saw me. He saw each one of us in Christ, and He turned His face away from Jesus Christ, His only Son, and let Him taste our second death. That is why the second death is no longer in our future. Jesus not only took your sin to the cross, He went to the cross as you. He not only died on the cross instead of you, He died on the cross as you. On the cross of Christ justice and mercy kissed each other. A tremendous collision took place on the cross of Jesus between God and man, where all of the pain was absorbed by the heart of God so that, whatever happened to Jesus, God now considers that it happened to you and me. In Christ, humanity died the second death penalty for sin.

Jesus was not a sinner, but He invited God to treat Him as if He was a sinner so that we who are sinners might be treated as if we were righteous. That's how God treats us. If you are contemplating to quit, leaving God and the church, please look at the cross of Jesus. Look at the love of God. You are loved with an everlasting love.

By this time Cynthia had switched her attention from Carlos to me. She said, "may I ask a question?" What about the Spirit? At first I thought she is questioning the Holy Spirit as a Person, but then realized that she meant the tongues since she was a Pentecostal Christian.

With a twinkle in my eye, I began to talk to her in tongues, in Russian and Armenian. She raised her hands in the air and cried out "O, Brother! You got the Spirit!"

I smiled at her and said, "I know but let me tell you something very simple. The tongues you have heard are real languages. I spoke to you in Russian and Armenian, I speak four languages. If I had shared that 60 Seconds and 5 Minute Gospel with you in Russian or Armenian, would you have been able to understand and appreciate it?"

She said, "No."

Then I added, "That was exactly the case with the disciples at Feast of Weeks/Pentecost. They were given the real existing languages to communicate the Gospel 'manna' with people who spoke those languages. At the time, there were people present who were from many different nations to observe the Feast of Pentecost. And that is why I communicated it to you in English."

We arrived to her workplace. It was the largest prison in Chicago area, where she works in the administration office. Now we are staying in touch with her to see if we can come and minister to the inmates the precious Gospel of Jesus, so they can take hold of the Power of God and to be set free.

Every person that comes to my door or calls my phone with advertising, I say to them: "This is not why you came or call me today. You may not sell to me what you offer, but you will get from me something more then what you expected." After sharing the 60 Seconds Gospel with them and assuring them that they are loved by the Creator, they say: "You have no idea how much I needed it today."

You meet people every day wherever you go. Every one of them has challenges in their lives. Most of them heard about God but do not know Him personally, (this is one of the big reasons we are losing our youth), and you can insert into any conversation The 60 Seconds Gospel with anyone. It is easier than you might think. As you share it a few times, you will find your way and you will have joy every time you share the Gospel.

Dear Father, my prayer is that everyone who reads this chapter will have the courage to share The 60 Seconds Gospel with the people You bring into their lives. The world is starving for this heavenly "manna" and many have never even heard it, or if they have, they have never applied it to themselves in such a direct way. I also pray that you send needy, hungry people to their encounter with these dear Readers as often as You choose to make their paths cross. Let this wonderful Good News be ever on their minds so that they are always ready to share. Time is so short, please use us in your Gospel work. In the precious name of Jesus we ask. Amen!

CLAIM YOUR CHILDREN BACK - PART II

BIBLICAL PRINCIPLES—SPIRITUAL WEAPONS TO RECLAIM YOUR CHILDREN AND LOVED ONES BACK

"The inspiration for this seminar arose out of personal experiences and disappointments in my own life and family. I can identify with and feel the pain of every grieving parent and grandparent of children who are no longer walking with the Lord." —Grant Agadjanian

CHAPTER 9

SUBMIT TO GOD

Today, Christian churches are losing up to 85% of young people to the world. Perhaps it's your children, grandchildren, siblings, or other family members, or just your church members. This phenomena has encompassed almost every family, and every church. This seminar/message came about out of personal struggle, disappointment, and grief. I can relate to each one of you. I want you to know that just because the salvation of our children may seem unlikely today does not mean that God will not grant it tomorrow. Don't lose heart and don't lose hope. The story of your beloved children and loved ones for whom you have been praying, perhaps for years now, is not yet fully told. As long as they have breath, there's every reason to persist in prayer that God will breathe new life into them. It could be in the concluding p.s of your child's story, perhaps long after you are dead and gone that the Gospel seed you planted in their hearts will spring up into a new and beautiful life. You may be thinking, "But I didn't come into the belief until later in life. I didn't bring my children up in church and plant the Gospel seed in them." Take heart. God has promised:

> "Behold, I will send you Elijah the prophet before the coming of the great and dreadful day of the Lord. He will restore the hearts of the fathers to their children and the hearts of the children to their fathers, so that I will not come and smite the land with a curse." (Malachi 4:5, 6)

No matter what your life was like when you were raising your children, your life today is the Gospel seed to them. God uses agricultural imagery to reassure His people:

> "I will make up to you for the years that the swarming locust has eaten…It will come about after this that I will pour out My Spirit on all mankind; and your sons and daughters will prophesy.." (Joel 2:25, 28)

The fact that you are reading this book means you are seeking ways to show your children that the Gospel has changed your life for the better and you regret the mistakes you may have made in the past.

Often when we talk about the salvation of our children, I hear the argument that God gives every person the freedom of choice. That is true. God does give us freedom of choice. But somehow, we forget the other side of the coin. Jesus said, *"For the Son of Man has come to seek and to save that which was lost."* (Luke 19:10)

There are three categories of lost people.

- **Category One:** Knows that they are lost but cannot find their way back
- **Category Two:** Does not know that they are lost.
- **Category Three:** They are Prodigals who have a distorted picture of God

The prodigal has made a choice against God based on a distorted picture of Him. They think they are fully informed, and want no part of God and the whole religion thing. They need help to discover and experience God's character and goodness/the Gospel so they can reconsider their choice against God.

That is why we must preach the Gospel/the undistorted picture of God, for a witness of what God's character is truly like. Then the individual can use his/her free will based on the true knowledge of God.

Let me share a thought with you.

Whoever does not belong to God belongs to another, and that other is Satan. There is no neutral. We could call that a form of possession. Jesus Christ came to seek and to save the lost. He came to reclaim every human being—every lost sheep. When Adam rebelled against God, he gave Satan what God had given him, "dominion." (Genesis 1:26) When Jesus died on the cross, He redeemed what was lost by Adam, so He is the rightful owner of all of us, including our children. He created and redeemed us. You belong to Him twice, as do your children.

Who can actually prove that when a person is away from God that it is their free will not to belong to God if they are enslaved by the ruler of darkness who has blinded them robbing them of the Gospel truth. And the Gospel is the revelation of the undistorted picture of God.

God is light! When a person does not see the light, that person is blind. Would you agree with me? Is it free will to be blind? Would you like to be blind? Of course not. None of you would like to be blind. This is not free will. What is it then that blinds the person? It is the lies of Satan that misrepresent God's character. Therefore we must reveal and proclaim the Gospel, for it is the Power of God unto salvation, and we must claim people back to God beginning with our children and loved ones. Jesus said: *"If I will be lifted up I will draw all peoples unto Myself."* (John 12:32) Lifting up His character and His Gospel will keep our children in the church and closer to God.

Some may disagree with me. All I can say is "you have a right to be wrong". Keep reading, keep seeking, and most of all keep praying for your children and loved ones.

THREE ENCOUNTERS OF JESUS

Let us visit three stories/encounters of Jesus in the Bible, and discover their meaning from a totally different perspective. These encounters will encourage you. But before you open your Bible, ask God for His presence and for the Holy Spirit to speak to you to bring conviction and comfort and to restore your hope and joy.

THE SYROPHENICIAN WOMAN

Our first story is found in the Gospel of Matthew.

> "Then Jesus went out from there and departed to the region of Tyre and Sidon. And behold, a woman of Canaan came from that region and cried out to Him, saying, 'Have mercy on me, O Lord, Son of David! My daughter is severely demon-possessed.' But He answered her not a word. And His disciples came and urged Him, saying, 'Send her away, for she cries out after us.' But He answered and said, 'I was not sent except to the lost sheep of the house of Israel.' Then she came and worshiped Him, saying, 'Lord, help me!' But He answered and said, 'It is not good to take the children's bread and throw it to the little dogs.' And she said, 'Yes, Lord, yet even the little dogs eat the crumbs which fall from their masters' table.' Then Jesus answered and said to her, 'O woman, great is your faith! Let it be to you as you desire.' And her daughter was healed from that very hour." (Matthew 15:21-28)

This was a pagan woman, yet she knows who Jesus is. She calls Him *"Lord, Son of David,"* and she knows and believes that He is the promised Messiah that was to perform miracles. Jesus had not spoken a word to her when His disciples came and urged Him to send her away. They were asking Jesus to: "Get rid of her; she's bothering us." But the woman was persistent, and we as parents and Christians must also be persistent. Jesus said to her:

"'I was not sent except to the lost sheep of the house of Israel.' Then she came and worshiped Him saying, 'Lord, Help me.' But He answered and said to her, 'It is not good to take the children's bread and throw it to the little dogs.'" (Matthew 15:24-26)

Right here at this very point, many people will point their fingers at Christians and say, "See who your Jesus is. He calls people dogs." The problem is they don't know the Word of God, they don't know God, and they don't know the custom of that region in the time of Jesus.

In the time of Jesus in that region, people had little pet dogs at home for children to play with. They were different from the packs of partially wild dogs that roamed the streets scavenging. When the family would gather together to eat at the table, the father would sit at the head of the table, and he would watch that everyone was fed, especially the children. And no one can get up from the table until the father gives the sign. Do you have a dog at home? Where is your dog at dinner time? It is usually at your feet, beside or under the table, right? Once the father saw that the children were fed, he would take his last piece of bread, wipe his plate, and give it to the little dogs to eat, signifying that dinner is over.

This woman knows the customs of that region, and she understood what Jesus was saying. She catches the ball, so to speak, and throws it back at Him saying, "I know, Lord, but even the little dogs are getting the crumbs from the children's table, and I want that crumb. Please give it to me." Jesus is disarmed. He makes a pivotal statement saying,

"'O woman, great is your faith! Let it be to you as you desire.' And her daughter was healed at once." (Matthew 9:28)

Did her severely demon-possessed daughter know that she needed restoration and deliverance? No. But even if she would have known, she had no way to do anything about it. Today your children and grandchildren or family members may not know that they need spiritual restoration. Yet through the faith of this mother, the child was restored. An individual doesn't have to be demon possessed. It could be restoration from sickness or unbelief. What would have happened if the mother had not come to Jesus in faith and pleaded with Him? The child would have remained in that condition, severely demon-possessed, spiritually sick. But through faith and persistence of the parent that would plead with Him, the child was restored.

Why do you suppose this story is in the Bible? The apostle Paul said,

"For whatever things were written before were written for our learning, that we through the patience and comfort of the Scriptures might have hope." (Romans 15:4)

This story is for us today. It is for you, dear parents and grandparents, that you might have comfort and hope. How is your faith today?

By the way, before Jesus came to the region of Tyre and Sidon to address the need of this Syrophoenician woman, He was in the region of Galilee. The distance between these two regions is approximately fifty miles. So Jesus says to His disciples, "Let's go for a hike." Jesus went fifty miles to address the need of this woman. He did this to demonstrate the faith of this pagan woman to teach His disciples. He addressed the need and immediately returned. How is your faith dear reader?

THE FATHER OF THE DEMON POSSESSED BOY

Our second story comes from the Gospel of Mark.

> "Now after six days Jesus took Peter, James, and John, and led them up on a high mountain apart by themselves and He was transfigured before them.... And when He came to the disciples, He saw a great multitude around them, and scribes disputing with them. Immediately, when they saw Him, all the people were greatly amazed, and running to Him, greeted Him. And He asked the scribes, 'What are you discussing with them?' Then one of the crowd answered and said, 'Teacher, I brought You my son, who has a mute spirit. And wherever it seizes him, it throws him down; he foams at the mouth, gnashes his teeth, and becomes rigid. So I spoke to Your disciples, that they should cast it out, but they could not.'" (Mark 9:2, 14-18)

In this story, Jesus has taken three of His disciples up to the Mount of Transfiguration and left the other nine behind. When they came down from the mountain, Jesus found these nine disciples surrounded by a crowd, and the Scribes and Pharisees were arguing with them. As Jesus approached them, He asked what it was they were discussing. Someone from the multitude answered Him, saying,

> "'Teacher, I brought You my son, who has a mute spirit. And wherever it seizes him, it throws him down; he foams at the mouth, gnashes his teeth, and becomes rigid. So I spoke to Your disciples, that they should cast it out, but they could not.'" (Mark 9:17-18)

The disciples had already been casting out demons prior to this. Why weren't they able to do it now? Let's not forget that only a short time before this, Jesus had taken three of His disciples up into the mount with Him, leaving behind the other nine. What do you think was going on in the minds of the nine? Wouldn't you expect that they were thinking, "Why not me?" How can you expect to cast out demons when your heart is filled with a spirit of jealousy? If a brother or sister in your congregation succeeds, we are all to rejoice with them. If anyone is hurting in your congregation, we are to be hurting with them. If this is not in place, I can tell you right now, it's not a healthy body. It is a numbed body. Please keep this in mind. Our churches should be so lovely that they will attract every sinner from the outside. Churches are to be a place where the sinner can find grace. People are hungering for this kind of church.

> "He answered him and said, 'O faithless generation, how long shall I be with you? How long shall I bear with you? Bring him to Me!'" (Mark 9:19)

Here is the solution for every parent regarding their prodigals: Bring your loved one to Jesus in your prayers.

> "Then they brought the boy to Him. And when he saw Him, the spirit immediately convulsed him, and he fell on the ground and wallowed, foaming at the mouth. So He asked his father, 'How long has this been happening to him?' And he said, 'From childhood.'" (Mark 9:20-21)

That points to the story of the human race which was kidnapped by the evil one, from its childhood.

This parent continued:

> "'And often he has thrown him both into the fire and into the water to destroy him. But if You can do anything, have compassion on us and help us!' Jesus said to him, 'If you can, believe, all things are possible to him who believes.' Immediately the father of the child cried out and said with tears, 'Lord, I believe; help my unbelief?'" (Mark 9:22-24)

The father tells Jesus that this had happened often and how he was thrown both into the fire and water to try to kill him.

> "And the father said, 'If you can do anything, have compassion on us and help us.'"

The word "Can" here in Greek is Dynamo—power. This parent is saying: "If you are of power"

> "And Jesus said, 'If you can believe.'" (Mark 9:22-23)

Jesus is asking the very same person that just said, "If you can do anything"— "can you believe?"

> "And Jesus said to him, 'All things are possible for the one who believes.'" (Mark 9:23)

How much does "all" include? Is that everything except our children or the prodigals? My friends, that includes all our children and our prodigals. Everything is possible to him who believes. How is your faith today? Right now you can rejoice with great hope and praise God for His power to save our children.

> "Immediately the father of the child cried out and said with tears, 'Lord, I believe, help my unbelief!' When Jesus saw that the people came running together, He rebuked the unclean spirit, saying to him, 'You deaf and unclean spirit, I command you, come out of him and enter him no more!' Then the spirit cried out, convulsed him greatly, and came out of him. And he became as one dead, so that many said, 'he is dead'. But Jesus took him by the hand and lifted him up, and he arose." (Mark 9:24-27)

How much faith did this father have compared to the Canaanite woman from Syrophoenicia? Not as much, right? He had only a little. And what happened? Jesus cast out the demon, and the child was restored. Some people say to me, "Oh, I don't have as much faith as my pastor or elder. This may not happen for me." Really? Why is this story in the Bible? Here is the answer again:

> "For whatever things were written before were written for our learning, that we through the patience and comfort of the Scriptures might have hope." (Romans 15:4)

Didn't Jesus say that if you have faith as little as a mustard seed, it will happen? When the Lord led me through all of this, we stopped crying. I stopped crying. I can relate to each one of you, but I stopped crying. Why? Because God revealed to me something so beautiful, so comforting, that gives me such a hope no matter what happens today. The devil doesn't want you to be encouraged. He wants to keep parents so wounded that they will be inactive in churches. These messages were meant to bring you healing. My desire and prayer for you is that when you go back to your churches, you will become an active parent and member of your church and bring parents together to reclaim their lost children back.

Let's not forget why we're here. The Lord called us to lift Jesus up and to share the Gospel.

JAIRUS' DAUGHTER AND THE WOMAN WHO TOUCHED IN FAITH

Our third story is found in the Gospel of Luke.

> "So it was, when Jesus returned, that the multitude welcomed Him, for they were all waiting for Him. And behold, there came

a man named Jairus, and he was a ruler of the synagogue. And he fell down at Jesus' feet, and begged Him to come to his house, for he had an only daughter about twelve years of age, and she was dying. But as He went, the multitudes thronged Him. Now a woman, having a flow of blood for twelve years, who had spent all her livelihood on physicians and could not be healed by any, came up from behind and touched the border of His garment. And immediately her flow of blood stopped. And Jesus said, 'Who touched Me?' When all denied it, Peter and those with him said, 'Master, the multitudes throng You and press You, and You say, 'Who touched Me?' But Jesus said, 'Someone touched Me, for I perceived power going out from Me.' Now when the woman saw that she was not hidden, she came trembling; and falling down before Him, she declared to Him in the presence of all the people the reason she had touched Him, and how she was healed immediately. And He said to her, 'Daughter, be of good cheer, your faith has made you well. Go in peace.'" (Luke 8:40-48)

Sometimes Jesus delays His coming. Sometimes, the answer to our prayer is delayed because there are some other things that need to be addressed. When Jesus stopped procession because of the woman, the ruler of the synagogue could have been anxious, upset, angry or jealous. He could have thought, "Would you please hurry? Couldn't you do this later?" We can only imagine the thought of Jesus, "but this woman is also My Daughter."

By the way, please notice that when the woman came to Jesus that touch of faith that she touched Jesus with was different from every other touch. That touch of faith drew power from the source, Jesus Christ. That power was the power of His life, and it supplied her need. Something real went out from Jesus into the woman. She received the life she did not have before, and that life came from Jesus Christ. How did she receive it?

"Jesus said, 'Your faith has made you well.'" (Luke 8:48)

That very power, my friends, is available to each one of us today through faith. When we pray for our loved ones, we are to pray with faith as touching that same power in order that the power of His life will flow into the lives of our loved ones who may be dead spiritually. Christ in His wisdom, allowed the delay to give a lesson of faith to this father, the ruler of the synagogue, through the faith of this unclean woman.

"While He was still speaking, someone came from the ruler of the synagogue's house, saying to him, 'Your daughter is dead. Do not trouble the Teacher.' But when Jesus heard it, He answered him saying, 'Do not be afraid; only believe, and she will be made

> well.' When He came into the house, He permitted no one to go in except Peter, James, and John, and the father and mother of the girl. Now all wept and mourned for her; but He said, 'Do not weep; she is not dead, but sleeping.' And they laughed Him to scorn, knowing that she was dead. But He put them all out, took her by the hand and called saying, 'Little girl, arise!' Then her spirit returned, and she arose immediately. And He commanded that she be given something to eat. And her parents were astonished, but He charged them to tell no one what had happened." (Luke 8:49-56)

We are not told why Jesus charged them not to tell anyone, but perhaps He was trying to protect the family from the anger of Sadducees who did not believe in the resurrection.

The ruler's daughter died while he was walking with Jesus. Today our children and grandchildren may be dead spiritually while we walk with Jesus. Who raised the child? – Jesus. Did the child know that she needed to be resurrected? No. The Bible tells us, *"The dead know nothing."* (Ecclesiastes 5:9) Our children, our prodigals, may not know that they need spiritual resurrection. What two things did Jesus expect from the parent in order to address the need? Take it right out of the text that we just read. *"Jesus told him, 'Do not fear."* What else? *"Only believe."* Just two things—do not fear, only believe. *Jesus is the same yesterday, today, and forever.* (Hebrews 13:8) Jesus expects these same things from us as parents today. Do not fear and only believe. God is still in control. So Jesus raised the child.

When we look at these three encounters of Jesus from a different angle, they give us hope.

Let's hear the scripture again.

> "For whatever things were written before were written for our learning, that we through the patience and comfort of the Scriptures might have hope." (Romans 15:4) This is meant for you and me today.

THREE PARABLES OF JESUS

Now let us look briefly at three of Jesus' parables found in Luke 15. Each parable is about something that was lost and then found. We can hear the good news in that already.

The first parable is the parable of the lost sheep. Sheep are the dumbest creatures. When the sheep goes astray, it knows that it is lost, but it can't find its way back. Who is it that finds the sheep? The shepherd finds the sheep. And when he finds it, what does he do? He places the sheep on his shoulders and carries it back rejoicing. A celebration takes place.

The second parable is the parable of the lost coin. The lost coin does not know that it is lost. Who was it that found the coin? It was the woman. What does a woman in the Bible represent? A woman represents the church. Did you know that women in Israel wore necklaces with precious coins? They would make a necklace or head band that included coins that were part of their marriage dowry and wear them. When one coin was lost, the woman was troubled. She was anxious to find it. Please hear this.

When this precious coin was lost, what does this woman do? This woman, representing the church, was troubled and anxious to find the lost coin. So she sweeps the house, lights a candle, finds the coin and rejoices. And then she throws a party.

The third parable is the story of the prodigal son. He comes to his father and says, "Dad, I wish you were dead. Give me the money now." So he gives the money to his son, and the son goes away and squanders it all. And when he returns to his father's house, he comes all beaten up. What was it that brought the prodigal back? He was hungry. He was in a desperate trial, and he had hit rock bottom. We can say the trials and difficulties brought him back to the father.

1. What was the father doing while the son was away? PRAYING
2. What was he praying for? FOR THE SON TO COME BACK
3. What brought the son back? THE TRIALS HE WAS GOING THROUGH

To what logical and radical conclusion does this bring us? If the father was praying for the son to come back, and the only thing that would bring him back was the trial, what should the father pray for?

Do you suppose that he was praying that he would hit rock bottom, and that his son would run out of his resources? What is more important for us, my friends? No caring parent prays for our children to succeed in this life at the cost of their eternity. It is safe to trust God not to allow our children more trouble than they can bear, so we can pray that they have a little shaking in their life, and come back to God. It's up to you. What's most important to you?

In every case the lost was found and recovered but it was not a passive recovery. Even in the case of the father, he was not just sitting and waiting. He was active in prayer. It was when the trials hit the prodigal, (which he knew were brought upon himself by his own choices) that he came back home to his father. The Bible doesn't say how long the father had been praying. The father was willing to pray as long as it took. Every case is different, so don't you ever give up.

Everything that was lost in these three parables was found and recovered. And in this recovery the Shepherd (Jesus) is involved, the woman (church) and the parent (Father). And in every recovery there was a celebration.

What did the father do when the prodigal came home? The son had taken his money and left home and squandered it. He knew his son wished that his father was dead and that he probably didn't even think about daddy. Yet daddy throws him a party. Why?

> "'It was right that we should make merry and be glad, for your brother was dead and is alive again, and was lost and is found.'" (Luke 15:32)

What does this tell us? When any prodigal bursts into your church, you may not know him. It may be my child, or it may be your child. Every person willing to come to Jesus is part of the church's marriage dowry, like the lost coin in the parable. If he is entering church somewhere, it is worth celebrating. He may look different. He may be tattooed with pierced ears or nose, or whatever. You name it. You've seen them all around. They don't look like us, and they don't smell like us. They enter the church like yours. What do we usually do? We say "Hi!" and go around them. Let's suppose that's your son, and he looks at the church members and says, "Nothing has changed." So he leaves forever.

Is that how we want to treat our prodigals? It could be your child. He did not come by himself. The Holy Spirit brought him, and we are not receiving him. What are we supposed to do, when the prodigal, the sinner, comes to church? We are supposed to throw a party for that person, my friends. Let him feel that he is back and welcomed at home, and he will never leave that church. Isn't that what you want for your children? Then do it for those who are not yours as well. God may do it through someone for your child in return, wherever they may be.

That is why, being mentored by Bill Liversidge, when I preach any sermon, I focus on two types of people in the congregation. I focus on the one who came for the first time to learn who God is, and the other is the one who came for the last time to give God just one more chance. And if you present the Everlasting Gospel – reveal the beauty of God's character for these two types of people, the whole congregation will be fed as well.

Before we go into the next two chapters of biblical principles, I would recommend that you act upon the law of forgiveness and consider James 4:7.

If we really believe in forgiveness, that the Lord has forgiven us, there are four things we must do:

FOUR ELEMENTS OF FORGIVENESS

1. We must forgive our parents for whatever wrong they have done to us. Research shows that most of our problems in our adult life are connected with the fact that we cannot or do not want to forgive our parents for the pain they caused to us or whatever they have not done for us that they should have done. We are psychologically healthy in proportion to the degree of our ability to freely forgive those who pained us.

2. We must forgive all people in our lives that have caused us pain. Forgiving never means you are approving the wrong. Release it, do not let the un-forgiveness make a nest in your mind. When you forgive you are the first beneficiary of it. It gives you peace and emotional, physical and spiritual health.

3. Forgive yourself for whatever mistakes and foolish things you have done in your past. Forgiveness releases yourself from the grip of guilt that paralyzes you. Forgive yourself one hundred percent as Jesus did. "Be of good cheer, your sins are forgiven you." (Matthew 9:2). If God has forgiven us, who do we make ourselves to be if we refuse to forgive ourselves. ("Forgive us our debts, as we forgive our debtors" Matthew 6:12) This is a form of blasphemy, because we are elevating ourselves above God.

4. Ask forgiveness from others whom you have caused pain. So many lives are destroyed because people do not have the courage to ask for forgiveness.

PREPARATION TO RECEIVE AND TO APPLY BIBLICAL PRINCIPLES AS SPIRITUAL WEAPONS IN RECLAIMING YOUR CHILDREN AND LOVED ONES BACK

Before we equip you with Biblical principles to claim your children back, I would like to share with you a Scripture and a statement from a Christian writer:

> "This is the preparation day. Set your own hearts in order and work earnestly for your children. An *unreserved surrender to God* will sweep away the barriers that have long defied the approaches of heavenly grace. When you take up the cross and follow Christ, when you bring your lives into conformity to the will of God, your

> children will be converted." (Ellen G. White, *The Adventist Review and Sabbath Herald*, July 15, 1902, Par.13, emphasis added)

"Surrender to God" without any reservations. Let your children see in you what you want to see in them. If you are only half-hearted with God or even 99% with God, this will result in your children to be 100% without God.

> "Therefore submit to God. Resist the devil and he will flee from you." (James 4:7)

"Submit to God." This is not a suggestion, it is a directive! "Submit" is not a passive act. It is an intentional surrender of every thought, decision and entire being to His Sovereign will. "Not my will, but Yours be done." (Luke 22:42). Thus you are aligned with the unshakable power of the kingdom of God.

To resist is to stand firm in the full armor of God. The devil will not walk away, he will flee in terror! A believer fully submitted to God is a terror to the forces of darkness. Why? Because submission grants you the access to Divine authority. Then when you resist the devil in the name of Jesus, you are not speaking as an ordinary human, you are speaking as ambassador of Heaven! Submission to God creates a fortress around your life. The enemy cannot dwell where obedience reigns. Submission to God is your shield and empowers you to resist the devil.

When you kneel in submission to God, Heaven stands with you. When you resist – you wield the authority of Christ Himself. Do not let fear hold you back. You are not only avoiding evil in your life, but advancing the Kingdom of God. The enemy flees not because of who you are but because of who resides in you.

> "...Greater is He who is in you than he that is in the world." (1 John 4:4)

> "Therefore submit to God. Resist the devil and he will flee from you." (James 4:7)

The victory over the enemy, over his power and sin, is through surrendering to God. And you are not fighting for the victory – you are fighting from an already victorious position. Remember this, the battle is the Lord's and the promise is yours. And you are more than conquerors through Him who loves you.

We are in a spiritual warfare, and we are in need of spiritual weapons.

> "For the weapons of our warfare are not carnal, but mighty in God, pulling down the strongholds." (2 Corinthians 10:4)

God gave us mighty weapons, and they are able to pull down the strongholds of the enemy. We will unfold and equip you with seven Biblical principles/spiritual weapons.

Let me ask you this. Would you say that light is stronger than darkness? Yes, light is stronger than darkness. Jesus said, *"You are the light of the world...."* (Matthew 5:14) What does that mean? It simply means that the darkness cannot withstand you. Wow!

CHAPTER 10

BIBLICAL PRINCIPLES– SPIRITUAL WEAPONS TO RECLAIM YOUR CHILDREN AND LOVED ONES BACK

PRINCIPLE NUMBER ONE – THE KEYS OF THE KINGDOM OF POWER

> "When Jesus came into the region of Caesarea Philippi, He asked His disciples, saying, 'Who do men say that I, the Son of man, am?' So they said, 'Some say John the Baptist, some Elijah, and others Jeremiah or one of the prophets.' He said to them, 'But who do you say that I am?' And Simon Peter answered and said, 'You are the Christ, the Son of the living God.' Jesus answered and said to him, 'Blessed are you, Simon Bar-Jonah, for flesh and blood has not revealed this to you, but my Father who is in heaven. And I also say to you that you are Peter, and on this rock I will build my church, and the gates of Hades shall not prevail against it.'" (Matthew 16:13-18)

The word "Peter" is *"Petros"* (Strong's G4074 Greek) meaning a piece of a rock or a small pebble. Can you build a church on a small rock? Some claim they did. Good luck; it will not stand. You cannot build a church on a small rock. Who is the rock then? Jesus is the rock, *"Petra"* (Strong's G4073 Greek) which means a mass of rock. There are more scriptures in the Bible than we can number that tell us Jesus is the rock. (Psalm 71:3; 2 Samuel 23:3; Deuteronomy 32:4; 1 Corinthians 10:14; Isaiah 17:10; Psalm 18:2; Ephesians 2:20) Jesus is the rock. He is the cornerstone. Jesus told

Peter that he was a little pebble, but that He would establish His church on this rock, referring to Himself. What is the church? It's people who believe in Jesus. We are the church.

Jesus says He will build His church on the rock, and the gates of Hades will never prevail against it. What that tells you and me is that no matter how terrible the assault of the enemy may be on us, he will never overpower us if Jesus is our rock. Doesn't that cause you to praise God? Jesus goes on to say,

> "And I will give you the keys of the kingdom of heaven;
> and whatever you bind on earth will be bound in heaven,
> and whatever you loose on earth will be loosed in heaven."
> (Matthew 16:19)

Jesus is handing to us the keys of the kingdom of heaven. In Mark 9:1 and 1 Corinthians 4:20, kingdom of heaven is referred to as the kingdom of power. The kingdom of heaven is the kingdom of power. Jesus is saying, "I am giving you the keys of the kingdom of power."

What does the keeper of the key have? If I were to give you the keys to my house, and you were to come to the door of my house with keys in hand, what do you have with my keys? You have access to my house and everything that is in the house, right? If you have the keys of the kingdom of power that Jesus gives to us, what do you have with them? You have access to the kingdom of power.

Many theologians consider that the New American Standard Bible is the best translation from Greek into English. If you've never studied Greek or Hebrew and you want to know what a word was in the original language, the closest to the original is the New American Standard Bible in English. Let me share with you what the Greek and the New American Standard Bible says on this verse.

> "I will give you the keys of the kingdom of heaven; whatever you bind on earth shall have been bound in heaven, and whatever you loose on earth shall have been loosed in heaven."
> (Matthew 16:19 NASB)

This tells me that the heavenly powers are involved on your behalf at that very moment when you bind or loose something on earth. Wow! I hardly know anyone who took Jesus's words here at face value.

Jesus said to His disciples:

> "If you forgive the sins of any, their sins HAVE BEEN FORGIVEN them; if you retain the sins of any, they HAVE BEEN RETAINED."
> (John 20:23, emphasis added)

My friends, the keeper of the keys has power and authority to "bind and loose". Jesus did not leave us helpless when He ascended to heaven. He knows that we are in the enemy's territory. He promised to be with us to the end of the age. (Matthew 28:20). And He gave us the keys of the kingdom of power.

When the devil injected sin into the human race, the kingdom of heaven was utterly shut against man. The door was shut, man was locked out and death came as a result of sin. It was the devil's plan that mankind would be shut out and locked up in death, not having access to heaven. By injecting sin into human race the devil made us powerless. But Jesus Christ came down from heaven with the keys of the kingdom of power and placed them in the hands of humanity, opened to us access to the kingdom of heaven once again. Jesus did not stop there. He went into the very stronghold of the devil, his prison of death. And when He came out of death, He ripped away the keys of death from Satan. Jesus says,

> "I am He who lives, and was dead, and behold, I am alive forevermore. Amen. And I hold the keys of Hades and of Death." (Revelation 1:18)

Satan no longer has those keys. Christ took those keys of death with Him when He went back to heaven, but He left the keys of the kingdom of heaven in the hands of His followers, and gave them the power to be the sons and daughters of God again. And Jesus took out of the hands of the devil the power to shut humanity – your loved ones, your children and all of us away from the kingdom of heaven. Praise God!

ANOTHER LOOK AT THE PLAN OF SALVATION

What did Jesus do that *entitled* Him to make humanity "the sons and daughters of God"? Even though God is more powerful than Satan, His justice will not allow Him to "bend the corners" of His law just because He wants to save sinners. God's law requires that "the soul who sins shall die." (Ezekiel. 18:4) The Godhead's plan to save fallen humanity must conform with God's own Law and requirements.

God announced His "law" regarding the Tree to Adam in the Garden of Eden:

> "in the day that you eat of it you shall surely die." (Gen 2:17)

PROBLEM ONE – CERTAIN IMMEDIATE DEATH

When Adam and Eve ate of the Tree, the law of God required that they would "surely die" on the day they ate. That would have met the demands of God's justice, but the human race would be dead. If God had resurrected them, the devil, as the accuser of the brethren, would have objected. He would have been correct, since the penalty for sin is the "second" death, (Rev. 21:8) which meant "good bye to life forever". God could not have resurrected them just because He felt sorry for them, and still meet the demands of His law of justice.

GOD'S SOLUTION TO PROBLEM ONE:

The Lamb slain from the foundation of the world.

> "As soon as there was sin, there was a Saviour. Christ knew that He would have to suffer, yet he became man's substitute. As soon as Adam sinned, the Son of God presented Himself as surety for the human race, with just as much power to avert the doom pronounced upon the guilty as when He died upon the cross of Calvary. (E. G. White, *The Advent Review and Sabbath Herald,* 3-12-1901; *In Heavenly Places,* p 13; *Faith I Live By,* p. 75; *The Desire of Ages,* p 210)

> "The plan for our redemption was not an afterthought, a plan formulated after the fall of Adam. It was a revelation of the 'mystery which hath been kept in silence through times eternal.' Romans 16:25, R.V. It was an unfolding of the principles that from eternal ages have been the foundation of God's throne. From the beginning, God and Christ knew of the apostasy of Satan, and of the fall of man through the deceptive power of the apostate. God did not ordain that sin should exist, but He foresaw its existence, and made provision to meet the terrible emergency. So great was His love for the world, that He covenanted to give His only-begotten Son, 'that whosoever believeth in Him should not perish, but have everlasting life.' (John 3:16)." (Ellen G. White, *The Desire of Ages,* p. 22)

PROBLEM TWO – IRRESISTIBLE SELFISHNESS IS SIN

In addition, Mankind now had another problem. Not only were they going to die forever, when Adam and Eve sinned they literally changed their nature to be self-centered, i.e. selfish. This means if God resurrected them, their selfish nature would cause them to sin naturally. Someone once said that "sin is the suicidal action of the human will against itself". Once we willingly commit sin, we are much more likely to sin again.

GOD'S SOLUTION TO PROBLEM TWO:

God needed to give them a new nature. He needed to resurrect them as a "new creation" to "newness of life", because we are dead to sin. Since God's *agape* (self emptying love) never forces His will on His creation, the solution must allow human beings to have a probationary life to make an informed choice whether they want that "newness of life".

> "Adam's sin plunged the race into hopeless misery; but by the sacrifice of the Son of God, a second probation was granted to man. In the plan of redemption a way of escape is provided for all who will avail themselves of it. God knew that it was impossible for man to overcome in his own strength, and he has provided help for him. How thankful we should be that a way is open for us, by which we can have access to the Father; that the gates are left ajar, so that beams of light from the glory within may shine upon those who will receive them! (E. G. White, *Christian Temperance and Bible Hygiene,* p 15)

> "They [Adam and Eve] earnestly entreated that they might remain in the home of their innocence and joy. They confessed that they had forfeited all right to that happy abode, but pledged themselves for the future to yield strict obedience to God. But they were told that their nature had become depraved by sin; they had lessened their strength to resist evil and had opened the way for Satan to gain more ready access to them. In their innocence they had yielded to temptation; and now, in a state of conscious guilt, they would have less power to maintain their integrity." (E. G. White, *Spirit of Prophecy,* Volume 1, p. 19)

God is entitled to extend grace to sinful humanity only because of the accomplishments of Christ.

> "The work was of God, and man should receive no glory. Precious Redeemer, thy grace was not given because of any man's merit nor as the result of any man's worth or righteousness, but the righteousness of Christ. The Sin-pardoning Saviour was holding forth the golden scepter of his matchless grace and mercy to wayward sinful souls....Let the efficacy of the blood of Christ avail in your behalf, and his righteousness become your righteousness." (E. G. White, *1888 Materials,* p. 63, 64)

Christ worked out righteousness for All of Humanity who take hold of it by faith

> "He worked out righteousness here in the flesh. What did he do it for? For himself? No, he did not have any need of it. He had riches to begin with. He had everything that he could have when he was in heaven. But here on earth, as a man, he worked out righteousness and eternal redemption *that he might give them to us.* That is the sole reason that brought him into the world. He has all

that righteousness he wrought out here, and he will and does give it to men. So he paid the penalty of the law, – for himself? No! He had no sin, consequently the law had no claim upon him. In the second letter to the Corinthians, chapter five, and verse twenty-one, the apostle Paul says: "For He hath made Him to be sin for us, who knew no sin; that we might be made the righteousness of God in Him." So it was that he suffered the penalty, not for himself, but for us. When we by faith lay hold on Christ, and become united with him, so that we are identified with him, then we have that life which he has to bestow." (E. J. Waggoner, *General Conference Daily Bulletin,* March 18, 1891, emphasis in original)

Jesus volunteered to become the Savior of the world (John 3:16) so that those who chose to "believe in Him" would not perish, but have everlasting life.

When "the Word was made flesh" (John 1:14) Jesus took humanity *in Him* and rewrote our history by living a sinless life *"in the likeness of sinful flesh."* (Romans 8:3) Then He took us, *in Him,* to the cross to pay the penalty for sin (the second death). That allowed God to impute the righteousness of justification to the human race since we were *in Him* when He went to the cross, and "on Him was laid the iniquity of us all." (Isaiah 53:6). It is therefore ethical for God to *"reckon yourselves to be dead indeed to sin, but alive to God in Christ Jesus our Lord."* (Romans 6:11)

When Adam sinned in the Garden of Eden, he had not yet had any children. When he sinned, his nature was changed to be self-centered, so mankind would find it almost impossible to resist the power of sin. In fact, scripture tells us that "all have sinned and fall short of the glory of God." (Romans 3:23). The plan devised by the Godhead solved all the objections that Satan, the accuser, could make. Since "through one man sin entered the world, and death through sin, and thus death spread to all men, because all sinned, (Romans 5:12), God's solution was that "one Man's righteous act the free gift came to all men, resulting in justification of life" (Romans 5:18). The righteousness that Christ worked out "in the likeness of sinful flesh" resulted in a righteousness that He can impart to the sinner who believes He will do what He said He would do.

What God did at the incarnation of Christ was to join all humanity in Jesus, so that everything He did "the likeness of sinful flesh, God could reckon that humanity also did, *in Him*. In Christ, we have lived His sinless life and overcome sin "in the flesh", and died the second death in Christ on His cross, and were resurrected in Him to newness of life.

At His ascension, He took humanity in Him and Paul can describe that He "raised us up together, and made us sit together in the heavenly places *in Christ Jesus."* (Ephesians 2:6, emphasis added) This is the incredible Good News of the Gospel of Christ.

Because of all that Christ Jesus has done, is doing, and will do in the future, the devil has no power to shut humanity away from the kingdom of heaven. That includes you, your children and loved ones. Praise God!

When we come together in prayer to reclaim our loved ones to God, do you believe that Jesus is right there with you in that moment? We are now the link in the chain thrown down from heaven for the salvation of men. We are to claim people back to God beginning with our children. If we do not claim our children we will not claim anyone.

> "Everything that came through Adam's fall is undone in Christ; or, better still, all that was lost in Adam is restored in Christ" (E. J. Waggoner, *Waggoner on Romans,* Section 5.100).

Many of us think that our loved ones are beyond hope, but believers know that if we are willing to believe, nothing is too difficult for the Lord. Because of Jesus, we have a right to claim our loved ones back. In this we are co-laborers with Christ. Just like the woman searching for the lost coin.

Just two chapters later, Matthew records this principle again. What does it mean when Jesus repeats something twice? It means this is something very important. It reminds me of repetition of the dream to Pharaoh. Something important is going to take place.

> "Truly I say to you, whatever you bind on earth shall have been bound in heaven; and whatever you loose on earth shall have been loosed in heaven. Again I say to you, that if two of you agree on earth about anything that they may ask, it shall be done for them by My Father who is in heaven. For where two or three have gathered together in My name, I am there in their midst." (Matthew 18:18-20, NASB)

When Jesus says, "Assuredly, or Truly, I say to you," It is Jesus' guarantee to us.

Whenever Jesus uses the 'I' pronoun it is to impress us with His power which He exerts on behalf of all who believe. He is the same One who spoke to Moses at the burning bush that calls Himself, *"I AM WHO I AM."* (Exodus 3:14) He is the same one who speaks to us today, saying, *"Truly I say to you."*

There are two categories of binding and loosing. In Matthew 16, the keys of the kingdom of power are given to us when we are dealing with the spiritual powers of darkness, to bind and loose them. In Matthew 18, the keys are given to us when we are dealing with the dark powers in the flesh. Apostle Peter said:

> "...as His divine power has given to us all things that pertain to life and godliness, through the knowledge of Him who called us by glory and virtue...." (2 Peter 1:3, NKJV)

You now have the keys of the kingdom of power. What are we doing with them? Take hold of it. Here is what you can do, I do it every day:

Come to God in prayer saying,

> "'Lord I take hold of the keys of the kingdom of power,' and you can visually turn the key, just as you would a key in a door. 'Jesus, I ask You to bind Satan from having any influence or access to me or my children, grandchildren, family members. If there is a spirit of unbelief, resentment, or un-forgiveness in them, or any spirit that is not from you Lord, cast it out, and fill them with the Spirit of Jesus. Forgive their iniquities, make them uncomfortable to live without You, and flood their hearts and minds with the Holy Spirit. If there are ungodly people in their circle of influence, I bind them from having influence upon my children. Please separate them from each other. Heal them and restore them from unbelief, for they belong to You, and I am claiming what is rightfully Yours. Lord I ask You to loose my child/family member, church member/from the enemy's deceptions so they can be free to hear God's word and respond to it. And I bind my child to the throne of Your grace with the cords of love. In the name of Jesus!'"

You can use your own words, but use the keys of the kingdom of power. Use them by faith. God cannot lie. It is important that you do it in the name of Jesus, because His name is the most powerful name in the universe. The devils tremble when you mention His name. Don't ever forget that. Don't miss a day. Do it every day for as long as it takes, and believe that the heavenly powers are involved at that very moment. Don't forget the woman who had been sick for 12 years that touched the hem of Jesus' garment. Power went out of Him immediately because in His government, faith is always rewarded automatically. Then, be at peace because God is in the redemptive business. When a sheep is lost, the shepherd gets involved.

> "The Lord is near to all who call upon Him, to all who call upon Him in truth. He will fulfill the desire of those who fear Him; He also will hear their cry and save them." (Psalm 145:18-19)

Dear Reader, in Matthew 16 and 18 Jesus gave those who believe in Him the keys of the Kingdom of Heaven. When believers claim this decree, there is power that can shake the foundation of the spiritual realm of darkness. When Jesus gave these words He was revealing a deep spiritual principle to His disciples. It is vital for us today. This is a profound truth:

You are entrusted with the keys of the kingdom of power! This power is real and active!

To bind is to forbid, to lock away, to render powerless. When you bind – you are exercising the authority bestowed upon you by Christ Himself. This is not an act of wishful thinking, but spiritual act that carries the weight of heaven's decree.

To loose is to release, to set free, to invite the blessings of God into someone's life.

When you bind and loose in the name of Jesus, you are enforcing the victory that He secured on the cross. He said, "It is finished"! So declare boldly: 'In the name of Jesus I bind every spirit of fear, confusion, darkness that seeks to dwell in my home and my children's home, my family members, church members… They are rendered powerless. I loose and invite the joy of the Lord and the presence of the Holy Spirit over my home, family, children, relatives, church and missing church members.

The authority to bind and to loose is not rooted in your human effort or your eloquence, but in the finished work of Jesus Christ. At the cross Jesus disarmed principalities and powers and triumphed over them. This must not be done with a prideful spirit, or taking any credit for it. Believers are called to intervene for our fellow men as faithful stewards of the blessings Jesus wants to bestow. The glory and credit must always be clearly identified as belonging solely to the Lord Jesus Christ.

Today there is no neutral ground in the universe. Every place, every home, every family, every church, every person is claimed by God or counter claimed by Satan. Your home, family, your children, your life, your church – these are the battlegrounds in the Great Controversy, the cosmic war. But be courageous, the victory has already been won! Our role is to enforce that victory by standing on the Word of God, His promises and walking in obedience to His commands.

THE AUTHORITY OF CHRIST IS IN YOUR HANDS YOU HAVE THE KEYS OF THE KINGDOM OF HEAVEN AND POWER.

When you speak in the authority of Jesus Christ heaven listens and hell trembles. Binding and loosing is not an act of fear but of faith. Align your life with the will of God, take hold of the keys of the kingdom of heaven and the forces of enemy will be pushed back. The enemy may claim some ground, claiming your children, but as a child of God you have the final say. This battle for our children and loved ones is real. But so is the victory! You are not alone in this battle and you will never be alone. Jesus said *"I will never leave you .... I will be with you always."* (Matthew 28:20)

The Word of God declares with certainty:

> "No weapon formed against you shall prosper..." (Isaiah 54:17)

This is not only a promise it is the assurance that God's protection is surrounding you like a shield. Every human being is created for the indwelling Glory of God. Your family, your children, grandchildren are set aside by God for that very purpose. By standing firmly on the authority of the Scriptures you are stepping into alignment with the ultimate victor Jesus Christ, who already triumphed over all the powers of the darkness. Allow the presence of Jesus to permeate your home and every corner of your life by submitting to Christ fully. Victory comes through surrendering fully to Jesus. Then take back what belongs to you. Your children and loved ones are not only yours, they belong to God. You are more than conquerors through Him who loves you! You are not just a survivor – you are the child of the King and heir of His promises.

So rise up in faith. CLAIM YOUR CHILDREN BACK! And walk in assurance of His love and power to save your children.

MISERY OF UNBELIEF

Have faith in God and His Word. Believe it. If you don't believe, you will be just as miserable as disciples when Jesus had risen from the dead. Let's look at this from the Bible in the Gospel of Mark 16.

> "Now when He rose early on the first day of the week, He appeared first to Mary Magdalene, out of whom He had cast seven demons. She went and told those who had been with Him, as they mourned and wept. And when they heard that He was alive and had been seen by her, *they did not believe.*" (Mark 16:9-11, emphasis added)

They were mourning and weeping while Jesus is alive! And when they heard that He is alive, they did not believe. They have chosen misery instead of belief! In verses 12-13 Jesus appeared to two other disciples and they went and told the rest of them, but they did not believe them either. They continued their mourning and weeping, in a state of misery and unbelief. Then Jesus appeared to all of them and rebuked them for unbelief and hardness of heart.

Dear reader, if we do not believe in the Word of God, His way and promises to save our children, we will end up in needless misery of mourning and weeping.

By the way, if the disciples had listened to Mary, they could have avoided all this misery. Mary saw something in the tomb that no one else saw, which is recorded in John 20: 11, 12.

> But Mary stood outside by the tomb weeping, and as she wept she stooped down *and looked into the tomb,* And she saw two angels in white sitting, one at the head and the other at the feet, where the body of Jesus had lain. Then they said to her, "Woman, why are you weeping?" She said to them, "Because they have taken away my Lord, and I do not know where they have laid Him. (John 20:11, 12)

If the disciples had understood and believed the symbolism that Mary was shown in the tomb, they would have thought of another symbol that had two angels on the top of the Mercy Seat, one at the head, and another at the feet. In the Most Holy Place of the Jewish Sanctuary, the Ark of the Covenant had the mercy seat on the top of it covering the Law of God. The Ark had two angels, one at each end covering the Mercy Seat. That Mercy seat was the revelation of the character of God that was embodied and revealed in Jesus Christ. And today Jesus is you merciful High Priest.

Here are a few additional scriptures for encouragement:

PETER WALKS ON WATER

Matthew describes the event. Jesus sent His disciples over to the other side of the lake ahead of Him, and after He had prayed, He caught up with them on the sea and came to them walking on the water. It's still stormy so the water is not still. The disciples are struggling, and when they saw Him walking on the sea, they were terrified:

> "And when the disciples saw Him walking on the sea, they were troubled, saying, 'It is a ghost!' And they cried out for fear. But immediately Jesus spoke to them, saying, 'Be of good cheer! It is I; do not be afraid.'" (Matthew 14:26-27)

When His disciples were in fear, how soon did Jesus respond? Jesus responded *immediately*. He is the same yesterday, today, and forever. *"Fear not,"* Jesus says to you and me. It is suggested that this sentiment, "fear not, do not be afraid" appears three hundred and sixty five times in the Bible, one for every day of the year. God does not want His children to live in fear, even for one day, period!

> "And Peter answered Him and said, 'Lord, if it is You, command me to come to You on the water.' So He said, 'Come.' And when Peter had come down out of the boat, he walked on the water to go to Jesus." (Matthew 14:28, 29)

Peter steps out of the boat from his safety zone into the stormy sea and begins to walk on the! Can you imagine this? When your overall body density is greater than that of the water, you will sink into the water. In this case, Peter is walking on the water. What is it that held Peter on the water?

Two big things we must see now:

The experience of Peter is the illustration of the teaching of Righteousness by Faith.

First: Peter was looking unto Jesus. There are unspeakable benefits to be derived from looking at Jesus. So long as Peter looked at Jesus he was able to walk on the water. He did the impossible by looking at Jesus.

Second: What else held Peter on the water? What did Jesus say to Peter? He told him to "Come." It was the word "Come" that held Peter on the water. We know this because when Peter began to sink, he cried out to the Lord to save him.

> "And Immediately Jesus stretched out His hand and caught him, and said to him, 'O you of little faith, why did you doubt?'" (Matthew 14:31)

What is it that Peter doubted? Peter doubted Jesus' Word. If we doubt the Word of God and His promises, we also will sink into fear, despair, and worries. Remember,

> "The Word of God is the truth and the channel through which God manifest His Spirit and power." (*Acts of the Apostles*, p. 520)

If you have not already done so, begin a private collection of Scripture verses that remind you in a special way of God's assurances and promises. (See also Chapter 12) Write them out and keep them in a place where you are reminded to read them on a daily basis. Whenever you are assailed with doubts and fears, train your mind to go to them and repeat them to yourself as if Jesus was standing right beside you and understands everything that is happening to you.

DEMONS CAST OUT

When Jesus sailed to the country of Gadarenes, which is opposite Galilee, a man who had many demons met Him.

"And Jesus asked him, saying, 'What is your name?' And he said, 'Legion', because many demons had entered him. And they begged Him that He would not command them to go out into the abyss." (Luke 8:30, 31)

Sin can make a person who was made in the image of God unrecognizable. Jesus asked his name. This demon possessed man said, legion, because many demons had entered him, and they begged Jesus that He would not command them to go into the abyss. The demons knew they were subject to Jesus' power. Even though He was in the flesh, they feared Him. I hope you are hearing this. When Jesus is living in you, the result is the same, because Jesus is the same always. So submit to God and the demons will be in fear.

"Then He called twelve disciples together and gave them power and authority over all demons and to cure diseases." (Luke 9:1)

Jesus said: "Behold, I give you the authority to trample on serpents and scorpions, and over all the power of the enemy, and nothing shall by any means hurt you." (Luke 10:19)

"So the Lord said, 'If you have faith as a mustard seed, you could say to this mulberry tree, 'Be pulled up by the roots and be planted in the sea' and it would obey you.'" (Luke 17:6)

Some versions say sycamore tree. Some say mulberry tree. Both trees are found in that region. Both are drought-tolerant trees and they develop very deep root systems, making them impossible to pull them out by the roots. And Jesus said, *"If you have faith as little as a mustard seed,"* you could do what? The impossible will be possible for you. Do you believe these things?

"'Most assuredly, I say to you, he who believes in Me, the works that I do he will do also; and greater works than these he will do, because I go to My Father'" (John 14:12)

Believe and have faith in God and in His word. If you don't, you will sink into worry, misery and despair. How can you counteract this? Take hold of another spiritual weapon/Biblical principle.

PRINCIPLE NUMBER TWO – BEGIN PRAISING AND THANKING GOD IN ADVANCE

Begin to praise and thank God for the victory before you even see it. Before you engage in a battle, begin to praise God for the victory because God inhabits the praises of His children, and He releases the power that breaks the strongholds of the enemy in your life and the lives of your loved ones.

This biblical principle is found in the Old and the New Testaments.

Turn in your Bible to 2 Chronicles 20. Three nations come together against Judah and Jerusalem. These three nations are related to Judah and Jerusalem. They are the Moabites and Ammonites, the descendants of the two daughters of Lot through incest, and the Meunites, descendants of Esau from Mount Seir. They came in such a large number that Judah and Jerusalem were trembling, and King Jehoshaphat gathered the whole nation together and came to the temple to pray to God.

> "O our God, will You not judge them? For we have no power against this great multitude that is coming against us; nor do we know what to do, but our eyes are upon You. Now all Judah, with their little ones, their wives, and their children, stood before the LORD...." (2 Chronicles 20:12,13)

On the spot God raises a prophet from the tribe of Levi:

> "Then the Spirit of the LORD came upon Jahaziel,...a Levite of the sons of Asaph, in the midst of the congregation; and he said, 'Listen, all you of Judah and you inhabitants of Jerusalem, and you, King Jehoshaphat! Thus says the LORD to you: Do not be afraid nor dismayed because of this great multitude, for the battle is not yours, but God's...You will not need to fight in this battle. Position yourselves, stand still and see the salvation of the LORD, who is with you, O Judah and Jerusalem! Do not fear or be dismayed; tomorrow go out against them, for the LORD is with you.'" (2 Chronicles 20:14, 15, 17)

Dear friends, the Lord is with you. Do not fear or be dismayed.

> "And they rose early in the morning and went out into the Wilderness of Tekoa; and as they went out, Jehoshaphat stood and said, 'Hear me, O Judah and you inhabitants of Jerusalem: Believe in the Lord your God, and you shall be established; believe His prophets, and you shall prosper.' And when he had consulted with the people, he appointed those who should sing to the Lord, and who should praise the beauty of holiness, as they went out before the army and were saying: 'Praise the Lord, for His mercy endures forever.' [Other translations put it this way: 'Give thanks to the Lord, for His faithfulness is everlasting.] Now when they began to sing and to praise, the Lord set ambushes against the people of Ammon, Moab, and Mount Seir, who had come against Judah; and they were defeated." (2 Chronicles 20:20-22)

Dear friend, begin to praise God for His power to deliver you before you are even delivered!

Here is what we need to see in this Bible record: When God's people began to sing and praise the Lord, He set ambushes against their enemies, and they were defeated. They got the victory by giving evidence of their faith by praising God for the victory, before they even had it. It is the same for us today. Begin to praise God for His power to save your children. Sing praises to God for the victory over your children because God inhabits the praises of His children, and He releases the power, that is actually stronger than an atomic explosion, that will break down the strongholds of the enemy in your life and the lives of your children.

It must be especially noticed that not until Israel began to sing and to praise, did the Lord set ambushes against the enemy. Who is our enemy? Who has blinded our children and loved ones? Yes, it is Satan, and God sets ambushes against the enemy when we begin to praise God. This signifies that our faith is real, and the promise is considered as good as if it has actually been accomplished. Because His promises (which you will discover as you continue to read this book) are His Word, and His Word has power in itself to do what it says. Are you hearing this?

"So they believed in the Lord, and thus they were established." They proved the scripture:

> "For whoever is born of God overcomes the world. And this is the victory that has overcome the world – our faith." (1 John 5:4)

This very principle is found in the New Testament as well. We find this in the story of Paul and Silas, who were bound in chains in prison (Acts 16:25, 26). While they were singing and praising God, God shook the prison, and the chains fell off and the doors were opened. God inhabits the praises of His children, and He releases the power that breaks the chains and the power of the enemy.

We don't praise God enough. Begin praising God because this is a strong weapon against the enemy. In a revised version it says,

> "Whoever offers the sacrifice of thanksgiving glorifies Me, and prepares a way that I may show him the salvation of God." (Psalm 50:23)

If God's people would praise God all the time, fear and discouragement will be unknown to them. And God will write victories on your behalf continuously.

You have received two spiritual weapons. Now go and use them!

CHAPTER 11

BIBLICAL PRINCIPLES–SPIRITUAL WEAPONS TO RECLAIM YOUR CHILDREN AND LOVED ONES BACK

SPIRITUAL WEAPON PRINCIPLE NUMBER THREE – THE GOODNESS OF GOD LEADS SINNERS TO REPENTANCE

Another beautiful principle can be found in Romans 2:4, where it says, "It is the goodness of God that leads you [all sinners] to repentance." Allow the goodness of God to flow through you to your children, grandchildren, and loved ones. Love them unconditionally and make no demands on your adult children. Let them see in you, what you want to see in them.

As parents, we often make mistakes in raising our children, and our mistakes affect our children. They are smart. They can see right through all of it. There is never a time that we can't learn new things. My wife and I have gone through our own trial with this, and it has been very painful. I praise God that when Pastor Bill Liversidge was alive, he would often share the Word of God with us and strengthen us through biblical principles. I was always taking notes, whether it was in his seminars or one-on-one with him. We learned that we don't need to punish ourselves for the mistakes that we made. Many of us did our best with as much as we knew. And then we asked ourselves, "What happened when our children left God?". We feel as if it is our fault. We may look at other parents and think they are better parents than us. Let me tell you why it happened. The devil snatched them out. But I have Good News for you. The devil may think he's got your children, but he is a defeated foe according to the Scriptures: Hebrews 2:14.

God says to us, "No weapon formed against you shall prosper...This is the heritage of the servants of the Lord..." (Isaiah 54:17) Do you believe it? Take it by faith, my friend. If you want to be a happy, hopeful Christian, take God at His Word. No weapon that is formed against you, my dear parents, shall prosper. We have done our best with what we knew at the time our children were young.

In 2 Samuel, Chapter 7, King David expresses a desire to build a temple for God. When he had gathered all of the materials to build the temple, he shared his desire with his friend, the prophet Nathan. Nathan told him to go ahead and do what he really wanted to do for the Lord. After Nathan had returned home, the Lord touched his shoulder and told him he had spoken on his own behalf. He instructed him to go tell David that he would not be the one to build a house for God, rather, his son, Solomon, would. In 1 Kings 8, there is something interesting added to this. Solomon said,

> "But the Lord said to my father David, 'Because it was in your heart to build a house for My name, *you did well that it was in your heart.*"
> (1 Kings 8:17, 18, emphasis added)

If you have done your best raising your children and with the best intentions, inasmuch as you had this in your heart, you did well. You don't need to punish yourself for the mistakes that you have made. God does not punish you because He is in the business of salvation.

> "For God did not send His Son into the world to condemn the world, but that the world [*you*] through Him might be saved." (John 3:17)

You will want to develop an appropriate attitude towards your children. Let your actions be from love, and no other motive. If you continue that way according to Galatians 6:9, *"...in due time, you will reap the reward."*

Make certain your level of forgiveness is complete by asking for God's grace in order to examine your conscience. You are only responsible for your actions. You are not responsible for the actions of your adult children. Don't carry that guilt.

Never defend yourself. Let God defend you, and it will end well. (See Exodus 14:13-14). Don't rush to point out their mistakes. Rather, be quick to acknowledge your own. Don't compare your children to yourself, especially spiritually. Remember how long it took you to be where you are today.

Allow yourself to grow in the things of the Spirit, and let them see in you what you would like to see in them. Love them unconditionally. Remember that the weapons God has given us, Biblical principles, are mighty in power, pulling down the strongholds of the enemy.

SPIRITUAL WEAPON PRINCIPLE NUMBER FOUR – BEGIN TO LIVE A HAPPY CHRISTIAN LIFE

A friend of ours told us about a woman who was a member of her church. This woman had an only daughter and raised her in a Christian Adventist home. Once the girl became an adult, she left the Lord and the church and began to drink, smoke, and sleep around with men. You can imagine the heartbreak of the mother. The woman became so broken hearted and miserable, it was practically impossible to be in her presence. Pastor Bill Liversidge was invited by the church to do a *Victory in Jesus* seminar. The woman was present at the seminar, and something happened to her. She rediscovered the Gospel and the goodness of God's character. It changed her attitude, and she became a happy Christian.

One day, the daughter came to visit her mother. The woman was so happy to see her daughter. She cooked for her and chatted with her with so much love. The daughter was shocked. She asked herself, "What happened to my mother?" The daughter visited her mother from time to time and on one occasion the mother was so happy to see her daughter again. She was cooking in the kitchen and floating through the living room like a butterfly, delighted and rejoicing in her daughter's visit. The daughter was sitting on the couch observing her mother and burst into tears, asking her mother, "What is it that you have that makes you so happy, that I don't have? I want what you have!"

My friends, if we are living an unhappy life, and oh, how many sad Christians there are, we are simply giving our prodigals the message that they made the right choice not to belong to God because God cannot keep His children happy. Do you realize what you are doing? We cannot afford to live a sad, Christian life! One day they are going to hit rock bottom in search of happiness in this world, but the world will never give that to them. I came from there with many scars. They will turn back home or back to the church that they left to see if they have missed something back there. If they find us, parents and church members, to be just as sad as they are without hope and joy, what do you think they are going to do? Why do you think there are so much suicide among young people in US?

We and our prodigals need to hear the Good News of the Gospel and the loving character of God to bring back a spark of hope and love for God.

After they hit rock bottom and are disappointed with the world, they need to see that we are the happiest people in the world in spite of all the trials we may be going through. Then, they are going to say, "Wait a minute, I missed something here. I want what they have."

Dear Reader our happiness does not depend on our circumstances. It depends on knowing and trusting the Lord.

I understand, there is a room for grief when our children leave the Lord and the church. We went through this. But grief is not where the Lord wants you to be all the time. It is the devil who wants you to be there so you become a disarmed, weak hopeless and inactive member of Christ's body.

Remember the story of David in 1 Samuel 28 through 30: A Philistine warlord asked David and his men to join forces with the Philistine army that was fighting against Israel's King Saul. David agreed and took his men to where the Philistine army was, but their commanders rejected David's help, concerned that they would not fight against their own people. When David and his men returned home they found that the savage Amalekites had raided and burned Ziklag, and had taken their children and women including two of David's wives. They were also grieving the loss of their loved ones... What did David do?

> "David strengthened himself in the Lord his God."(1 Samuel 30:6)

We too can find strength in the Lord, for He is the same always and forever. David was subjected to God:

> So David inquired of the LORD, saying, "Shall I pursue this troop? Shall I overtake them?" And He answered him, "Pursue, for you shall surely overtake *them* and without fail recover *all*." (1 Samuel 30:8)

If we want the victory, the same thing is required of us:

> "Therefore submit to God. Resist the devil and he will flee from you. Draw near to God and He will draw near to you." (James 4:7, 8)

When you are submitted to God you align yourself with the unconquerable power of God.

> "So David recovered all that the Amalekites [enemies of God's children] had carried away, and David rescued his two wives. And nothing of theirs was lacking, either small or great, sons or daughters, spoil or anything which they had taken from them; David recovered all." (1 Samuel 30:18, 19)

Why is this story in the Bible?

> "For whatever things were written before were written for our learning, that we through the patience and comfort of the Scriptures might have hope." (Romans 15:4)

Never forget that our God is the God of love. Love casts out fear. Where there is fear, there is no God. So when we fear about our loved ones – there is no God. Stop fearing about their destiny. Begin to praise God for His power to save them.

There are great books that will draw you closer to the Lord, strengthen your faith and give you much joy: *Victory in Jesus* by Bill Liversidge and *Lessons on Faith,* by Jones and Waggoner. You can find them on our website. Read them!

SPIRITUAL WEAPON PRINCIPLE NUMBER FIVE – CLAIM YOUR CHILDREN BACK BY CLAIMING THE PROMISES OF GOD

Now, I'm going to give you a Big Gun in the spiritual warfare arsenal. And no-one can take this one from you. Here it goes. Claim your children back! How? By claiming the promises of God.

There is an encouraging article written by Ellen White in the *Review and Herald* about a mother who was praying for a wayward son. She opened the scriptures, found a promise, pointed her finger to the promise, and prayed earnestly to God, and God granted her request. (See Chapter 12)

Did you know that God's promise is like a signed check? God can not lie, so take the check and cash it. Only those who believe it will cash the check. When you claim your children back, you are simply claiming what is rightfully yours. There is a prerequisite, though. Jesus said:

> "If you abide in Me, and My Words abide in you, ask what you desire, and it shall be done for you." (John 15:7)

Make sure you have this in place. Your children belong to God. The devil wants you to think that he's got your children. But according to God's Word, he's a defeated foe. Jesus rendered him powerless.

> "Inasmuch then as the children have partaken of the flesh and blood, He Himself likewise shared in the same, that through death He might destroy him who has the power of death, that is, the devil." (Hebrews 2:14) [Some versions say, the devil was rendered powerless]

Can a defeated foe hold your children? No. But he can under a certain condition. If you don't know, don't remember or believe that the devil is a defeated foe, and if you don't claim your children back, he will continue to hold them. How is your faith today? Do you believe the Word of God? Then count on it. The Word of God works effectively in those who believe.

> "For this reason we also thank God without ceasing, because when you received the Word of God which you heard from us, you welcomed it not as the word of men, but as it is in truth, the Word of God, which also effectively works in you who believe." (1 Thessalonians 2:13)

Many people want to believe the Word of God and that it applies to them personally, but have never had an experience when they can honestly say God came through with something they were asking for. They are not sure if the good that happened to them was the result of a prayer request or just coincidence. They may say the words "I believe" but deep down they know they really do not believe. What they believe is more like a hope or wish rather than genuine belief. A wise writer described it this way:

> "What you need to understand is the true force of the will. This is the governing power of the nature of man, the power of decision, or of choice. Everything depends on the right action of the will. The power of choice God has given to men; it is theirs to exercise. You cannot change your heart, you cannot of yourself give to God its affections; but you can choose to serve Him. You can give Him your will; He will then work in you to will and to do according to His good pleasure. Thus your whole nature will be brought under the control of the Spirit of Christ; your affections will be centered upon Him, your thoughts will be in harmony with Him." (*Steps to Christ*, p 47, emphasis in the original)

Every time you pray for your children or loved ones, ask the Lord to work in you to give you *belief in His ability* to give what you are praying for. Persist in this even if you can detect little or no change. Keep reminding God of His promises and claiming them in the name of Jesus.

In *Christ's Object Lessons* p. 38, there is a statement that is so profound, it is my favorite statement.

> "In every command and in every promise of the word of God is the power, the very life of God, by which the command may be fulfilled and the promise realized. He who by faith receives the word [that is believes it] is receiving the very life and character of God."

Wow! Are you able to grasp that? That power in the Word, it says, is the very life of God. And it is by the life of God in the Word, every promise

CAN be realized and the command CAN be fulfilled. By receiving His Word (believing IT) you receive His very life and the character of God which is the power that overcame the world.

The Word of God Works effectively in you who believe.

Perhaps you've been striving to reach and obtain for the character of God. This is a shortcut. And this is the way.

God spoke the promise to Abraham and Sarah. It was His Word, but Abraham and Sarah tried it their way. They did not let the Word of God do the work to fulfill the promise. And when they came to the end of their own resources, they depended on the Word only.

> "By faith Sarah herself also received strength to conceive seed, and she bore a child when she was past the age, because she considered Him faithful who had promised. Therefore from one man, and him as good as dead, were born as many as the stars of the sky in multitude – innumerable as the sand which is by the seashore." (Hebrews 11:11-12)

Sarah's womb was dead. Abraham was as good as dead. Through the faith of two who were as good as dead, God raised up a nation.

> "Is anything too hard for the Lord?" (Genesis 18:14; *cf.* Jeremiah 32:17, 27)

Today, your children may be spiritually as good as dead. You have no resources to save them. Nothing whatsoever except we have the Word of God. And here is what the Word of God says:

> "But thus says the Lord: 'Even the captives of the mighty shall be taken away, and the prey of the terrible will be delivered; For I will contend with him who contends with you, and I will save your children.'" (Isaiah 49:25)

Note, He does not say "might be delivered" but "WILL BE DELIVERED".

> "Thus says the Lord: 'Restrain your voice from weeping, and your eyes from tears; For your work shall be rewarded,' says the Lord, 'And they shall come back from the land of the enemy. There is hope in your future,' says the Lord, 'That your children shall come back to their own border.'" (Jeremiah 31:16-17)

The Lord said to me through this passage, "Grant, you have just one prodigal. I have millions. Why don't you go get one for Me, and I'll take care of yours?" I don't do this to deserve something. I believe God's promise. When we go through this trial of loosing our children to the world, we become the people after God's own heart of pain. Can you feel His pain? The old devil snatches the child from the family. It wounds the parents so deeply that they become inactive in the church. This is one of the biggest reasons why so many Christians are inactive. But there is hope, my friends. The Lord says your work will be rewarded. Go get one for Me, and I'll take care of yours. They shall come back from the land of the enemy.

God is telling us that there is hope in our future. Our children shall come back to their own border. Hope is not a wish. Hope is an expectation. And the Lord says there is an expectation in your future that your children will come back to their own border. This promise is a delicious piece of cake, isn't it? Dear friend, the Lord has given us so many promises. I have only shared a few with you. (*cf.* Isaiah 43:5-7, Isaiah 29:22-24).

Now let me add some icing on the cake:

> "For as the rain comes down, and the snow from heaven, and do not return there, but water the earth, and make it bring forth and bud, that it may give seed to the sower and bread to the eater, so shall My Word be that goes forth from My mouth; it shall not return to Me void, but it shall accomplish what I please, and it shall prosper in the thing for which I sent it.'" (Isaiah 55:10-11; *cf.* Isaiah 46:9-11; Ezekiel 36:36)

The Lord gave us promises to save our children. (And there are many in the Bible). Then He says, His Word will not come back to Him void. It will accomplish the very thing for which it was sent. Are you feeling better?

Do you like cherries? I love cherries. I travel to Washington every summer just so that I can get enough cherries to eat. Alright, let's put a cherry on the top of the cake with the icing.

Abraham's faith came to maturity, and we read:

> "He did not waver at the promise of God through unbelief, but was strengthened in faith, giving glory to God, and being fully convinced that what He had promised He was also able to perform. And therefore 'it was accounted to him for righteousness.'" (Romans 4:20-22)

What was promised to Abraham? He was promised a son. Did he get a son? Yes, he got a son because he believed. What else did he get with a son? He got righteousness. He was counted righteous. If you believe God's promises, what is He promising you? He is promising you that the

Word that came out of His mouth will never return to Him void. It will accomplish the very thing for which He sent it.

If you believe the promises of God, then you are Abraham's seed. (Galatians 3:29) And if you believe the promises of God, not only are you going to get your children back, but He counts you righteous. What a generous God we serve. The world needs to know about this kind of God. If we don't believe what God has promised, we don't give Him permission to do what He promises to do. It's that simple.

Jesus said:

> "...Do not be afraid, only believe." (Mark 5:36)

> "According to your faith let it be to you." (Matthew 9:29)

> "Not a word failed of any good thing which the LORD had spoken to the house of Israel. All came to pass." (Joshua 21:45)

How many of the blessings that God has given to us are lost simply because our faith does not grasp them? Do you believe that Jesus is the same yesterday, today, and forever? Not one good thing that He promised to Spiritual Israel will fail. It will all come to pass. How's your faith? Do you see why we stopped crying? I pray you also will stop crying and that you will live a happy Christian life. Our happiness does not depend on our circumstances, but in knowing and trusting the Lord!

It is not for us to speculate as to how and when His promises will be fulfilled. It is enough for us to know that God said it and that He is able to make every promise good. We need faith, and faith comes by hearing the Word of God. Without the Word of God, there can be no faith. Where the Word of God is, faith will demonstrate total trust and dependence upon the Word for the accomplishment of what it says to us. Based upon this simple truth, it is clear, that in order for us to ask in faith, we must first of all be sure that we have God's Word for what we ask. And when you have God's Word for what you ask, promise which you want to claim, then you can ask/pray with confidence in perfect faith.

> "Now this is the confidence that we have in Him, that if we ask anything according to His will, He hears us." (1 John 5:14)

When you pray this way, you know that you are asking according to the will of God, because you know that you have the plain Word of God for it, which is the expression of His will.

> "Therefore I say to you, whatever things you ask when you pray, believe that you receive them, and you will have them." (Mark 11:24)

This is a blank check. Take it to the bank.

Therefore, you know that God hears you, and knowing that God hears you, you can believe you have what you are asking for, because the sole basis of your hope is the Word of God which spoke it. And that is the basis of your asking.

Happy is the one who learns to wait as he prays and never loses his patience, for God's time is the best time.

Here is an encouraging statement found in

> "Not because we see or feel that God hears us are we to believe. We are to trust His promises. When we come to Him in faith every petition enters into the heart of God. When we have asked for His blessing, we should believe that we receive it, and thank Him that we have received it. Then we are to go about our duties, assured that the blessing will be realized when we need it most. When we have learned to do this, we shall know that our prayers are answered. God will do for us "exceeding abundantly," "according to the riches of His glory," and "the working of His mighty power." (Desire of Ages, p. 200; *Signs of the Times,* January 20, 1904)

SPIRITUAL WEAPON PRINCIPLE NUMBER SIX – A SPECIAL PRAYER BOMBER

Now I want to bring out the B-52. Do you know what a B-52 is? It's the largest bomber in the US Air Force. If you have a prodigal child, you can fly this bomber and drop some bombs on the path of your prodigal.

My friend and mentor shared the story of how he prayed a special prayer for his teenage children who were trying to go their way.

One day he announced to his children that he will begin to pray for them a special prayer.

A few weeks later his older son came up to his father and asked him: "Dad, please stop praying for me."

This prayer works.

> "Before I was afflicted I went astray, but now I keep Your word." (Psalm 119:67)

When does a person learn to keep God's word?

> "It is good for me that I have been afflicted, that I may learn Your statutes." (Psalm 119:71)

When did he begin to keep God's Word and learn His statutes, before or after affliction? He began keeping God's Word and His statues after he was afflicted.

> "I will return again to My place till they acknowledge their offense. Then they will seek My face; In their affliction they will diligently seek Me." (Hosea 5:15)

Perhaps you have read the book about the sheep. (Phillip Keller, *A Shepherd Looks at the 23rd Psalm*, Zondervan Publishing) A pastor friend of mine gave me the book, and I was absolutely fascinated with it. It was written by a former shepherd who became a pastor. What I took away from this book was that when a wandering sheep continually goes astray, and cannot or will not learn to stay close to safety, the knows that one day, the sheep will be completely lost, and wild animals will tear it to pieces. So the shepherd takes that sheep, and with deep pain in his heart, he breaks the legs of the sheep. Then he puts a cast on the broken legs and carries the sheep on his shoulders until it is healed. When the sheep is healed, he lets it go, but it never walks away from the shepherd, it becomes like a pet.

In the story of the prodigal son, the father was praying for the son to come back. He knew that while everything was good and that the son had erased his father from his mind, he wouldn't come back. He knew that the only thing will bring his son back would be trials. So this wise father most likely was praying a special, radical prayer. I have parents during these seminars that stand with tears in their eyes shouting, "Lord, whatever it takes." "My daughter wouldn't speak with me for thirty-eight years. Lord, whatever it takes." Other parents can't even bring themselves to pray a radical prayer.

What is more important for us? Do we want our children to have the whole world with the scars and suffering that it brings, as well as losing eternity, or to have some trials and to gain eternity? Keep in mind, our God is a very gentle God. He may crack the nut, but He will not crush it. "A bruised reed He will not break, and smoking flax He will not quench." (Isaiah 42:3; Matthew 12:20).

Are you, Dear Friend, willing to fly the bomber, trusting the Lord? I'll leave this principle on the table for you.

SPIRITUAL WEAPON PRINCIPLE NUMBER SEVEN – UNITED PRAYERS OF THE BELIEVERS

Here's another big gun. This one is so big and powerful that it must be handled by a group of people. The devil dreads this so much that he will try to do everything possible to prevent you from use and the power of it. Don't allow him to do this. Organize a special prayer ministry in your church, and claim your children back.

CLAIM YOUR CHILDREN BACK PRAYER MINISTRY

I was at a Washington camp meeting some years ago. That was the first time I presented this seminar, it was a much shorter version then. There was a couple sitting on the front pew every morning at nine o'clock. At the last session, the whole class, over fifty people, came together and held each other's hands while we prayed for all of our children. At lunchtime, I was standing under a tree on the sidewalk waiting for my colleague to come so we could go to the cafeteria for lunch. This same couple passed me by. There were two young women following them. They went about fifteen yards. They were laughing and chatting, and everyone was so happy. Suddenly, the man turned around and ran towards me with a big smile on his face. He said, "Grant, I have to share this with you. These two ladies are our daughters. They left the church thirteen years ago, and haven't stepped in the door of a church since. After we prayed in the morning together, they showed up for church at Camp Meeting for the first time since they left."

Many of the churches where we have done this seminar are establishing a prayer ministry. The overjoyed leaders of the groups are texting me, emailing me, and sending pictures.

Recently I got another text with the pictures of the two prodigals that had come back. They are being baptized. From other parts of the country, I'm receiving calls saying that as we pray, our children are coming back. They are coming with their spouses and their children and taking them to Sabbath School. They are also bringing their friends to the church.

I want to give you a couple of statements that give us some insight into why this is happening.

> "The promise is made on condition that the united prayers of the church are offered, and in answer to these prayers there may be expected a power greater than that which comes in answer to private prayer. The power given will be proportionate to the unity of the members and their love for God and for one another." (Letter 32, 1903, p. 6, (To Brother and Sister Farnsworth, January 28, 1903))

When members come together in unity, in love for God, in love for one another and pray together in unity, when these three things are in place you can expect a greater power in answer to your prayers.

We can't do this alone. To borrow Paul's analogy of the body working together, one finger or one wrist alone cannot do much. But if the wrist is attached to the elbow, then to the shoulder, and to the whole body, the whole body can do a lot. It is the united body of Christ that will reveal the fullness of who God is. We should never forget that we all need each other.

> "I saw the cruel power of Satan that has afflicted us of late and bound us to keep the truth from coming out in the paper, that meant to have taken the life of little Edson [James Edson White], *but our united prayer drove him back and weakened his powers; ....*" (The Ellen G. White *Letters and Manuscripts*: Volume 1, p. 222, 1850)

I hope you are hearing this. Our united prayers drive Satan back and weaken his power, his grip on our children!

As parents, we may have raised our children in the church, but they left. The other parents' children are in the church, and we are ashamed to share our grief, we go into a shell. We're very vulnerable. We feel like we are not good enough as parents, and we feel inferior to the others. We feel that if we open up, they may look down on us. We have enough pain already and can't take any more. So, we don't open up. We carry the burden alone. We pray alone, and things seem to drag. Take a risk and come together. Become a body with love for one another. Be committed to one another. If you pray together, you will become the backbone of the church. When the members are united in love for God and for one another, the prodigals will come back. Do you want this to happen in your church?

Here are three more statements to encourage you.

> "Prayer and faith will do what no power on earth can accomplish." (*Ministry of Healing*, p. 509)

> "Appeals, petitions, entreaties, between man and man, move men and act a part in controlling the affairs of nations. But prayer moves heaven." (*In Heavenly Places*, p. 75)

> "It is a wonderful thing that we can pray effectually; that unworthy, erring mortals possess the power of offering their requests to God. What higher power can man desire than this,—to be linked with the infinite God? Feeble, sinful man has the privilege of speaking to his Maker. We may utter words that reach the throne of the Monarch of the universe. We may speak with Jesus as we walk by the way, and He says, I am at thy right hand. [See Psalm 16:8.] We may commune with God in our hearts; we

> may walk in companionship with Christ. When engaged in our daily labor, we may breathe out our heart's desire, inaudible to any human ear; but that word cannot die away into silence, nor can it be lost. Nothing can drown the soul's desire. It rises above the din of the street, above the noise of machinery. It is God to whom we are speaking, and our prayer is heard. Ask, then; ask, and ye shall receive. Ask for humility, wisdom, courage, increase of faith. To every sincere prayer an answer will come." (*Gospel Workers*, p. 258)

How often we neglect prayer. Friends, many do not value the power and efficacy of prayer as they should. When we ask something from God in prayer, – we express our belief that He can do it. That is faith. When we don't ask God, – we express that we do not believe that He can bring it to pass. But when you ask – ask without doubting – don't be like a wave on the sea tossed by the wind. (*cf.* James 1:6)

And we are told that united prayer adds power to our prayers. We see the power of God taking over where the church members unite in prayer. If you want a revival in your church, and healing for parents, and you need help, you can go to our website to get our contact phone number. We'll be there for you, we will come to your church and help to establish that prayer ministry. It can be done as a Revival and Outreach to the community. All other churches have the same problem and they are helplessly waiting for the solution. Invite your neighbors and friends. The community will love you for it.

When God's people come into unity of purpose, God is present in the midst of them. Satan looks at it as a dark cloud above him and he will try to do everything possible to prevent you from doing it.

Come together dear parents and grandparents as a body. Show to God that you are serious about salvation of your children and loved ones. You are the ones that are experiencing same pain as God in the loss of the children. You have become a people after God's own heart of pain.

> "And He put all things under His feet, and gave Him to be head over all things to the church, which is His body, the fullness of Him who fills all in all." (Ephesians 1:22-23)

Everything that is true of the body is true because of the head – Jesus Christ! The body is the fullness of Jesus Christ.

> "To know the love of Christ which passes knowledge; that you may be filled with all the fullness of God." (Ephesians 3:19)

This means that the fullness of God and His power is available to His body! When God's people coming together in unity of purpose – God is present, for:

"Where two or three come together in My name, I am in the midst of them." (Matthew 18:20)

As we said before, when you do this, Satan looks at it as if a dark cloud gathers over him. He will try to discourage or distract you from getting together.

Take courage from the parables of Jesus, *everything* that was lost was recovered. Even the father of the prodigal, did not sit passively. He was praying radical prayers. *All* of the lost things were recovered. God is serious about it. The question is, "Are we serious about the salvation of our loved ones, our children?"

When you pray, pray with expectation. Do you recall how many times Elijah prayed for the rain to come? Seven times. Nothing happened after the first time. Then the second time and the third time, and still, nothing happened. Did he stop praying? No! He prayed seven times. Then the servant came with a report that there was a little cloud on the horizon, about the size of a man's hand. When Elijah saw it, he proclaimed, "Get up, let's run. The rain is coming."

My friends, we have clouds of God's promises, and it's going to rain!! The answers to our prayers will happen. It may happen quickly, it make take time. But it will happen. It may even take a lifetime. Perhaps even when we are dead and gone. Why do I believe it will happen? Because God said it, and He cannot lie. I can begin to live a happy life.

In many churches after seminars, people would come up to me to say that they were prodigals but they came back to God after their parents died. Many of them are serving as elders and other positions in the church. Imagine the joy of these parents being united with their precious children when Jesus returns and all are resurrected together. Why do you think the prodigals came back? Because parents and sincere church members were praying. This same joy is waiting for you if you will not give up on praying for your prodigals. Have faith in God and His word. There is no such thing as faith without His word. His word is solid rock. The rock is Christ. And Christ is the Word. (*cf.* John 1:1, 14). So the Word is as substantial as God Himself. True faith accepts the Word of God no matter what it says, without doubt or questioning. Jesus Christ said:

"Therefore I say to you, all things for which you pray and ask, believe that you have received them, and they shall be granted you. (Mark 11:24, NASB). But when you have faith you will ask according to God's will, and God will always hear such request and answer it, for faith always rests on God's word, which is the expression of His will. "...If you will not believe, surely you shall not be established." (Isaiah 7:9)

I was in one of the churches in Washington State. A woman and her son came up to me after a seminar and introduced themselves as Karla and Jeff. Jeff was about thirty years old. She told the story, saying, "This is my son. He was a prodigal and just came back. His father, my husband, passed away, and he came back during my husband's last illness. My husband and I had been praying for him to return. The young man told me later that one thing he always knew deep down was that his parents loved him, and continued to love and pray for him while he was playing the prodigal. Jeff's father was loving and fearless, and not afraid to die. He had a strong faith and was secure in Christ. During the father's final illness he told Karla that if his brain tumor had anything to do with Jeff returning to the Lord, he would be willing to go through this condition a thousand times. Karla told me that Jeff was amazed by his father's faith and fearlessness and wanted what his father had.

Jeff asked me where I lived. This was during COVID time. I told him where I lived, and he told me that he lived not far away in Loma Linda and worked in the hospital there. He was a head nurse in the emergency room. He told me he wanted to catch up with what he had lost and missed out on. He asked if I had a Bible study group and if he could join it. I invited him to join our study group. This was during the time that most of the churches were closed. We met through the entire pandemic. I often was traveling to wherever churches were open and speaking during this time. And whenever I was free I was leading the Bible study. Sabbath was an all-day affair for us, from morning until evening. We had worship, songs, and Bible studies, and this young man began to grow.

He worked in the emergency room with COVID patients, and he contracted COVID. It hit him hard. The mother came down to help care for him. He recovered, and they came together for the Sabbath in our friends' home meetings. I noticed that he was struggling with depression. We sat across the table from each other eating our lunch. I asked him what was going on, and tears began streaming down his face. He told me he wasn't sure what had happened. The depression came on, and it was like he was in a fog with a lot of bad feelings and guilt for the death of his dad.

He asked if he could be anointed. He asked if he could have it done in my home, so he and his mother and my wife and I, drove to our home. I took him again through the character of God. I never do anointing without a study that reveals the character of God. I shared my personal testimony of how I was anointed three different times with Pastor Bill Liversidge. I had fallen into that condition three times, largely because I was working too hard and suffering from exhaustion. Every time I was anointed, I would come out of the depression immediately. We read James chapter five together and pointed out that anointing is not just for physical healing, but that physical healing was secondary to spiritual restoration. When Christ healed people, He first dealt with the spiritual and then the physical. This is biblical anointing. He understood this, and we knelt to pray. After I anointed him, we opened our eyes to see him smiling from ear to ear. He was as happy as he could be.

I checked on him the next day and asked how he was doing. He said he was better than ever. I called him again later and asked how he was doing, and the Lord rebuked me: "Why are you of little faith? Don't you remember what happened to you? "

One day this young man told me there was no literature in the emergency room at Loma Linda Hospital. I was shocked! And I told him to do whatever the Lord put on his heart. He began spending his own money to buy literature, and stocked the emergency room where people were the most vulnerable. He spent a lot of money on that ministry.

Don't forget this was a former prodigal. He called me one day and told me that they had a patient, a man in his late forties in critical condition and on a ventilator in the emergency room, and the doctor said he wasn't going to make it. The family wanted to have him anointed, and they couldn't find anyone available at this crucial time in the hospital to anoint him. He was puzzled about what they should do. Because I was traveling, I told him, "Jeff, you're going to do the anointing." He said, "But I'm not an elder." I told him, "That's all right. I'll be the one doing the anointing, and you'll be an extension of my hand." Sometimes you have to be radical when it comes to God's children and the souls of men. I told him, "Just do what I tell you to do, and make sure you have the oil." The family gathered around this man. He was intubated and almost unconscious. We unfolded the beauty of the character of God. I shared the cross. The wife had the phone on speaker where the man could hear. She shouted, "Pastor, Pastor please keep talking. He's smiling. He's getting it." Then we quickly visited James chapter five and prayed over this man. Then I told Jeff to go ahead and anoint him. Then I hung up. Guess what happened? A miracle happened, and the man survived. In a few days he went home.

Why am I telling you this story? Jeff was a prodigal. You may have a prodigal today, but your prodigal may be in ministry tomorrow. Don't underestimate the power of God, no matter what condition they are in. Begin to apply these principles, and begin to live a happy life.

THE PROMISE OF POWER

We can repeat what the prophet Jeremiah told the Lord:

> "You created heaven and earth by your mighty power and your outstretched arm. Is there anything too difficult for you?" (Jeremiah 32:17)

> "Then the Word of the Lord came to Jeremiah, saying, 'Behold, I am the Lord, the God of all flesh; is anything too difficult for Me?'" (Jeremiah 32:26,27)

We are tempted not to take God at His Word and say, "But my child's case is different." I hope you're not one of those. We are to trust God and His infinite love and power that created this world. That same power is involved in the salvation of our loved ones. At creation when God said, *"Let there be..."* it came into existence. His Word alone is sufficient to establish it. Remember that every promise of God is His Word to us. Its power is never diminished. It is able to save our loved ones as simply as it was able to create. Do you believe it? The same Word that commanded, *"Let the earth bring forth grass....and trees,"* is still causing the earth to bring forth grass and trees. If the power in His Word were only effective for that time when He spoke it, we would not see any grass and trees today. What does that tell you?

The Word of God abides and endures forever. It means that the power in His Word abides and endures forever! And it works effectively in those who believe. (*cf.* 1 Thessalonians 2:13) This is not a theory, it is a fact.

It is timely to bring this quote:

"In every command and in every promise of the word of God is the power, the very life of God, by which the command may be fulfilled and the promise realized. He who by faith receives the Word is receiving the very life and character of God." (*Christ's Object Lessons*, p. 38)

Please HEAR what it says.

In every *command* and in *every promise* of the Word of God is the power. That power is the very life of God. By the life of God in His word, the command may be fulfilled and the promise realized. He who by faith receives the Word is receiving the very life and character of God.

The Word of God that created all things is upholding all things. The power in the Word at creation is the same power that is involved in the salvation of our children. That power is available to you today. All heaven is geared and anxious to release its power on our behalf.

> "The power of God awaits their demand and reception." (*Testimonies to Ministers*, p. 175)

> "The Spirit awaits our demand and reception." (*Christ's Object Lessons*, p. 121)

> "The whole heavenly treasure awaits our demand and reception." (*Testimonies to Ministers*, p. 510)

> "The inexhaustible supplies of Heaven are at their command… In their human weakness they are enabled to do the deeds of Omnipotence." (*Gospel Workers*, p. 112)

Dear Friend, God has inexhaustible supplies at our command to be used in our human weakness. All heaven is geared and anxious to release its power. How is your faith today?

Jesus said:

> "And I say to you, ask, and it will be given to you; seek, and you will find; knock, and it will be opened to you., For everyone who asks receives, and he who seeks finds, and to him who knocks it will be opened." (Luke 11:9-10; *cf.* verses 11-13)

> "If you ask anything in My name, I will do it." (John 14:14)

I pray that you will take God's word and these Biblical principles to heart and apply them to your life. The knowledge of these principles will be useless to you unless you, with faith, put them into practice.

SEVEN SPIRITUAL WEAPON PRINCIPLES

1. Take hold of the keys of the kingdom. Begin to bind and loose. Ask Jesus to bind the devil from having access to your children and loved ones. Loose your children to be set free from the deception of the enemy, so they can hear the Word of God and respond to it. Bind them with the cords of love to the throne of God's grace. Do it all in the name of Jesus. The demons tremble at the name of Jesus.

2. Begin to praise God before you even see victory in their lives. Praise God for His power to save your children because God inhabits the praises of His children and releases the power on your behalf that can break the strongholds of the enemy in their lives and yours.

3. Allow the goodness of God to flow through you to your loved ones.

4. Begin to live a happy life.

5. Claim your children back by claiming the promises of God.

6. Fly the bomber if needed. Pray that radical prayer.

7. Unite your prayers in love for God and one another. Remember, united prayers drive Satan back and weaken his powers.

> "When the storm of persecution really breaks upon us, the true sheep will hear the true Shepherd's voice. Self-denying efforts will be put forth to save the lost, and many who have strayed from the fold will come back to follow the Great Shepherd." (*Testimonies to the Church*, Volume 6, p. 401)

> "The love of God still yearns over the one who has chosen to separate from Him, and He sets in operation influences to bring him back to the Father's house... A golden chain, the mercy and compassion of divine love, is passed around every imperiled soul. "I have loved thee with an everlasting love; therefore with loving-kindness have I drawn thee." (*Christ's Object Lessons*, p. 202)

> "Heaven is waiting and yearning for the return of the prodigals who have wandered far from the fold. Many of those who have strayed away may be brought back by the loving service of God's children.." (*In Heavenly Places*, p. 10)

You can demonstrate your loving service through prayer ministry in your church to claim your children back. Unite your prayers in love for one another and in love for God and by doing so, Satan will be driven back and his power over your children will be weakened. Pray not just for your own child, but for all children. Take hold of each other and show that you belong to the body of Jesus. Feel each other's pain. Pray for one another. Tell God that your hearts are heavy and how much you love your children. Ask the Lord to help you embrace His forgiveness for past mistakes that you cannot change, and to help you grow in your walk with Jesus. By faith, take hold of the keys of the kingdom of power and use your privilege to bind and loose.

Ask for a hedge of protection around your loved one from the deceitfulness and temptations of Satan and the temptations of the world. Ask that they will not find peace until they find the Lord. Ask that they will feel the emptiness of this life without Him, and if need be, give God permission to do whatever is necessary to bring them to Him. Claim His promises to bring your children back and thank Him for those promises. Include your relatives, your friends, and missing church members in your prayers (there are so many missing members!). Praise Him and thank Him for hearing and answering your prayers and understanding your grief. Profess that you believe it is an accomplished fact, and ask Him to heal you from unbelief you may have. Pray for the Holy Spirit to pour His love into your hearts and in your children's hearts. Pray these things in Jesus's all powerful name.

> Thus says the LORD: "Refrain your voice from weeping, And your eyes from tears; For your work shall be rewarded, says the LORD, And they shall come back from the land of the enemy. There is hope[expectation] in your future, says the LORD, That *your* children shall come back to their own border." (Jeremiah 31:16,17)

Begin to live a happy Christian life!

If you need this series come to your church to help establish a powerful prayer ministry and to have an outreach to the community at the same time (because all Christian churches are having the same pain and looking for solutions), you may contact us:

CREATIVE MEDIA MINISTRIES
P.O. BOX 837
MURRIETA, CA 92564

WEBSITE: www.CreativeMediaMinistries.org
EMAIL: victoryinjesus1@verizon.net
PHONE: 951-440-7688

GOD'S ENCOURAGING PROMISES TO SAVE OUR CHILDREN, AND MORE TOOLS FOR INDIVIDUALS AND PRAYER GROUPS TO RECLAIM OUR LOVED ONES TO GOD

Jesus teaches and commands us to:

ASK, BELIEVE and CLAIM answers to our prayers. In addition Scriptures teaches us to praise God in advance for the victory over the forces of the enemy that are against us.

ASK:

MATTHEW 7:7 "ASK, and it will be given to you; seek, and you will find; knock, and it will be opened to you"

JOHN 15:7 "If you abide in Me, and My words abide in you, you will ASK what you desire, and it shall be done for you.."

JOHN 14:13 "And whatever you ASK in My name, that I will do, that the Father may be glorified in the Son."

BELIEVE:

MARK 11:24 "Therefore I say to you, whatever things you ask when you pray, BELIEVE that you receive them, and you will have them."

HEBREWS 10:23 "Let us hold fast the confession of our hope WITHOUT WAVERING, for He who promised is faithful."

CLAIM AND PRAISE GOD IN ADVANCE

JOHN 11:41 "Then they took away the stone from the place where the dead man was lying. And Jesus lifted up His eyes and said, 'Father, I thank You that You have heard Me.'"

Notice, Lazarus is still in the grave, and the thanksgiving precedes the miracle of resurrection. As humans we express thanksgiving after seeing miracles, but Jesus is giving us a faith model: He gives thanks IN ADVANCE for what He is about to receive. The gratitude breaks forth BEFORE the bounty has arrived, in the assurance that it is certainly on the way.

The song of victory is sung BEFORE the battle has been fought (see 2 Chronicles 20)

Give thanks to the Loving Almighty Father before the miracle! Praise changes things. "It is a good thing to give thanks unto the Lord."

MATTHEW 8:8,10 "The centurion answered and said Lord, '..But only speak a word, and my servant will be healed..' When Jesus heard it, He marveled, and said to those who followed, 'Assuredly, I say to you, I have not found such great faith, not even in Israel!'"

Even though your eyes may not see the answer, let your heart believe God is answering. Choose to look beyond the dark clouds and be filled with His rays of goodness as you rest in knowing Him. Live in the reality of God's love and care for you, and in the knowledge of His faithfulness when you don't see the way.

GOD'S ENCOURAGING PROMISES AND MORE FOR CLAIMING OUR CHILDREN AND LOVED ONES BACK:

ISAIAH 49:25 "But thus says the LORD: 'Even the captives of the mighty shall be taken away, and the prey of the terrible be delivered; for I will contend with him who contends with you, and I WILL save your children.'"

JEREMIAH 31:16-17 "Thus says the LORD: 'Refrain your voice from weeping, and your eyes from tears; for your work shall be rewarded, says the LORD, and they shall come back from the land of the enemy. There is hope [expectation] in your future, says the LORD, that your children shall come back to their own border.'"

ISAIAH 55:11 "So shall My word be that goes forth from My mouth; it shall not return to Me void, but it shall accomplish what I please, and it shall prosper in the thing for which I sent it."

ROMANS 4:19-22 "And not being weak in faith, he did not consider his own body, already dead (since he was about a hundred years old), and the deadness of Sarah's womb. He did not waver at the promise of God through unbelief, but was strengthened in faith, giving glory to God, and being fully convinced that what He had promised He was also able to perform. And therefore 'it was accounted to him for righteousness.'"

MATTHEW 24:35 "Heaven and earth will pass away, but My words will by no means pass away."

ISAIAH 46:11 "...Indeed I have spoken it; I will also bring it to pass. I have purposed it; I will also do it."

JEREMIAH 32:27 "Behold, I am the LORD, the God of all flesh. Is there anything too hard for Me?"

LUKE 1:37 "For with God nothing will be impossible."

NUMBERS 23:19 "God is not a man, that He should lie, nor a son of man, that He should repent. Has He said, and will He not do? Or has He spoken, and will He not make it good?"

PSALMS 37:4 "Delight yourself also in the LORD, and He shall give you the desires of your heart."

PSALMS 62:8 "Trust in Him at all times, you people; pour out your heart before Him; God is a refuge for us. Selah."

1 KINGS 8:56 "Blessed be the LORD, who has given rest to His people Israel, according to all that He promised. There has not failed one word of all His good promise, which He promised through His servant Moses."

MAKE GOD'S PROMISES THE FOUNDATION ON WHICH YOUR PRAYER STANDS

HEBREWS 4:15 "For we do not have a High Priest who cannot sympathize with our weaknesses, but was in all points tempted as we are, yet without sin. Let us therefore come boldly to the throne of grace, that we may obtain mercy and find grace to help in time of need."

EPHESIANS 3:14-20 "For this reason I bow my knees to the Father of our Lord Jesus Christ from whom the whole family in heaven and earth is named, that He would grant you, according to the riches of His glory, to be strengthened with might through His Spirit in the inner man, that Christ may dwell in your hearts through faith; that you, being rooted and grounded in love, may be able to comprehend with all the saints what is the width and length and depth and height—to know the love of Christ which passes knowledge; that you may be filled with all the fullness of God. Now to Him who is able to do exceedingly abundantly above all that we ask or think, according to the power that works in us,..."

JAMES 5:16 "Confess your trespasses to one another, and pray for one another, that you may be healed. The effective, fervent prayer of a righteous man avails much."

1 JOHN 3:22 "And whatever we ask we receive from Him, because we keep His commandments and do those things that are pleasing in His sight."

JOHN 15:7 "If you abide in Me, and My words abide in you, you will ask what you desire, and it shall be done for you.."

PHILIPPIANS 4:6-7 "Be anxious for nothing, but in everything by prayer and supplication, with thanksgiving, let your requests be made known to God; and the peace of God, which surpasses all understanding, will guard your hearts and minds through Christ Jesus."

ISAIAH 54:10 "'For the mountains shall depart and the hills be removed, but My kindness shall not depart from you, nor shall My covenant of peace be removed,' says the LORD, who has mercy on you."

HEBREWS 13:5 "Therefore by Him let us continually offer the sacrifice of praise to God, that is, the fruit of our lips, giving thanks to His name."

DEUTERONOMY 31:6 "Be strong and of good courage, do not fear nor be afraid of them; for the LORD your God, He is the One who goes with you. He will not leave you nor forsake you."

JEREMIAH 31:3 "The LORD has appeared of old to me, saying: 'Yes, I have loved you with an everlasting love; Therefore with loving-kindness I have drawn you.'"

JEREMIAH 29:11 "'For I know the thoughts that I think toward you,' says the LORD, 'thoughts of peace and not of evil, to give you a future and a hope.'"

ROMANS 8:32 "He who did not spare His own Son, but delivered Him up for us all, how shall He not with Him also freely give us all things?"

DEUTERONOMY 1:30, 31 "The LORD your God, who goes before you, He will fight for you, according to all He did for you in Egypt before your eyes, and in the wilderness where you saw how the LORD your God carried you, as a man carries his son, in all the way that you went until you came to this place."

PSALMS 145: 14 "The LORD upholds all who fall, and raises up all who are bowed down."

2 CHRONICLES 16:9 "For the eyes of the LORD run to and fro throughout the whole earth, to show Himself strong on behalf of those whose heart is loyal to Him."

PSALMS. 94:14 "For the LORD will not cast off His people, nor will He forsake His inheritance."

ISAIAH 49:16 "See, I have inscribed you on the palms of My hands; Your walls are continually before Me."

FURTHER ENCOURAGING PROMISES

DEUTERONOMY 30:4, 6 "If any of you are driven out to the farthest parts under heaven, from there the LORD your God will gather you, and from there He will bring you...And the LORD your God will circumcise your heart and the heart of your descendants, to love the LORD your God with all your heart and with all your soul, that you may live.."

JEREMIAH 24:7 "And I will give you ______________________________ (your child's name) a heart to know Me, that I am the Lord: and ________________________(your child's name) shall be my people, and I will be (his/her/their) God; for____________________________ (your child's name) shall return unto Me with their whole heart."

JEREMIAH 31:9 "They shall come with weeping, and with supplications I will lead them. I will cause them to walk by the rivers of waters, in a straight way in which they shall not stumble; for I am a Father to Israel, and Ephraim is My firstborn."

ISAIAH 43:5-6 "Fear not, for I am with you; I will bring your descendants from the east, and gather you from the west;"

ISAIAH 44:3 "For I will pour water on him who is thirsty, and floods on the dry ground; I will pour My Spirit on your descendants, and My blessing on your offspring;"

ISAIAH 54:13 "All your children shall be taught by the LORD, and great shall be the peace of your children."

ISAIAH 59:21 "'As for Me,' says the LORD, 'this is My covenant with them: My Spirit who is upon you, and My words which I have put in your mouth, shall not depart from your mouth, nor from the mouth of your descendants, nor from the mouth of your descendants' descendants,' says the LORD, 'from this time and forevermore.'"

EZEKIEL 36:27 "And I will put My Spirit within_______________________(your child's name), and cause_________________________ (your child's name) to walk in My statues, and _________________________ (your children's names) shall keep My judgments and do them."

HOSEA 14:4 "I will heal their backsliding, I will love them freely, for My anger has turned away from him."

PSALMS 72:4 "He will bring justice to the poor of the people; He will save the children of the needy, and will break in pieces the oppressor."

ISAIAH 42:16 "I will bring the blind by a way they did not know; I will lead them in paths they have not known. I will make darkness light before them, and crooked places straight. These things I will do for them, and not forsake them."

PROVERBS 22:6 "Train up a child in the way he should go, and when he is old he will not depart from it."

ZEPHANIAH 3:17 "The LORD your God in your midst, the Mighty One, will save; He will rejoice over you with gladness, He will quiet you with His love, He will rejoice over you with singing."

2 TIMOTHY 1:12 "For this reason I also suffer these things; nevertheless I am not ashamed, for I know whom I have believed and am persuaded that He is able to keep what I have committed to Him until that Day."

MATTHEW 18:14 "Even so it is not the will of your Father who is in heaven that one of these little ones should perish."

2 CHRONICLES 20:15 "...Do not be afraid nor dismayed because of this great multitude, for the battle is not yours, but God's."

PSALMS 121:4 "Behold, He who keeps Israel, shall neither slumber nor sleep."

LUKE 19:10 "for the Son of Man has come to seek and to save that which was lost."

1 PETER 2:6 "Behold, I lay in Zion a chief cornerstone, elect, precious, and he who believes on Him will by no means be put to shame."

PHILIPPIANS 4:19 "and my God shall supply all your need according to His riches in glory by Christ Jesus."

EZEKIEL 34:16 "I will seek what was lost and bring back what was driven away, bind up the broken and strengthen what was sick; but I will destroy the fat and the strong, and feed them in judgment."

EZEKIEL 34:11-12 "For thus says the Lord GOD: 'Indeed I Myself will search for My sheep ________________(your child's name) and seek them out. As a shepherd seeks out his flock on the day he is among his scattered sheep, so will I seek out My sheep ______________________ (your child's name) and deliver them from all the places where they were scattered on a cloudy and dark day.'"

LUKE 4:18-19 "The Spirit of the LORD is upon Me, because He has anointed Me to preach the gospel to the poor; He has sent Me to heal the brokenhearted, to proclaim liberty to the captives and recovery of sight to the blind, to set at liberty those who are oppressed;"

PSALMS 145:19 "He will fulfill the desire of those who fear Him; He also will hear their cry and save them."

PROVERBS 14:26 "In the fear of the LORD there is strong confidence, and His children will have a place of refuge."

JEREMIAH 29:11-12 "For I know the thoughts that I think toward you, says the LORD, thoughts of peace and not of evil, to give you a future and a hope."

JEREMIAH 30:17 "'For I will restore health to you and heal you of your wounds,' says the LORD,"

PSALMS 147:1, 3 "For He has strengthened the bars of your gates; He has blessed your children within you."

ISAIAH 57:18 "I have seen his ways, and will heal him; I will also lead him, and restore comforts to him And to his mourners."

PROVERBS 16:3 "Commit your works to the LORD, and your thoughts will be established."

ISAIAH 37:3-5 "And they said to him, Thus says Hezekiah: 'This day is a day of trouble and rebuke and blasphemy; for the children have come to birth, but there is no strength to bring them forth. It may be that the LORD your God will hear the words of the Rabshakeh, whom his master the king of Assyria has sent to reproach the living God, and will rebuke the words which the LORD your God has heard. Therefore lift up your prayer for the remnant that is left.' So the servants of King Hezekiah came to Isaiah."

PSALMS 107:20, 27, 28 "He sent His word and healed them, and delivered them from their destructions.... They reel to and fro, and stagger like a drunken man, and are at their wits' end. Then they cry out to the LORD in their trouble, and He brings them out of their distresses."

JEREMIAH 33:6 "Behold, I will bring it health and healing; I will heal them and reveal to them the abundance of peace and truth."

2 TIMOTHY 1:7 "For God has not given us a spirit of fear, but of power and of love and of a sound mind."

JEREMIAH 33:3 "Call to Me, and I will answer you, and show you great and mighty things, which you do not know."

JAMES 1:5-6 "If any of you lacks wisdom, let him ask of God, who gives to all liberally and without reproach, and it will be given to him. But let him ask in faith, with no doubting, for he who doubts is like a wave of the sea driven and tossed by the wind."

PSALMS 34:17 "The righteous cry out, and the LORD hears, and delivers them out of all their troubles."

PSALMS 37:32-33 "The wicked watches the righteous, And seeks to slay him. The LORD will not leave him in his hand, nor condemn him when he is judged."

PSALMS 37:40 "And the LORD shall help them and deliver them; He shall deliver them from the wicked, and save them, because they trust in Him."

JOHN 14:27 "Peace I leave with you, My peace I give to you; not as the world gives do I give to you. Let not your heart be troubled, neither let it be afraid."

HEBREWS 4:16 "Let us therefore come boldly to the throne of grace, that we may obtain mercy and find grace to help in time of need."

ISAIAH 65:24 "It shall come to pass, that before they call, I will answer; and while they are still speaking, I will hear."

PSALMS 57:2 "I will cry out to God Most High, to God who performs all things for me."

DEUTERONOMY 1:30 "The LORD your God, who goes before you, He will fight for you, according to all He did for you in Egypt before your eyes."

PSALMS 112:7 "He will not be afraid of evil tidings; His heart is steadfast, trusting in the LORD."

ISAIAH 54:17 "'No weapon formed against you shall prosper, and every tongue which rises against you in judgment, you shall condemn. This is the heritage of the servants of the LORD, And their righteousness is from Me,' Says the LORD."

PSALMS 62:8 "Trust in Him at all times, you people; pour out your heart before Him; God is a refuge for us. Selah"

PHILIPPIANS 4:19 "And my God shall supply all your need according to His riches in glory by Christ Jesus."

PSALMS 62:8 "Trust in Him at all times, you people; pour out your heart before Him; God is a refuge for us. Selah"

PSALMS 145:18-19 "The LORD is near to all who call upon Him, To all who call upon Him in truth. He will fulfill the desire of those who fear Him; He also will hear their cry and save them."

DEUTERONOMY 31:6 "Be strong and of a good courage, do not fear nor be afraid of them; for the Lord your God, He is the One who goes with you, He will not leave you [and your children] nor forsake you [and your children]"

Because:

PSALMS 121:4, 5 "Behold, He who keeps Israel shall neither slumber nor sleep. The LORD is your keeper; the LORD is your shade at your right hand."

PSALMS 119:154 "Plead my cause and redeem me; revive me according to Your word."

HEBREWS 13:5 "For He Himself has said, 'I will never leave you nor forsake you.'"

PSALMS 124:8 "Our help is in the name of the LORD, Who made heaven and earth."

PSALMS 91:9-10 "Because you have made the LORD, who is my refuge, even the Most High, your dwelling place, no evil shall befall you, nor shall any plague come near your dwelling;"

PSALMS 91:11-12 "For He shall give His angels charge over you, to keep you in all your ways. In their hands they shall bear you up, lest you dash your foot against a stone."

PSALMS 91:14-15 "Because he has set his love upon Me, therefore I will deliver him; I will set him on high, because he has known My name. He shall call upon Me, and I will answer him; I will be with him in trouble; I will deliver him and honor him."

2 CHRONICLES 20:12 "O our God, will You not judge them? For we have no power against this great multitude that is coming against us; nor do we know what to do, but our eyes are upon You."

PSALMS 108:13 "Through God we will do valiantly, for it is He who shall tread down our enemies."

2 TIMOTHY1:7 "For God has not given us a spirit of fear, but of power and of love and of a sound mind."

PSALM 145:14 "The LORD upholds all who fall, and raises up all who are bowed down."

EXODUS 14:13-14 "And Moses said to the people, 'Do not be afraid. Stand still, and see the salvation of the LORD, which He will accomplish for you today. For the Egyptians whom you see today, you shall see again no more forever.'"

JOSHUA 1:9 "Have I not commanded you? Be strong and of good courage; do not be afraid, nor be dismayed, for the LORD your God is with you wherever you go."

MORE PROMISES FOR INDIVIDUAL AND PRAYER GROUPS TO RECLAIM YOUR CHILDREN, FAMILY MEMBERS AND MISSING CHURCH MEMBERS BACK TO GOD

ISAIAH 59:19 "So shall they fear the name of the LORD from the west, and His glory from the rising of the sun; when the enemy comes in like a flood, the Spirit of the LORD will lift up a standard against him."

2 CORINTHIANS 10:4-5 "For the weapons of our warfare are not carnal but mighty in God for pulling down strongholds, casting down arguments and every high thing that exalts itself against the knowledge of God, bringing every thought into captivity to the obedience of Christ,"

PSALMS 107:14 "He brought them out of darkness and the shadow of death, and broke their chains in pieces."

PSALMS 107:16 "For He has broken the gates of bronze, and cut the bars of iron in two".

PSALMS 107: 17 – 19, 21 "Fools, because of their transgression, and because of their iniquities, were afflicted. Their soul abhorred all manner of food, and they drew near to the gates of death. Then they cried out to the LORD in their trouble, and He saved them out of their distresses. He sent His word and healed them, and delivered them from their destructions."

ISAIAH 42:16 "I will bring the blind by a way they did not know; I will lead them in paths they have not known. I will make darkness light before them, and crooked places straight. These things I will do for them, and not forsake them."

2 PETER 3:9 "The Lord is not slack concerning His promise, as some count slackness, but is long-suffering toward us, not willing that any should perish but that all should come to repentance."

PSALMS 35:1 "Plead my cause, O LORD, with those who strive with me; fight against those who fight against me."

EPHESIANS 1:19 "...and what is the exceeding greatness of His power toward us who believe, according to the working of His mighty power."

DEUTERONOMY 1:30 'The LORD your God, who goes before you, He will fight for you, according to all He did for you in Egypt before your eyes,..."

EPHESIANS 3:20-21 "Now to Him who is able to do exceedingly abundantly above all that we ask or think, according to the power that works in us, to Him be glory in the church by Christ Jesus to all generations, forever and ever. Amen"

ISAIAH 54:17 "'No weapon formed against you shall prosper, and every tongue which rises against you in judgment, you shall condemn. This is the heritage of the servants of the LORD, And their righteousness is from Me,' Says the LORD."

EPHESIANS 3:16 "...that He would grant you, according to the riches of His glory, to be strengthened with might through His Spirit in the inner man...."

1 JOHN 5:16 "If anyone sees his brother sinning a sin which does not lead to death, he will ask, and He will give him life for those who commit sin not leading to death. There is sin leading to death. I do not say that he should pray about that."

1 JOHN 5:14-15 "Now this is the confidence that we have in Him, that if we ask anything according to His will, He hears us. And if we know that He hears us, whatever we ask, we know that we have the petitions that we have asked of Him."

EZEKIEL 36:26 "I WILL GIVE YOU ______________________________ (YOUR CHILD'S NAME) A NEW HEART AND PUT A NEW SPIRIT WITHIN YOU ______________________________ (YOUR CHILD'S NAME); I WILL TAKE THE HEART OF STONE OUT OF YOUR______ ______________________________ (YOUR CHILD'S NAME) FLESH AND GIVE YOU (YOUR CHILD'S NAME) ________________________ ________A HEART OF FLESH"

When the answer to your prayer delays, do not let Satan discourage you. Continue to strengthen yourself with God's promises. Though the fulfillment of the promise terries it will be fulfilled, because God can not lie. God's timing is the best!

Remember Joseph when he was a slave In Egypt. He was waiting for God to fulfill His promises (the dreams that he had as teenager). He endured that waiting time of trials, until the Word of God was fulfilled: Psalm 105:19 "Until the time that his word came to pass, the Word of the Lord tested him." That time of waiting was a trial for him. See now James 1:2-4.

JAMES 1:2-4 "My brethren, count it all joy when you fall into various trials, knowing that the testing of your faith produces patience. But let patience have its perfect work, that you may be perfect and complete , lacking nothing."

HEBREWS 11:1 "Now faith is the substance of things hoped for, the evidence of things not seen."

HEBREWS 11:6 "But without faith it is impossible to please Him, for he who comes to God must believe that He is, and that He is a rewarder of those who diligently seek Him."

HEBREWS 10:23 "Let us hold fast the confession of our hope without wavering, for He who promised is faithful."

HEBREWS 10:35-36 "Therefore do not cast away your confidence, which has great reward. For you have need of endurance, so that after you have done the will of God, you may receive the promise:"

1 KINGS 8:56 "Blessed be the LORD, who has given rest to His people Israel, according to all that He promised. There has not failed one word of all His good promise, which He promised through His servant Moses."

PSALMS 37:5 "Commit your way to the LORD, trust also in Him, and He shall bring it to pass."

JAMES 4:7 "Therefore submit to God. Resist the devil and he will flee from you."

MATTHEW 18:19 "Again I say to you that if two of you agree on earth concerning anything that they ask, it will be done for them by My Father in heaven."

"GOD'S TREASURE BOX FOR YOU" HAVE THE FAITH OF JESUS "PUT YOUR TRUST IN THE LORD AND YOU WILL BE ESTABLISHED"

2 CHRONICLES 20:20 "Hear me, O Judah and you inhabitants of Jerusalem: Believe in the LORD your God, and you shall be established; believe His prophets, and you shall prosper."

CORINTHIANS 5:7 "FOR WE WALK BY FAITH, NOT BY SIGHT"

– Faith is taking God at His Word.

– Faith is not belief without evidence. It is belief on the very best of evidence – the Word of Him "that cannot lie" (Titus 1:2). Faith is so rational that it does not need any other evidence than all sufficient evidence – the Word of God that has power to do what it says. And to ask or look for other evidence than the Word of Him who can not lie is not rationalism, but consummate irrationalism.

– Faith is like setting a sail towards what we do not see. We are departing the shores of sight and feelings. It is saying "good-bye" to feelings and signs. We are now on the ocean of divine love, believing in God and steering for Heaven by the direction of the Word of God as our compass.

HEBREWS 11:1 "Now faith is the substance of things hoped for, the evidence of things not seen."

HEBREWS 11:6 "But without faith it is impossible to please Him, for he who comes to God must believe that He is, and that He is a rewarder of those who diligently seek Him."

1 JOHN 5:4 "For whatever is born of God overcomes the world. And this is the victory that has overcome the world—our faith."

HEBREWS 6:12 "That you do not become sluggish, but imitate those who through faith and patience inherit the promises."

PSALMS 62:8 "Trust in Him at all times, you people; pour out your heart before Him; God is a refuge for us. Selah."

HEBREWS 10:35-36 "Therefore do not cast away your confidence, which has great reward. For you have need of endurance, so that after you have done the will of God, you may receive the promise:"

JOHN 14:12-13 "Most assuredly, I say to you, he who believes in Me, the works that I do he will do also; and greater works than these he will do, because I go to My Father. And whatever you ask in My name, that I will do, that the Father may be glorified in the Son."

MATTHEW 9:28-29 "And when He had come into the house, the blind men came to Him. And Jesus said to them, 'Do you believe that I am able to do this?' They said to Him, 'Yes, Lord.' Then He touched their eyes, saying, 'According to your faith let it be to you.'"

MATTHEW 21:22 "And whatever things you ask in prayer, believing, you will receive."

JAMES 1:6 "But let him ask in faith, with no doubting, for he who doubts is like a wave of the sea driven and tossed by the wind."

MATTHEW 9:22 "But Jesus turned around, and when He saw her He said, "Be of good cheer, daughter; your faith has made you well." And the woman was made well from that hour."

LUKE 7:50 "Then He said to the woman, 'Your faith has saved you. Go in peace.'"

1 KINGS 8:56 "Blessed be the LORD, who has given rest to His people Israel, according to all that He promised. There has not failed one word of all His good promise, which He promised through His servant Moses."

ISAIAH 50:10 "Who among you fears the LORD? Who obeys the voice of His Servant? Who walks in darkness And has no light? Let him trust in the name of the LORD And rely upon his God."

GOD'S DESIRE FOR US TO BELIEVE HIM BEFORE WE GET THE ANSWER, HE IS GROWING IN US THE FAITH THAT CAN NOT BE SHAKEN, SO WE CAN WALK EVEN IN DARKNESS HAVING HIS WORD AS THE LIGHT UNTO OUR PATH. KEEP YOUR FAITH IN CHRIST AND NOT IN HOW WELL OR NOT SO WELL YOUR CHILDREN ARE DOING..

DEAR READER, IF YOU ARE IN FEAR, THE FOLLOWING SCRIPTURES ARE FOR YOU

1 JOHN 4:18 "There is no fear in love; but perfect love casts out fear, because fear involves torment. But he who fears has not been made perfect in love."

FEARFULNESS IS IN THE CATEGORY OF SIN.

REVELATION 21:8 "But the COWARDLY, unbelieving, abominable, murderers, sexually immoral, sorcerers, idolaters, and all liars shall have their part in the lake which burns with fire and brimstone, which is the second death." No wonder the Word of God repeats the statement "FEAR NOT", "DO NOT BE AFRAID" 365 times. Why? Because God does not want His people to leave in fear even for one day. Please do not forget this. The Almighty God said to us: "I will never leave you nor forsake you."

JESUS TOOK OUR SIN OF FEAR AND BORE THE CONSEQUENCE OF IT ON THE CROSS. NOW HIS VICTORY OVER FEAR IS YOURS.

SURRENDER YOUR FEARS TO HIM.

BELIEVE THAT JESUS IS ANXIOUS TO GIVE YOU VICTORY OVER FEAR AND EVERY SIN. CLAIM IT AND RECEIVE IT. IT IS YOURS FOR TAKING. NEVER LET FEELINGS DECEIVE YOU. DARE TO BELIEVE GOD AND BE CHANGED!

ISAIAH 41:10 "Fear not, for I am with you; Be not dismayed, for I am your God. I will strengthen you, Yes, I will help you, I will uphold you with My righteous right hand."

2 CHRONICLES 20:15 "And he said, 'Listen, all you of Judah and you inhabitants of Jerusalem, and you, King Jehoshaphat! Thus says the LORD to you: 'Do not be afraid nor dismayed because of this great multitude, for the battle is not yours, but God's.'"

1 CHRONICLES 28:20 "And David said to his son Solomon, 'Be strong and of good courage, and do it; do not fear nor be dismayed, for the LORD God—my God—will be with you. He will not leave you nor forsake you, until you have finished all the work for the service of the house of the LORD.'"

EXODUS 14:13 "And Moses said to the people, 'Do not be afraid. Stand still, and see the salvation of the LORD, which He will accomplish for you today. For the Egyptians whom you see today, you shall see again no more forever.'"

2 KINGS 6:16 "So he answered, 'Do not fear, for those who are with us are more than those who are with them.'"

ISAIAH 35:14 "The wilderness and the wasteland shall be glad for them, And the desert shall rejoice and blossom as the rose;"

2 TIMOTHY 1:7 "For God has not given us a spirit of fear, but of power and of love and of a sound mind."

ISAIAH 41:13 "For I, the LORD your God, will hold your right hand, Saying to you, 'Fear not, I will help you.'"

PSALMS 121:4 "Behold, He who keeps Israel Shall neither slumber nor sleep."

ROMANS 8:15 "For you did not receive the spirit of bondage again to fear, but you received the Spirit of adoption by whom we cry out, 'Abba, Father.'"

PROVERBS 3:25-26 "Do not be afraid of sudden terror, Nor of trouble from the wicked when it comes; For the LORD will be your confidence, And will keep your foot from being caught."

PSALMS 31:24 "Be of good courage, And He shall strengthen your heart, All you who hope in the LORD".

ISAIAH 43:2 "When you pass through the waters, I will be with you; And through the rivers, they shall not overflow you. When you walk through the fire, you shall not be burned, Nor shall the flame scorch you."

In Acts 27 the Apostle Paul reveals the highest level of faith. He believed God's word having all circumstances speaking contrary. (See vs 20) And Paul exercised faith:

ACTS 27:25 "Be of good cheer, for I believe God, that it shall be even as it was told me"!!!

May God give us faith to trust His Word fully, even though everything else witness contrary to it.

JOHN 14:27 "Peace I leave with you, My peace I give to you; not as the world gives do I give to you. Let not your heart be troubled, neither let it be afraid."

Stop fearing for your children and loved ones. Remember there is an almighty God who is watching over your children and over you as well.

Praise and give thanks to God for His power to save our children and loved ones.

Praise Him in advance for His victory in their lives before you even see any evidence of it. God inhabits the praises of His children and He is releasing the power that will break the strongholds of the enemy in their lives.

2 CHRONICLES 20:20-23 "So they rose early in the morning and went out into the Wilderness of Tekoa; and as they went out, Jehoshaphat stood and said, 'Hear me, O Judah and you inhabitants of Jerusalem: Believe in the LORD your God, and you shall be established; believe His prophets, and you shall prosper.' And when he had consulted with the people, he appointed those who should sing to the LORD, and who should praise the beauty of holiness, as they went out before the army and were saying:

'Praise the LORD, For His mercy endures forever'

Now when they began to sing and to praise, the LORD set ambushes against the people of Ammon, Moab, and Mount Seir, who had come against Judah; and they were defeated. For the people of Ammon and Moab stood up against the inhabitants of Mount Seir to utterly kill and destroy them. And when they had made an end of the inhabitants of Seir, they helped to destroy one another."

ACTS 16:25,26 "But at midnight Paul and Silas were praying and singing hymns to God, and the prisoners were listening to them. Suddenly there was a great earthquake, so that the foundations of the prison were shaken; and immediately all the doors were opened and everyone's chains were loosed."

PHILIPPIANS 4:6-7 "Be anxious for nothing, but in everything by prayer and supplication, with thanksgiving, let your requests be made known to God; and the peace of God, which surpasses all understanding, will guard your hearts and minds through Christ Jesus."

COLOSSIANS 4:2 "Continue earnestly in prayer, being vigilant in it with thanksgiving;"

1 THESSALONIANS 5:18 "...in everything give thanks; for this is the will of God in Christ Jesus for you."

PSALMS 107:8 "Oh, that men would give thanks to the LORD for His goodness, And for His wonderful works to the children of men!"

PSALMS 40:3 "He has put a new song in my mouth—Praise to our God; Many will see it and fear, And will trust in the LORD."

PSALMS 89-15-16 "Blessed are the people who know the joyful sound! They walk, O LORD, in the light of Your countenance. In Your name they rejoice all day long, and in Your righteousness they are exalted."

HEBREWS 3:18 "And to whom did He swear that they would not enter His rest, but to those who did not obey?"

PSALMS 33:21 "For our heart shall rejoice in Him, because we have trusted in His holy name."

JOHN 16:22 "Therefore you now have sorrow; but I will see you again and your heart will rejoice, and your joy no one will take from you."

1 PETER 2:9 "But you are a chosen generation, a royal priesthood, a holy nation, His own special people, that you may proclaim the praises of Him who called you out of darkness into His marvelous light;"

HEBREWS 13:15 "Therefore by Him let us continually offer the sacrifice of praise to God, that is, the fruit of our lips, giving thanks to His name."

ALL PROMISES GOD MADE ARE "YES" IN CHRIST

2 CORINTHIANS 1:20 "For all the promises of God in Him are Yes, and in Him Amen, to the glory of God through us."

Since the promises of God are definite, our prayers should be definite.

Search the Word, choose the promise that will fit your case. Read it to Him. PROVE HIM! Back of the Word of Lord is the person and character of God Himself, the God who cannot lie.

GOD HONORS THE PERSON WHO TRUSTS HIM IMPLICITLY

It is not your worth, but Christ's, which secured for us immediate access to the Throne of God. With such assurance and invitation from God Himself, why hesitate to claim the things the Lord has already provided?

HEBREWS 4:14-16 "Seeing then that we have a great High Priest who has passed through the heavens, Jesus the Son of God, let us hold fast our confession. For we do not have a High Priest who cannot sympathize with our weaknesses, but was in all points tempted as we are, yet without sin. Let us therefore come boldly to the throne of grace, that we may obtain mercy and find grace to help in time of need."

A MOTHER'S PERSISTENCE

"God has promised to give wisdom to those that ask in faith, and he will do just as he said he would. He is pleased with the faith that takes him at his word. The mother of Augustine prayed for her son's conversion. She saw no evidence that the Spirit of God was impressing his heart, but she was not discouraged. She laid her finger upon the texts, presenting before God his own words, and pleaded as only a mother can. Her deep humiliation, her earnest importunities, [persistence] her unwavering faith, prevailed, and the Lord gave her the desire of her heart. Today he is just as ready to listen to the petitions of his people. "His hand is not shortened that it cannot save, neither his ear heavy that it cannot hear;" and if Christian parents seek him earnestly, he will fill their mouths with arguments, and for his name's sake, will work mightily in their behalf in the conversion of their children." (*Testimonies for the Church*, Volume 5, 322, 323)

CLAIM YOUR CHILDREN BACK BY CLAIMING THE PROMISES OF GOD!

"Do as You have said, that Your name may be magnified." (1 Chronicles 17:23-24)

"Remember the word unto Your servant, on which You have caused me to hope." (Psalms 119:49)

This is the most persuasive pleading. You have here a double argument:

1. **It is Your Word.**
2. **Will You not keep it? Why have You said it if You will not make it good? Lord, You caused me to hope in it, will You disappoint the hope which You have planted in me?**

"Being absolutely certain that whatever promise He is bound by, He is able also to make good." (Romans 4:21 Weymouth's Translation).

The everlasting faithfulness of God makes a Bible promise "exceeding great and precious".

REMEMBER, ALL PROMISES OF GOD ARE BUILT UPON PILLARS THAT CAN NOT BE SHAKEN:

- God's Justice and Holiness, which will not allow Him to deceive;
- His Grace and Goodness, which will not allow Him to forget;
- His Truth, which will not allow Him to change;
- These pillars of His character enable Him to accomplish it with absolute certainty.

These same pillars of His character enable *us* to have the confidence that He will fulfill his promises with absolute certainty.

MARK 11:24 "Therefore I say to you, whatever things you ask when you pray, believe that you receive them, and you will have them."

"The very time to exercise faith is when we feel destitute of the Spirit. When thick clouds of darkness seem to hover over the mind, then is the time to let living faith pierce the darkness and scatter the clouds. True faith rests on the promises contained in the Word of God, and those only who obey that Word can claim its glorious promises." (Ellen G. White, *Early Writings*, p. 72-73)

JOHN 15:7 "If you abide in Me, and My words abide in you, you will ask what you desire, and it shall be done for you."

1 JOHN 3:22 "And whatever we ask we receive from Him, because we keep His commandments and do those things that are pleasing in His sight."

INTERCEDE FOR YOUR LOVED ONES AND MISSING CHURCH MEMBERS

ACTS 12:5 "Peter was therefore kept in prison, but constant prayer was offered to God for him by the church."

Today your children, loved ones or your missing church members may be in different kind of prisons: addiction, unbelief, resentment, alienation, sin, etc. It is not a hopeless situation. The Bible tells us: "BUT FERVENT PRAYER WAS MADE BY THE CHURCH" And what happened?

Fervent Prayer Moved Heaven!

"And behold, an angel of the Lord suddenly appeared." (see Acts 12:7). The deliverance took place! The prisoner was set free!! Please hear this!!!

Look at the full story: The prison open, the prisoner set free, the enemies baffled, the wicked king eaten by worms and the Word of God rolling on in greater victory!

Today God is not waiting to have great men, He is waiting for men and women who will dare to prove the greatness of their God.

DO NOT FEAR GIANTS ON THE WAY

NUMBERS 13:33 "There we saw the giants (the descendants of Anak were giants); and we were like grasshoppers in our own sight, and so we were in their sight."

We see here the fear of giants on the way.

NUMBERS 14: 8-9 "If the LORD delights in us, then He will bring us into this land and give it to us, a land which flows with milk and honey. Only do not rebel against the LORD, nor fear the people of the land, for they are our bread; their protection has departed from them, and the LORD is with us. Do not fear them."

And here we see Courage and Faith. What are you choosing?

1 JOHN 5:4 "For whatever is born of God overcomes the world. And this is the victory that has overcome the world—our faith."

2 TIMOTHY 1:7 "For God has not given us a spirit of fear, but of power and of love and of a sound mind."

Let us have the spirit of faith and power and love, and a sound mind. See God and not giants. He will take care of the giants (the difficulties). For He said: "I will never leave you, nor forsake you." "Be not afraid, only believe."

And remember, when we go through hard places in life, it is a school of faith and building of the character.

THERE IS NO STRENGTH IN UNBELIEF!

Question was asked by those of little or no faith: "Can God?" (Psalm 78:19, Mark 9:22)

Let us never ask that question. We are rather to say: "God Can!" That will bring you through many difficulties and clear up many problems in your life. Make the Lord your confidence. He CAN surpass all our expectations!

1 CORINTHIANS 2:9 "Eye has not seen, nor ear heard, Nor have entered into the heart of man The things which God has prepared for those who love Him."

"For those who love Him" includes love, revere and trust.

MARK 9:23 "Jesus said to him, 'If you can believe, all things are possible to him who believes.'"

That faith is a culmination of growing stages. God first must put us through the process of faith growth, where there must be room for:

1. The trial of faith, (great trials produce great faith)
2. The discipline of faith,
3. The courage of faith and number of other stages, until we arrive to the end of faith growth,
4. Which is the VICTORY OF FAITH.

That is why the apostles wrote:

JAMES 1:2-4 "My brethren, count it all joy when you fall into various trials, knowing that the testing of your faith produces patience. But let patience have its perfect work, that you may be perfect and complete, lacking nothing."

2 CORINTHIANS 4:17 "For our light affliction, which is but for a moment, is working for us a far more exceeding and eternal weight of glory."

ROMANS 8:18 "For I consider that the sufferings of this present time are not worthy to be compared with the glory which shall be revealed in us."

ROMANS 5:3-5 "And not only that, but we also glory in tribulations, knowing that tribulation produces perseverance; and perseverance, character; and character, hope. Now hope does not disappoint, because the love of God has been poured out in our hearts by the Holy Spirit who was given to us."

1 PETER 4:12 "Beloved, do not think it strange concerning the fiery trial which is to try you, as though some strange thing happened to you;"

1 PETER 1:5-7 "...who are kept by the power of God through faith for salvation ready to be revealed in the last time. In this you greatly rejoice, though now for a little while, if need be, you have been grieved by various trials, that the genuineness of your faith, being much more precious than gold that perishes, though it is tested by fire, may be found to praise, honor, and glory at the revelation of Jesus Christ...."

DELAYS ARE NOT DENIALS

HABAKKUK 2:3 "For the vision is yet for an appointed time; But at the end it will speak, and it will not lie. Though it tarries, wait for it; Because it will surely come, It will not tarry."

There are secrets of love and wisdom of God in His Delayed Blessings Department, of which we may not be aware. We are like little children often want to pluck the fruit that is not fully ripe yet, and it tastes sour. The Lord waits, so when He gives it to you ripened you can experience the fullness of the taste and sweetness of God's blessing. "Therefore will the Lord wait, that He may be gracious to you.." (Isaiah 30:18)

Sometimes the Lord waits until the dross is consumed, and then He comes to pluck you out of the fire just in time! (Malachi 3:3) He knows how long the silver must be in the fire. It is until He sees His image/reflection in it. He will never allow the silver to be in fire longer than it should be. He will never allow more trials in our lives than we can handle.

Dear friend, let us not grieve the Lord by doubting His Love. Lift up your head, and begin to praise Him for the trial and for the deliverance which is on the way to you. You will be abundantly rewarded for the delay which has tried your faith. God will not fail you.

BE NOT AFRAID OF GOD'S SILENCE

JOHN 11:6 "So, when He heard that he [Lazarus] was sick, He stayed two more days in the place where He was."

There was seemingly no answer to the friends of Jesus. Only silence. But that very silence was an answer – and that silent far-away-ness of Jesus, being away from Bethany, was itself the nearness of God. Martha and Mary asked for too little, they had asked only for the life of Lazarus. They were to get the life of Lazarus and a revelation of Eternal Life as well! (see vs 25-26)

Some of our prayers are followed by a Divine silence because we are not yet ripe for all that we have asked. Some prayers are answered quickly because we are ripe for more. We do not always know the full strength of our own capacity; we have to be prepared for receiving greater blessings than we have ever dreamed of.

Mary came to the entrance of the tomb where the body of Jesus was laid. She begged with tears for the dead body of Jesus. We are answered by silence because we are to get something greater – a Living Lord!

Dear Readers, when the Lord wants to lead a soul to great faith, He for a time delays the answer to our prayer.

Believe that your prayers offered in the name of Jesus will not be in vain. You never find that Jesus Christ rejected one needy supplicant who came to Him for mercy.

PSALMS 62:5 "My soul, wait silently for God alone, for my expectation is from Him."

DO NOT BE ANXIOUS NOR DISCOURAGED

PHILIPPIANS 4:6 "Be anxious for nothing, but in everything by prayer and supplication, with thanksgiving, let your requests be made known to God;"

A discouraged soul is helpless. He cannot resist the wiles of the enemy nor prevail in prayer for others. And what is the use of worrying or being anxious? It never made anyone strong. It does not help anyone to get out of perplexity. It only spoils lives. People can see when you are in the realm of anxiety and worry. It shows up on your face through wrinkles, through your eyes, tone of your voice, low key in your life, lack of joy in your spirit. Consider the freedom and the heights of a life that is abandoned to God's care, then you will look down on the clouds beneath your feet.

Be still and know that Jehovah is God!

ISAIAH 54:10 "'For the mountains shall depart And the hills be removed, But My kindness shall not depart from you, Nor shall My covenant of peace be removed,' Says the LORD, who has mercy on you."

LAMENTATIONS 3:22, 23 "Through the LORD's mercies we are not consumed, They are new every morning; Great is Your faithfulness. Because His compassions fail not. They are new every morning; Great is Your faithfulness."

LAMENTATIONS 3:57 "You drew near on the day I called on You, And said, "Do not fear!"

HEBREWS 4:9 "There remains therefore, a rest to the people of God"

The rest includes Victory

JOSHUA 21:44 "The LORD gave them rest all around, according to all that He had sworn to their fathers. And not a man of all their enemies stood against them; the LORD delivered all their enemies into their hand."

PSALM 149:4 "For the LORD takes pleasure in His people; He will beautify the humble with victory".

PSALMS 34:1 "I will bless the LORD at all times; His praise shall continually be in my mouth."

THANK GOD IN ADVANCE FOR WHAT YOU ARE ABOUT TO RECEIVE

Let's take another look at the story of resurrection of Lazarus as recorded in John 11.

John 11:41 "Then they took away the stone from the place where the dead man was lying. And Jesus lifted up His eyes and said, 'Father, I thank You that You have heard Me. And I know that You always hear Me, but because of the people who are standing by I said this, that they may believe that You sent Me.' Now when He had said these things, He cried with a loud voice, 'Lazarus, come forth!'"

This is an unusual sequence. Notice, Lazarus is still in the grave, and the thanksgiving precedes the miracle of resurrection. As humans we express thanksgiving after seeing miracles, but Jesus is giving us a faith model: He gives thanks for what He is about to receive.

The gratitude breaks forth **BEFORE** the bounty has arrived, in the assurance that it is certainly on the way.

The song of victory is sung **BEFORE** the battle has been fought (see the full story in 2 Chronicles 20). It is when God's people begin to thank and praise God in advance for the fulfillment of the promise, God sets ambushes for their enemy and breaks the power of the enemy in our lives and the lives of our children.

Give thanks to the Loving Almighty Father before the miracle! Praise changes things. "It is a good thing to give thanks unto the Lord."

IF GOD'S PEOPLE WOULD PRAISE GOD CONTINUOUSLY—HE WILL WRITE VICTORIES FOR THEM CONTINUOUSLY; FEAR AND DISCOURAGEMENT WILL BE UNKNOWN TO THEM.

MATTHEW 8:8, 10 "The centurion replied, 'Lord, I do not deserve to have you come under my roof. But just say the word, and my servant will be healed'....When Jesus heard this, he was amazed and said to those following him, 'Truly I tell you, I have not found anyone in Israel with such great faith.'"

Even though your eyes may not see the answer, let your heart believe God is answering. Choose to look beyond the dark clouds and be filled with His rays of goodness as you rest in knowing Him. Live in the reality of God's love and care for you, and in the knowledge of His faithfulness when you don't see the way.

May the Faith of Jesus be yours.

> "The Lord bless you and keep you; The Lord make His face shine upon you, and be gracious to you; The Lord lift up His countenance upon you, and give you peace." (Numbers 6:24-27)

TWO BOOKS RECOMMENDED FOR FURTHER READING FOR EVERY FAMILY WITH YOUNG PEOPLE

FIRST BOOK – OVERCOMING THROUGH JESUS
by Bill Liversidge

During the time of COVID, many churches around the country were closed down. People began to order a book written by Pastor Bill Liversidge called Overcoming Through Jesus. In one of the churches in Oregon, they used the book to start small Bible study groups in their homes, and revival began to take place. When the churches reopened, the people came back to church and shared their testimonies about the revival they had experienced. Other members were inspired by their testimonies to study the book. One hundred and thirty people signed up for a study group. The whole church experienced revival. It was the impact the book was having on the lives of those who were hearing the Gospel message.

Later, a young man came to visit his parents, who were members of this church. For the past 12 years he had not been attending church during which time he had fallen away from the Lord. He was living in California at that time and had gotten involved in drugs. He decided to join his parents on the Sabbath when the members from their home study group were sharing their testimonies. He was moved as he heard the testimonies of the members and his father's testimony of how the message in Overcoming Through Jesus had impacted their lives.

When he returned to his parent's home, he found the book on his father's desk. He picked it up and began reading it. He told me later he couldn't put it down, and he finished the entire book before he returned to California. He purchased twenty five copies of the book and gave a book to each of his drug-using friends on his way home. Sad to say, many of them were from Adventist homes. A few months later, he called me and told me that he was free from drugs, and that he wants to go into ministry.

I had to ask myself what had happened here? He was raised in a Christian home. He went to church and church school. He knew all of the biblical teachings, yet he walked away from it all. What brought him back? Read that book "Overcoming Through Jesus", and you will understand for yourself. Your prodigals need this book. They need to hear the simplicity of the Gospel presented in a practical way that they have not heard before. They will see the undistorted picture of God through this book. Your youth in your church need to read this book. When they hear the Gospel, it will safeguard them from the enemy's attempts to wrestle them out of the hands of the Lord, and away from their family and the church. Over 50 of Christian academies and Andrews University, just recently obtained this book for all their graduates. In addition, the book has been given to every pastor in over 20 conferences in the North American Division. It was also given to over 1000 pastors in the country of India. The book was translated into Spanish and 2,740 pastors in the Inter-American Division received copies.

SECOND BOOK – GOD SO LOVED THE WORLD BIBLE STUDY GUIDES IN THE LIGHT OF THE GOSPEL

This is a Christ-centered series of 25 studies that presents the beauty of God's character and our Seventh-day Adventist doctrines in the light of the Gospel. You will not be able to resist the beauty of God's character that comes out with these studies. Great for family Bible study as well as for small groups.

Both are available at: www.CreativeMediaMinistries.org